The Complete Guide to
DESIGNING YOUR
LAW OFFICE

uzette S. Schultz and Jon S. Schultz

ABA LawPracticeManagementSection

MARKETING • MANAGEMENT • TECHNOLOGY • FINANCE

Commitment to Quality: The Law Practice Management Section is committed to quality in our publications. Our authors are experienced practitioners in their fields. Prior to publication, the contents of all our books are rigorously reviewed by experts to ensure the highest quality product and presentation. Because we are committed to serving our readers' needs, we welcome your feedback on how we can improve future editions of this book.

Cover design by Kelly Book, ABA Publishing.

© 2005 American Bar Association. All rights reserved.
Printed in the United States of America.

Library of Congress Cataloging-in-Publication Data
The Complete Guide to Designing Your Law Office. Suzette S. Schultz and Jon S. Schultz: Library of Congress Cataloging-in-Publication Data is on file.

ISBN 1-59031-481-6

09 08 07 06 05   5 4 3 2 1

Contents

CHAPTER 4
Checklists and Schedule   **25**

CHAPTER 5
Trends in Law Firm Designs   **39**

CHAPTER 6
Determining Your Square Footage Requirements   **45**

CHAPTER 7
Shopping for the Space   **77**

CHAPTER 8
Lease and Work Letter Analysis and Negotiations   93

CHAPTER 9
Technology and Law Firm Design   103

CHAPTER 10
Utilities, Lighting, and Security   111

CHAPTER 14
Public Areas

CHAPTER 15
Finishes in the Lawyer Environment

CHAPTER 16
Moving to the New Space

About the Authors

Suzette S. Schultz is president of Interior Space Design, Inc. (ISD), a firm specializing in law firm design throughout the United States and abroad. Her credits include personally designing more than four million square feet of law firm space, as well as a broad portfolio of corporate executive offices. She joined the ISD Inc. firm in 1979, designing law firms and corporate offices in the New York, Los Angeles and Houston offices. She acquired the Houston office in 1991, and now operates ISD from its offices on Galveston Island, Texas.

Jon S. Schultz is a professor of law at the University of Houston, a law library expert, and a registered builder. A former senior associate dean for information technology and for libraries at the University of Houston Law Center, he served as chair of the committee to develop the ABA's standards for law school libraries. A prolific author, he joined Suzette S. Schultz to produce this book, *The Complete Guide to Designing Your Law Office*, for the ABA. As a consultant, Professor Schultz provides advice on buildings and disaster planning to law firm, court, and academic libraries.

Preface

This book is about making the most of an opportunity to build or change the space that houses your law practice. As in so many other endeavors, planning makes the difference between a smashing success and mediocrity, whether the office is large or small. Even the casual observer has seen tremendous changes in law practice and law firms in the past decade. New law offices need to reflect these changes and maintain the flexibility to embrace the next decade's developments in the firm's practice and their clients' changing requirements.

Designing big law firm spaces is more complicated than designing small spaces, yet the planning and building processes for big and small firms follow the same order and share the same issues. From the huge to the solo, there is much similarity in the available ways to tackle the processes. Given the universal rule that budgets are generally underestimated, there are similar ways to stretch budgets. In this book we try to present principles, trends, and solutions that apply to firms of all sizes. Where it is feasible, we cover issues from the point of view of very small firms and solo practitioners, while also providing information for midsized and larger firms. We include a chapter just for small firms (Chapter 17). We also include a comprehensive checklist (see Chapter 4) and some appendices and examples from bigger firms' projects. We included these examples not because we intend to direct the book toward big firms as our primary audience, but because they suggest issues and solutions for you to discuss with your designer and project team, no matter what the size of your firm.

If you view your office as a marketing tool and see it as something that can make you more profitable by increasing your firm's effectiveness, the extra thought you give to the design in the early stages will reward the firm for as long as it stays in the space.

We owe thanks to many people who have helped us with ideas and comments for the book. We specifically want to thank Marty Festenstein and Chris Murray of Gensler who took the time to look deeply into the process and spent hours with us, giving us the benefit of their experience and providing opportunities to compare our reactions and responses to trends we see in recent law firm designs. Throughout the early stages of the book, we were fortunate to have the help of Rebecca Morecraft, who helped us maintain order in the drafts. Chenglin Liu and Harriet Richman of the University of Houston O'Quinn Law Library provided important assistance, and we thank researcher Mikal Colby Lewis for his work on the bibliography.

Beginning the Project

For law firm offices, planning makes all the difference. Projects start with planning work that can be tedious, but it makes a huge difference in the business and aesthetic success of the project. Whether it is a room renovation or a multistory high-rise law firm office, the planning effort produces two products: (1) the drawings or graphic representation, and (2) the specifications, a written list of the requirements for construction. A plan and its specifications provide the information necessary to estimate office construction and furnishing costs with acceptable accuracy. The plan has a continuing life as it becomes the document by which the project is constructed. For guidance in maintenance, repairs, and future construction, the plan provides a record of what is behind the walls.

Before the drawings and specifications are produced, the preparation begins. Preparation may have varying degrees of formality, depending upon the size of the project. Throughout this book, we discuss four distinct kinds of areas, each of which carries highly specific requirements for location, level of design detail, and level of finishes. Cost and appearance for each type of area or space depend on these requirements. The four areas are:

1. Public areas, the areas that the clients and general public see. These include the reception area, conference rooms, guest phone rooms, and visitor offices. These areas typically have the highest level of detail and finishes.
2. The lawyer environment, primarily lawyer offices located on the perimeter window wall in a typical office building.
3. The support personnel environment, including space for paralegals and legal secretaries.

4. Space for all other support functions, such as library, accounting, information technology, human resources, and administrative functions and staff.

Once we have the idea to do a law office project, we need to be able to sell the concept to other people. Whether the idea is to investigate the need for an expanded office or to go full-bore to house a new office by a deadline, we need a package of information that tells people what we would like to accomplish, and whether the project makes economic sense. In addition to creating marketing information for getting approvals inside and outside the firm, this package saves time for both the firm and the space designer. Ideally, it helps the design professional, engineers, and your builder get more things done right the first time. Whether the project is large enough to require very formal planning documents or small enough to be conveyed verbally, preparation saves money. The same rationale applies to the selection of a new building or to the refurbishing of an existing office.

Later on in this book we look at a substantial building criteria report as we go through the process of locating law office space. The report cumulates information from internal and external sources, and allows comparative studies of available spaces.

There are plenty of things to think about, but we begin with what you need to communicate to people outside the firm, as well as some things that need to be communicated and understood within the firm at an early stage in order to make the project a success.

What Is Driving the Process of Changing Your Office Space?

It is seldom a single issue that results in a desire to change your space. An inventory of the driving forces can help you establish the framework for the project. Your firm's experience and the combined experience of your advisors will guide your vision for the next iteration of your firm. Typically, consider these sorts of issues:

- Practice is just starting
- Upcoming lease expiration
- Firm has too much space
- Firm has run out of space
- Lack of space for expansion
- Increase in rent cost
- Need to become more space efficient
- Existing space is "tired" (needs renovation)
- Upcoming merger or acquisition

- Upcoming spin-off
- Need for a satellite office

Growth Patterns and Work Patterns Within the Firm

These patterns affect the use of your firm's space. The past few years have seen very significant changes in the way law firms use lawyers and staff, and the way they bill for their services. Your new space should accommodate recent changes and be flexible enough to handle expected changes with plenty of room for adjustments along the way. Consider, for example:

- Increasing associate to partner ratios
- Increasing lawyer to secretary ratios
- Increasing use of paralegals and more effective use of paralegals
- New profit centers
- New client base
- Redirecting support and overhead costs
- Outsourcing administrative tasks
- Moving administrative functions to administrative floor or off site
- Reevaluating internal support functions
- Reorganizing by practice group
- Keeping things flexible
- Adopting a one-size office policy
- Using standard-issue furniture

External Factors and Longer-Term Business Projections

These will be important to your designer as you search for the appropriate space for your office. Share as much information with your project team as you can. Consider such factors as economics, neighborhood changes, personnel projections, and overhead cost control.

Competition strategies and economics need to be clearly articulated. Your need to serve specific clients, groups, or geographic areas should trigger research and investigation by members of your project team. This will likely affect your choice of building type, style, and technology, whether you are a solo lawyer working out of a home office with a laptop, a larger firm developing extranets to support work for specific clients, or an international practice centralizing support functions for a multioffice firm.

Neighborhood and building changes provide reasons to leave, as well as opportunities to expand into contiguous or nearby space. The arrival or departure of a client base in the area or other tenants' exercise of options on space in your building can present problems or opportunities for the firm and your project team.

Long-term personnel projections help your space planner figure out how much building space you need. Changes or developments in the partnership structure of your firm are important indicators of the type and location of office space and support space necessary to carry out your plan. An egalitarian trend in the firm may promote such things as one-size offices and standardized furniture.

Overhead cost control has led to some distinct changes in the way law firms operate, and one of the most significant is moving support functions to less-expensive space. Off-site storage and document management are common solutions to the high cost of office space. "Out-spacing" (moving selected support functions or departments off site), digital imaging, space sharing, and other techniques discussed in Chapter 5 provide some relief by targeting the functions that do not require high-cost space and are not frequented by clients or the public.

What Image Do You Want to Portray?

Who are we? Analyzing, articulating, and portraying the image you want to project helps you establish the personality of your firm and its home. It is easy to confuse the quality level of finishes with the firm's image, but even the dress-for-success books tell us that the cost-neutral choices we make for many aspects of our appearance have predictable effects on other people. In the twenty-first century, there is no standard look for law firms, so we need to be sure that the image we create affects people in the desired way, and this analysis should happen long before we develop our budget.

If there is one factor that should influence your style and image, it is your firm's relationship with your clients. Your clients should see their expectations of quality legal services reflected in your offices. What should your office say about your firm? As you work with your advisors on the look of your offices, you will find it much easier to convey your wishes about the characteristics and the feel of your offices if you have developed a general concept of the message you want to present. If it is a difficult matter for you to verbalize the way your offices should represent you, consider other law offices you have visited. Imagine the way you think other offices must appear to their clients, and how they would appear to your intended audience. Depending on the attitudes of your clientele, you may want to consider one or more of these common image types for your description:

- Lean and mean image
  - Downgraded finishes in lawyer areas
  - Solo or small firm in shared office suite building
  - Spartan public areas

- o Firm appears to be active
- o No library
- Cutting-edge image
  - o Attracts a younger and less-staid client base
  - o Uses latest technology
  - o Better for a younger-aged group of partners
- Corporate image
  - o Solid, established base that can handle all of clients' needs
  - o Conference facilities available to corporate clients
  - o Firm facilities on an equal level with the image its corporate clients portray to their clientele
- Comforting image
  - o Appropriate for concentration in trusts, wills, estates
  - o Reassuring to aging clientele
  - o Clients meet with lawyers in an environment that resembles their own living rooms
- Neighborhood lawyer image
  - o Located for convenience of clientele
  - o For clients who are intimidated by going downtown
  - o Not out to impress
  - o Gives a warm, friendly feeling
- Legal services office image
  - o "Public official" style
  - o Accommodates broad range of ages

Within each of these types of images, you can have a variety of design styles: traditional, transitional, contemporary, or eclectic. Whatever image you want your firm's offices to project, consider the cost of maintaining it. Like a dress code, the quality design features of a law office can fade in effectiveness over time, so your commitment to maintaining your chosen image may require some reinforcement as time passes. In our chapter on moving, we offer some suggestions for maintaining a commitment to quality in appearance, regardless of the style you adopt.

Organizing for Decision Making

2

Establishing the Team

The firm needs to select a building committee to be responsible for the hard work of planning and executing the project, and to represent the firm's interests as members of the project team. The project team is made up of the representatives of the firm, the design professionals, and the consultants and advisors who make decisions, provide communication for the project, and keep the project on track. On the law firm side, the team typically consists of an executive director, administrative manager, legal administrator or office manager, and several partners representing a broad cross section of the firm. This could be a partner from each of the firm's practice groups, or it could be the senior members who have the most ownership. It is good to have one or two younger members to bring fresh perspective to today's law firm planning.

Delegating Authority

The committee needs to be empowered by the partnership to have full representation of the firm. The firm needs to expressly delegate this authority to the committee. One person should be charged to head up this committee. This job takes a lot of time, so often the committee head is an administrator so that billable time is not lost.

Making Everyone Feel Involved

Up and down the organization, ask people in the firm to send e-mails to the head of the building committee with a list of five things that they do not like about the existing space, and five things that they would like to see in the new space. Everyone in the firm knows something that would make the firm work better.

Organizing the Team

At this earliest point the firm needs to hire a design professional. This design professional should be a licensed, degreed individual or firm, either an interior designer or an architect. Find someone with *plenty* of law firm planning experience. Learning about law firms takes a long time, and you do not want someone going to school on your project while doing their first law firm design.

Start with eight or ten design firms. Have them make twenty-to-thirty-minute presentations in your offices, showing you examples of their law firm work and presenting their qualifications for your project. Shorten your list to about three candidates. Then have the remaining candidates do a one-hour presentation. In this longer presentation, the designers have more time to show you what they can do for your firm. By the time these presentations have been made, you should have a lot of information for comparing the candidates and their approaches to your project. Before you hire a designer, visit some of their law firm projects and talk with the legal administrators of those projects.

Design fees today can range anywhere from $1 per square foot up to $9 per square foot, depending on the complexity and the timing. The lowest rate might buy you advice on carpet colors and finishes, whereas the other extreme includes the full range of services described in this book. As we write this, full services generally cost about $5 to $10 per square foot. Design fees are affected by the size of the project and by the number of consultants used. Drawings for design services are required to be stamped by a licensed, degreed professional, so this is not the sort of job to be done in-house by the law firm.

The other consultant to be brought on board at this time is the broker or brokerage firm who represents the firm's real estate issues. Some firms elect not to use a broker because they feel that a partner in their real estate department can perform this service. One thing to keep in mind is that this takes many, many hours of legwork and negotiations that take away a partner's billable time. Brokers also know local buildings, are aware of comparable rental rates, and know the landlords. Brokers are paid by the landlord, so their costs are never apparent to the client. They typically get 4.5 percent of every penny of rent that you pay over the life of the lease.

An additional member of the team may be added at this point: a manager who represents the interests of the firm in quickly settling issues that arise among the players. Known as an owner's representative or an owner's construction manager, this is someone whose interest in the project is to keep the project on track and on time and to interpret the firm's interests when issues and disputes arise during the construction process. The practice of a law firm using an owner's construction manager is more prevalent in some areas of the United States than in others, but there are many who consider a construction manager to be essential, especially when the firm's administrator lacks the time to devote to such a big project. The firm needs to be represented in construction meetings and in settling issues that affect timing, budgets, and other matters. It is not unusual for one of the firm's lawyers on the building committee to attend construction meetings. The lawyer generally has more fiscal authority than an owner's representative would have, so issues can be solved more quickly with a lawyer committee member present. Firms that do not use a construction manager generally rely on a stronger presence from the design professional for administration of the construction process. For these firms, hiring a design professional with considerable experience in construction and contract administration is crucial. The construction contract itself is critical for settling disputes and establishing authority for resolving issues.

Legal Representation

Most firms agree that the best practice for legal representation is to hire outside counsel for a building project. Find people with relevant experience in the varied aspects of commercial real estate leases, contracting, work letter negotiation, and construction issues. In most cases, this amounts to two specialists, one for the real estate issues and another for the work letter and construction issues. In the rare instance that your firm might be able to spare the time and talents of a lawyer with this sort of background, consider the effect of diverting his or her efforts away from your clients. Keep your own lawyer billable and out of the nearly inevitable political issues that arise within the firm when inside lawyers are assigned to the project.

Visiting Other Firms

After your design professional is hired, the first thing you should do is tour other law firms for the purpose of getting ideas about your preferences and dislikes. Your designer can offer tours of his or her projects, or you may have favorite law firms that you would like to compare. Your partners on the committee should talk to partners of other law firms or administrators to set up

. We highly recommend that you tour approximately ten law nmittee and the designer should be the people taking the tour. ally be met by the administrator, executive director, or a part- that they are visiting.

The following is a checklist of things to observe and write down during a tour. When you set up the tour, ask the other firm for permission to take digital photos.

- Layout of offices by practice group
- Size of lawyer offices
- Location of secretaries to lawyers
- Location of secretaries, lawyers, and paralegals to each other
- Size and height of secretarial stations
- Acoustics at the secretarial units
- Storage within the secretarial unit
- Size of paralegal offices
- Type of paralegal space (private office or work station)
- Size of paralegal space, furniture, built-ins, systems furniture
- Technology
- Use of wireless versus hardwired network
- Phone system location
- Number of printers
- Acoustics
- Lighting
- Ceiling
- Design style or design features
- Design features within the space
- Use of wood or stone
- Materials
- Furniture
- Carpet
- Colors
- Wall coverings
- Durability of finishes
- Upgrading of flooring finishes
- Security in the reception area
- Method of vertical transportation (for multifloor firm)
- Employee lounge
- Satellite coffee area and coffee bars
- Catering pantry or food service
- Method of soft-drink dispensing
- Use of centralized or decentralized filing

- Method of litigation filing (files in lawyer offices, paralegal offices, or secretarial stations)
- How much outsourcing is done by this firm
- What functions (if any) they have taken off site
- Project workrooms
- Project workroom layout
- Library
- Use of high-density shelving
- Number of carrels versus the number of tables
- Name of general contractor
- Name of millwork contractor
- Would they recommend these contractors again?
- Length of their office construction project
- What they would do and not do again

Most firms are not willing to give out detailed costs, but they may be willing to give a range, such as whether the build-out cost was between $60 and $70 per square foot or $70 to $80 per square foot. If you do not feel comfortable asking these questions, consider other firms who might share their information.

Immediately after the tour, even while you are riding down the elevator, record your reactions, both positive and negative. The reason to record them right away is that after you have seen a couple of firms they will start running together in your mind. It is very important to record as much as possible as quickly as possible, so a hand-held recorder may be useful for a recap after each tour.

Budgets and Schedules

A Realistic Estimate

The three main concerns of projects—the price, the timing, and the project quality—are enemies of each other. Speedy construction costs more and it forces expediencies that detract from the quality. To keep costs down, lead times need to be longer and the amenities fewer. As for quality of the project, it comes from better designs, better materials, and enough time to do things the right way.

As we write this, a typical law firm build-out costs from $60 to well over $100 per square foot. A low-end build-out is from $35 to $45, a moderate one is $45 to $65, and a high-end build-out costs from $70 to over $100 per square foot. These figures, of course, vary by geographic areas; New York City, for example, can easily be 20 percent higher. These build-out prices are for construction costs only, and include walls, ceiling, finishes, lighting, mechanical, electrical, and plumbing. This does not include furniture costs, fees, or costs for computer equipment. It may or may not include cabling. Materials costs fluctuate, and they have a significant effect on overall cost. We examine budgets more thoroughly in Chapter 7.

The firm typically does not have to immediately absorb 100 percent of build-out costs. The landlord may contribute substantially to those costs, which are amortized in the rent over the life of the lease. This is an area where a broker can be very helpful in negotiating what the landlord pays.

A Realistic Schedule

Ideally, you should have about thirty-six to forty-eight months for a medium-sized law firm. This would be from the start of programming to move-in.

Projects can be done on fast-track basis. A one-floor law firm could conceivably be planned and built out in a year. Fast track is about six months. The faster the project has to go, the more expensive it will be, with more chances for hiccups along the way. We cannot urge you strongly enough to budget enough time so that the job can go at a normal pace.

We have had overnight projects where suddenly a law firm opened an office in another city, because another firm disbanded and they were looking to acquire people in that vicinity. So, yes, you can do it. Using rental furniture and a good broker who can find you immediate space, you could literally establish an office in a few days.

In any case, a law firm project goes through distinct phases, following a necessary process to produce its result.

An Overview of the Planning and Building Process

3

This chapter gives you a concise look at the whole process of conceiving, locating, designing, and building your law office, as well as a time frame for the work.

The purpose of this section is to identify all stages of the project, to present the order in which the stages occur, to identify the deliverable products, and to explain who is generally responsible for what. We mention some of these phases in other chapters, and focus here on those that we do not cover in depth elsewhere in the book.

A law firm project requires five distinct phases.

Phase I: Project Requirements

The critical first phase consists of defining the objectives, creating the program, finding the space, negotiating the lease and work letter, and executing the lease. Because this is the phase where the law firm needs to do its analyses and make the decisions that drive the project, we have devoted several chapters to covering these issues in detail. Our brevity at this stage should not be taken as a lack of emphasis.

The deliverables that your design professional should provide in Phase I include the program, test-fit plans of the various buildings being considered, an in-depth building analysis study including an estimate of expected cost, and help in work letter negotiations. Several chapters and exhibits in this book contain examples of these products.

As a general rule, the broker is responsible for finding all available space options, and negotiating and executing the lease and work letter.

Phase II: Schematic Design

This phase is called schematic design or conceptual design. The design professional prepares a conceptual design for the space that the law firm has selected. A conceptual design is by no means cast in stone, and is subject to change. The design professional should bear in mind comments made by the law firm's committee during Phase I when design styles and preferences were discussed. A conceptual design includes a floor plan and organizational elements of the space, such as where and how lawyer files are accommodated. At this stage, the designer prepares a preliminary plan and elevation drawings to illustrate concepts for the reception, conference, and other public areas. The designer likewise illustrates locations and layouts for the core area and administrative functions, as well as for secretarial stations and paralegal offices. The plan proposes layouts of the perimeter window wall for lawyer offices, as well as design elements within the lawyer-secretarial corridor. A schematic design for the reflected ceiling plan (lighting plan) is included. The conceptual plans and drawings should relate the overall feeling that the project is expected to convey. For example, is it traditional, transitional, contemporary, or eclectic? A sampling of furniture forms proposed should also be presented, as well as a conceptual discussion of where art and signage are to be located. An estimated budget for the cost of the design wraps up the package.

A presentation of the design should be made to all members of the committee. Committee members should make every effort to adjust their schedules to attend the full length of the meeting with no interruptions. Sometimes it is best to hold these meetings out of the office in a neutral site such as a hotel conference room.

The committee should have a few days or a week to respond to the design professional's presentation. The landlord may require that the schematic design plans be submitted for review and approval. If this is the case, time needs to be built into the schedule to accommodate this review process, since theoretically the designer cannot proceed to the next step of design (design development) without these approvals. It will save some time if the drawings are issued to the landlord at the same time they are issued to the contractor for preliminary pricing. We have seen instances where the overall project schedule can increase by six weeks because of the landlord's review process in Phase II, Phase III, and Phase IV.

Phase III: Design Development

This phase of design expands on the design concepts started and presented in Phase II. Assuming that the firm's committee approves the schematic design, the designer refines and further develops the design. It may be beneficial to engage the services of the engineers (mechanical, electrical, plumbing, and structural) at this time, so they can write a preliminary scope of work to enable contractors to price their scope of work. It should be the intent at this stage to have one general contractor price the preliminary plans. Not surprisingly, these are referred to as the preliminary pricing plans. A contractor usually performs these services for no monetary reward, although he gains an opportunity to become very familiar with the project before it goes out for final pricing, which helps him prepare for the competition. If the contractor has already been established, try to negotiate this free preliminary pricing. Preliminary pricing is something that you can not absolutely count on, but it is usually within 15 to 20 percent of the final pricing.

The design professional should submit the following information in drawings and schedules for preliminary pricing:

- Partition types, door and frame types, hardware
- Ceiling, floor, wall, and base finishes
- Typical electrical and voice/data outlets
- Quantities and locations of equipment (appliances and plumbing fixtures that the contractor is to provide)
- Typical lighting layouts, including a lighting schedule
- Manufacturers and model numbers
- Location of built-in millwork and case goods
- Materials for the millwork (plastic laminate, stained wood, or painted wood)
- Pertinent details that affect pricing

Approximately two weeks should be allowed for the contractor to perform the preliminary pricing, depending on the scope of the project. Another three or four days may be needed to assimilate this into a meaningful budget format.

In addition to the architectural design concepts, the furniture and free-standing millwork designs should be presented at this stage. This includes secretarial stations, reception desks, reception area furniture, and administrative area furniture. Typically this furniture budget includes all furniture except partner offices, unless the firm has decided to provide new furniture for partners as well.

Phase IV: Contract Documentation

The purpose of this phase is to finalize the contract documents, issue them for pricing, and to award contracts.

The firm needs to determine whether the project is to be bid or negotiated. At this stage, determine which general contractors are qualified and interested in the project, and determine what form of contract and general conditions are to be used.

At this stage, the design professional continues to develop the drawings that were started in the previous phases. The designer completes power and communication plans, including locations of all equipment items, the reflected ceiling plan, a partition plan indicating all partition types and plumbing locations, finish plans indicating all ceiling types, furniture plans indicating all furniture layouts, the equipment schedule, the lighting schedule, and the plumbing schedule. These are issued to the mechanical, electrical, and plumbing (MEP) engineers for the project. Any areas requiring floor loading or structural modifications for stairways or dumbwaiters are issued to the structural engineers. It is beneficial to have a kick-off meeting with the engineers a few days after issuing them the plans.

The law firm should also review the design professional's drawings when they are about 50 percent complete, and again at 100 percent.

Over the course of the next few weeks to a few months (depending on the scope of the project), the designer and engineers complete the drawings and written specifications. There will probably be several different packages of drawings and specifications issued, depending on the type of work. These may include the following:

- General construction
- Trades with contracts separately held by the law firm (rather than being under the general contractor's contract), such as:
  o Freestanding loose millwork
  o Cabling
  o Paging system
  o Audiovisual
- Furniture
- Library shelving

- Moveable shelving
- Window coverings
- Special floor coverings (area rugs)
- Signage and graphics
- Plantings and plant containers
- Artwork
- Accessories
- Telephone system
- Computer hardware
- Reproduction equipment

The drawings and specifications that should be issued for pricing include

- Site plans (if required)
- Demolition plans (if applicable)
- Partition plans
- Reflected ceiling plans
- Power and communication plans
- Finish plans
- Enlarged plans to illustrate details
- Elevations
- Details/sections
- Schedules: equipment, reflected ceiling, finish, plumbing, hardware, doors, door frames, accessories
- Specialty items such as stairs, restrooms, etc.
- Furniture plans
- Electrical lighting plans
- Electrical power plans
- Mechanical plans
- Plumbing plans
- MEP schedules and details
- Structural plans
- Written specifications for all sections represented in the drawings

The bid form should include all alternates that the contractors are being asked to price (see the examples in Exhibit 3.1).

After the drawings have been issued for pricing and about a week before pricing is due, the design professional, MEP engineers, landlord representative, and the law firm should have a pre-bid meeting, preferably at the site where the project is to be built. All general contractors as well as all subcontractors should be invited and should be present. Provide a sign-in sheet. A statement of quality-level expectations and schedule should be discussed. Questions should be addressed at this time. Later, meeting notes should be sent to all attendees indicating answers that were verbally given to the questions asked at the meeting.

After pricing is received, a bid analysis needs to be compiled by either the design professional or the law firm's representative. Questions should be raised when there are disparate bids. Many variables and questions can occur here that are unique to the project.

At this point you may want to narrow competitors to a short list of two general contractors. Their representative work should be toured and references should be checked.

Contracts are awarded and signed, and the general contractor issues the drawings for permit.

Phase V: Contract Administration

This phase of the project deals with building the space, controlling the process and cost issues, and moving and post-move issues.

Construction is often a process of argumentative finger-pointing and delays. You should go into it knowing that a paper trail needs to be established in case there is a formal dispute resolution farther down the road.

At the beginning of this phase, a preconstruction meeting should take place. This meeting is to review the administrative process of how paperwork is handled in this phase, and to discuss the schedule and lead times of materials.

Construction Meetings

Construction meetings should be scheduled on a weekly basis. Before the meeting, the job site (the area where construction is taking place) should be walked and weekly progress noted in a field report prepared by the design professional. The construction meeting should be attended by the design professional, law firm representative, the general contractor's project manager and superintendents, subcontractors, and (when necessary) the MEP and structural engineers, cabling vendor, and audiovisual vendor. The agenda of the weekly meeting should include:

- Review of the meeting notes from the previous meeting. These meeting notes are prepared by the general contractor and issued via e-mail to all attendees before the next meeting.
- Old business.
- Review of request for information (RFI) log. Contractors issue RFIs in writing to the design professional or engineers, asking for information that they cannot interpret from the drawings or specifications. An RFI could be about an unexpected field condition where the contractor is

looking for direction in how to handle the situation. The response should be given in writing and in a timely manner so as not to slow or interrupt construction.

- Review of item of change (IOC) log. IOCs become directives to the contractor to change something due to a conflict, or because the law firm wants to change something. IOCs are assigned consecutive numbers and are logged. Periodically, several IOCs are lumped into a change order, which is a vehicle for changing the price of the contract.

- Review of submittal and shop drawing log. All materials used on the project are submitted to the design professional or engineers for review and comment to insure that they match the design intent. The subcontractors first submit them to the general contractor, who then checks them for accuracy with field conditions, compatibility and interface with other trades' work, compliance with codes, and compliance with the design intent. Examples are paint, carpet, wall covering, stone, millwork, ceiling materials, hardware, special finishes, electrical, mechanical, and plumbing. In addition, many subcontractors are required to submit shop drawings. These drawings show more detail and means and methods than the designer's drawings. These are the drawings from which the items are actually manufactured. Examples are millwork, stone, plastic laminate case goods, and structural steel. The design professional or engineers have ten working days to review these submittals and shop drawings and return them to the general contractor. The submittals and shop drawings are either returned to the contractor as approved, approved as noted, revise and resubmit, or rejected. If the subcontractor has to resubmit the drawings, it must be done in a timely manner so as not to affect the project schedule. The submittal process can take a few weeks to a few months and can affect the project schedule, so timely submittals are critical.

- Review of material lead time. Material lead time has a direct effect on the project schedule. For example, if a manufacturer cannot ship the product until four weeks after it is needed on the job site, what are the solutions?

- Review of any outstanding change orders. Change orders are the paperwork that amends the contract price. Change orders need to be priced, reviewed, and responded to in a timely manner so as not to disrupt the schedule.

- Review of application for payment. Every month the contractor submits an application for payment. Each application is based on work completed that month, and materials that may be in storage for the project. The application is reviewed by the design professional and submitted to the owner, who then has a given number of days (a previously agreed-upon amount of time) to submit payment. This all has to happen like clockwork so that subcontractors do not walk off the job because they are not being paid. Typically, contractors submit a lien release for previous work for which they have been paid.

- Review of current schedule. The schedule needs to be updated by the contractor and reviewed on a weekly basis. If something falls short that week, it needs to be immediately remedied. Waiting a month is too late.
- Pre-move status. As the project gets closer to completion, areas requiring early move-in need to be closely tracked. For example, the librarian wants to move in a week before the firm is scheduled to move. How is the construction progress in that area? Will it be cleaned and ready to receive the library shelving?
- Move status. The move-in date needs to be carefully monitored. There are too many players involved to treat this lightly.

Punch List

At the end of construction, the general contractor should prepare a punch list of all incomplete or unsatisfactory work and give the list to the subcontractors for them to correct their work. Following this, the design professional prepares a punch list of unsatisfactory work. The subcontractors are given a specific period of time in which to correct their work. The reality of this process is that the punch list is done just before move-in, and the subcontractors have to come back outside of business hours to complete or repair their work.

Post-move Problems

After move-in, there will be issues that need attention. Someone's office is too hot; someone else's is cold; another person has trouble with the door lock. The law firm staff should be given a page in the move-in book where they can respond to items that may or may not have appeared on the designer's punch list. This list should be e-mailed to the law firm's representative, and then collectively sent to the general contractor.

Project Closeout

About two to three months after move-in, it is time to have a project close-out meeting with the contractor. At this time the contractor should have completed all punch list items, and the subcontractors should have prepared "as-built" drawings that show if any work was not installed according to the contract drawings. This is especially true of any MEP work, so that if maintenance is required on something such as a variable air volume (VAV) box, the base building engineer or janitor can see that the VAV was really installed over room 2204, not room 2210 as the drawing indicates. The contractor should provide three sets of the closeout materials. The firm keeps one, one is sent to the landlord, and the third is sent to the designer. The project closeout materials should also include all maintenance and warranty information. Examples are millwork maintenance guidelines from the manufacturer, or the maintenance operations guide for the ice maker.

Warranty

The contractor should warrant the work for a minimum of one year, or according to the contract specifications. Just before the one-year period ends, the design professional should do a walk-through of the space to determine if items need to be adjusted and if products are performing as intended.

Exhibit 3.1
BID ANALYSIS

SAMPLE BID ANALYSIS					
Item No.	Description	Company A		Company B	
Division 1	General Conditions	$ 68,947.00		$ 75,521.00	
Section 01010	Floor Stoning/ Grinding	$ 12,000.00	Allowance	$ 120,000.00	
Section 02060	Selective Demolition			$ 25,000.00	
Section 05500	Metal Fabrication	$ 18,000.00			
Section 06100	Rough Carpentry	$ 8,792.00		$ 3,500.00	
Section 06400	Architectural Woodwork	$ 618,553.00	Subcontractor (name)	$ 661,553.00	
Section 07951	Joint Sealants				
Section 08116	Aluminum Door Frames	$ 8,091.00		$ 2,705.00	
Section 08700	Hardware	$ 25,860.00		$ 29,043.00	
Section 09210	Glass Reinforced Gypsum		W/09260	$ 22,705.00	
Section 09260	Gypsum Wallboard Systems	$ 160,798.00	Subcontractor	$ 191,279.00	
Section 09510	Acoustical Ceilings	$ 60,593.00	Subcontractor	$ 19,164.00	
Section 09520	Acoustical Wall Treatment	$ 93,042.00	Subcontractor	$ 78,460.00	
Section 09610	Interior Stone and Tile	$ 212,742.00	Subcontractor	$ 212,742.00	
Section 09650	Resilient Flooring		W/09680	$ 1,350.00	
Section 09680	Carpeting	$ 50,769.00	Subcontractor	$ 49,419.00	
Section 09900	Painting	$ 68,128.00	Subcontractor	$ 29,090.00	
Section 09950	Wallcovering		W/09900	$ 44,100.00	
Section 10150	Marker boards	$ 2,300.00		$ 1,600.00	
Section 11470	Kitchen Equipment	$ 47,000.00	Subcontractor	$ 47,200.00	

Exhibit 3.1 **23**

Exhibit 3.1 Bid Analysis (continued)

Item No.	Description	Company A		Company B	
Section 12306	Plastic Faced Casework	$ 44,290.00	Subcontractor	$ 44,290.00	
Section 15320	Sprinkler System	$ 16,215.00	Subcontractor	$ 16,215.00	
Section 15400	Plumbing	$ 28,434.00	Subcontractor	$ 28,134.00	
Section 15800	HVAC	$ 173,500.00	Subcontractor	$ 173,500.00	
Section 16400	Electrical	$ 200,313.00	Subcontractor	$ 191,515.00	
Section 16720	Fire Alarm System (Smoke Detectors, Fire Speakers, & Fire Strobes)		W/16400	$ 18,754.00	
	Security Allowance	$ 1,800.00		$ 10,100.00	
	Miscellaneous (Indicate)	$ 8,850.00	Blackout Shades	$ 3,049.00	Blackout Shades
	Miscellaneous (Indicate)	$ 990.00	Fire Extinguishers	$ 3,350.00	Relocate Elevator
	Miscellaneous (Indicate)	$ 3,750.00	Elevator Controls	$ 2,000.00	Fireproofing
	Miscellaneous (Indicate)	$ 6,149.00	Permit		
Overhead & Profit	Overhead & Profit	$ 78,247.00		$ 168,507.00	
	TOTAL	$ 2,018,153.00		$ 2,274,845.00	

Item No.	Description	Company A		Company B	
Alternate #1		$ 4,125.00		$ (3,750.00)	
Alternate #2		$ (1,600.00)		$ (1,600.00)	
Alternate #3		$ (38,496.00)		$ (41,850.00)	
Alternate #4		$ (15,646.00)		$ (15,130.00)	
Alternate #5		$ (56,171.00)		$ (54,760.00)	
Alternate #6		$ (93,568.00)		$ (102,481.00)	Painted Walls
Alternate #7		$ (4,879.00)		$ (9,916.00)	
Alternate #8		$ (3,800.00)		$ (3,800.00)	
Alternate #9		$ (57,584.00)		$ (55,623.00)	
Alternate #10		$ (20,143.00)		$ (28,410.00)	
Alternate #11		$ (7,528.00)		$ (8,432.00)	
Alternate #12		$ 24,600.00		$ 18,757.00	

Checklists and Schedule

4

The timing of projects, however truncated, depends on getting things done in the right order and being prepared for the next task. Because this preparation is the most important part of getting your office built within a reasonable time and budget, we place our comprehensive checklist here in a separate chapter near the beginning of the book. In addition to serving as a resource for keeping track of the sequence of tasks, it can serve as a record of progress on your project.

This chapter includes a checklist to provide perspective on the timing, effort, and issues you can expect to face. The checklist is a document you can use throughout your project, and it provides a time-based outline of the contents of this book. The topic of each section is discussed in more depth in subsequent chapters.

A comprehensive checklist is equally important for small and large firms. The time frames given below can be compressed, although we caution against underestimating them.

Phase I: Building Selection, Lease and Work Letter Negotiation

36 to 24 months before move-in (48 to 36 months for large firms); the following can easily take one year:

Checklist Item	Start Date	Complete Date	Who Is Responsible?	Date Completed
1. Establish objectives and goals of the relocation, renovation, or expansion.				
2. Establish budget and schedule objectives.				
3. Determine who will be decision-makers.				
4. Establish committee, their responsibilities and voting power.				
5. Establish subcommittees: secretarial, paralegal, library, etc.				
6. Determine day-to-day contact.				
7. If design professional is involved, prequalify, interview, and select design professional.				
8. If broker is involved, prequalify, interview, and select broker.				
9. Tour existing facilities.				
10. Review lease expiration dates for equipment, copiers, furniture, plants, etc.				
11. Other consultants: technology, telecommunications, office automation, MEP, structural.				
12. Agree to consultants' fees, responsibilities, contracts, and terms of payment.				
13. Arrange tours of other law firms.				
14. Distribute programming questionnaire to selected staff.				
15. Solicit wish list from lawyers and staff.				

Checklist Item	Start Date	Complete Date	Who Is Responsible?	Date Completed
16. Analyze and assess the wish list.				
17. Interview committee and selected staff.				
18. Determine office sizes.				
19. Prepare space program and long-range personnel projections.				
20. Review and comment on preliminary program draft.				
21. Review revised program.				
22. Review options for available space: lease, lease with equity share, build-to-suit, buying a building.				
23. Review building conditions and systems.				
24. Design professional does test fits of available options.				
25. Evaluate building space analysis comparison studies.				
26. Review and update schedule and budget.				
27. Lease and work letter negotiations.				
28. Determine final building.				
29. Fine-tune lease and work letter.				
30. Execute lease.				
31. Obtain loan, if required.				
32. Verify utilities and availability.				

Mistakes firms typically make during this phase:

- Not starting the process soon enough
- Underestimating the time for lease and work letter negotiations
- Underestimating the budget
- Not thinking outside the box (not willing to change the way things are currently done)
- Not dotting your *I*'s and crossing your *T*'s (be sure to leave a paper trail documenting who, what, when, where, and how)
- Not thinking through technology issues soon enough

Phase II: Planning Work Areas, Beginning the Design Process, and Schematic or Conceptual Design

24 to 18 months before move-in (now that a building has been selected):

Checklist Item	Start Date	Complete Date	Who Is Responsible?	Date Completed
1. Re-review building conditions and systems.				
2. Prepare furniture inventory.				
3. Prepare equipment inventory.				
4. Determine and prioritize desirable and undesirable views.				
5. a. Re-review planning considerations				
• Conference center location and requirements				
• Office sizes				
• Offices for retired partners and of counsel				
• Desired location and proximity of secretaries and paralegals to lawyer offices				
• Clustering of offices				
• Identical footprint of offices on each floor?				
• Grouping by practice group				
• Practice groups near which core functions				
• Project workrooms				
• Litigation support				
• Transactional support				
b. Re-review likes and dislikes from law firm tours.				
c. Re-review likes and dislikes of existing space.				
d. Aesthetics				
• Image				
• Design style preference				
• Colors, materials, and finishes preferences				
• New or re-used furniture?				
• Standardization or nonstandardization of individual office furniture				

Checklist Item	Start Date	Complete Date	Who Is Responsible?	Date Completed
e. Technology				
• Electrical capacity				
• Cabling: wireless or hardwired, or both?				
• New versus used systems (telephone, word and data processing, computers, file servers, printers, scanners, fax, copiers, food service, appliances, audiovisual, mail equipment); if new equipment will be used, send out RFPs				
• Temperature control				
• Lighting				
• Security				
• Life safety				
• Review code requirements				
f. Consultant coordination				
• Space planner/designer				
• Technology				
• MEP (select)				
• Structural (select)				
• Building code (select if required)				
g. Administrative support functions				
• On site				
• Off site				
• In less expensive space in building				
• Out-sourcing				
• Relationship to practice groups or individual lawyers				
• Desired adjacencies				
• Special work area needs				
h. Rethink support areas				
• Library				
• Records management (filing)				
• Accounting				
• Information technology				

Checklist Item	Start Date	Complete Date	Who Is Responsible?	Date Completed
• Human resources				
• Food service areas				
• Service center:				
σ Mail				
σ Copy				
σ Deliveries				
σ Messengers and runners				
σ Supplies				
σ Outsourced services				
σ Satellite service centers				
σ Satellite coffee areas				
σ Satellite printing areas				
σ Word processing:				
• Centralized or decentralized				
• On site or off site				
• Outsourced				
σ Backup receptionists				
σ Backup secretaries				
σ Specialized secretaries				
σ Telephone operators				
σ Specialized clerks				
σ Housekeeping staff				
i. Code review				
j. Obtain technical cut sheets from all equipment manufacturers and transmit to designers				
6. Conceptual or schematic design				
a. Relay information to design professional				
b. 33% review with design professional				
c. Update program, and compare program to final plans				
d. 66% review with design professional				
e. Revise and update schedule and budget				
f. Schematic design presentation				

Checklist Item	Start Date	Complete Date	Who Is Responsible?	Date Completed
g. Issue preliminary plans to landlord for review and comment.				
h. Review and comment to design professional about schematic design.				
i. Present plans and budget to partnership.				
7. Issue RFPs for MEP and structural engineering.				

Mistakes firms typically make during this phase:

- Not deciding on equipment needs soon enough (for example, new telephone system or not; new or re-used computer equipment?)
- Not paying enough attention to things designer is presenting, thinking, "Oh, we can change that later." Changes cost money!

Phase III: Design Development and Preliminary Pricing

Checklist Item	Start Date	Completion Date	Who Is Responsible?	Check Here When Complete
1. Consultant coordination				
• Food service (select, if required)				
• Art (select, if required)				
• Acoustical (select, if required)				
• Space planner (designer)				
• MEP				
• Structural				
• Technology				
• Code				
• Audiovisual (if required)				
• Lighting (select, if required)				

Checklist Item	Start Date	Completion Date	Who Is Responsible?	Check Here When Complete
2. Continue design development.				
• Determine what furniture will be reused.				
• Develop new furniture options.				
3. 50% review of design development.				
• Finishes				
• Millwork details				
• Built-ins				
• Typical electrical and voice/data outlets				
• Typical lighting layouts				
• Typical furniture layouts				
• Specialized lighting				
• Specialized conference room features				
• Specialized technology features				
4. Issue for preliminary pricing:				
• General construction: structural upgrades; walls; partitions; doors; frames; hardware; all ceiling, wall and floor finishes; mechanical; electrical, plumbing; appliances; fire and life safety systems				
• MEP and structural outline notes for preliminary pricing				
• Cabling (voice, data, backbone, termina-tions, and testing)				
• Audiovisual equip-ment, electronics, wiring				
• Free-standing millwork				
• Specially designed area rugs				

Checklist Item	Start Date	Completion Date	Who Is Responsible?	Check Here When Complete
• Owner-provided items				
• Update budgets for:				
• Furniture and furnishings				
• Signage, art, plants, accessories				
• Custom work walls in offices				
• Custom reception desk				
• Custom secretarial stations				
• Custom conference tables				
• Custom credenzas				
• Custom podiums				
5. Prepare renderings.				
6. Receive and review preliminary pricing.				
7. Revise budget and schedule.				
8. Final design development presentation to committee.				
9. Review and comments to design team.				
10. Present final design and budget to partnership.				
11. Release design team to continue contract documents.				
12. Landlord coordination				
13. Obtain new telephone numbers.				
14. Confirm mailing address and ZIP code with post office.				
15. Code review				
16. Install mock-ups.				
17. Final sign-off of plans so designers can prepare final working drawings.				

Phase IV: Contract Document Preparation, Bids, and Pricing

20 to 10 months before move-in:

Checklist Item	Start Date	Completion Date	Who Is Responsible?	Check Here When Complete
1. Determine whether the project will be bid or negotiated.				
2. Determine bid list (general contractors).				
3. Determine what contract form and general conditions will be used.				
4. Firm needs to review and approve the following:				
• Issue plans for MEP engineering (lighting, switching, electrical, voice, data outlets, equipment locations, special air-conditioning needs).				
• Issue plans for structural engineering (heavy floor loading, internal stairs).				
• 50% review architectural and MEP plans.				
• Complete working drawings and specifications for all consultants, architectural, MEP, structural.				
• Prepare cabling plans and specifications, and issue for bids.				
• Prepare furniture drawings and specifications, and issue for bids.				

Checklist Item	Start Date	Completion Date	Who Is Responsible?	Check Here When Complete
• Prepare free standing millwork drawings and specifications, and issue for bids.				
• Prepare signage and graphics drawings and specifications, and issue for bids.				
• Prepare plant and plant container drawings and specifications, and issue for bids.				
• Receive and evaluate bids, prepare bid analysis for each contract.				
• File construction documents with city for permit.				
• Award bids, prepare and execute contracts.				
• Revise and update schedule and budget.				
• Present final budget to firm.				

12 to 6 months before move-in:

Checklist Item	Start Date	Completion Date	Who Is Responsible?	Check Here When Complete
5. Firm needs to order (if needed):				
• New telephone system				
• Any other new equipment				
• New furnishings, signage				
• Have weekly in-house meetings if more than one person is responsible for in-house coordination				
• Determine food service vendor				

Phase V: Construction and In-House Coordination

Construction

10 to 6 months before move-in:

Checklist Item	Start Date	Completion Date	Who Is Responsible?	Check Here When Complete
1. Conduct preconstruction meeting with general contractor, all subcontractors and design consultants, cabling contractor, audiovisual contractor, and any other separate contractors.				
2. Establish schedules and means of payment with contractors and vendors.				
3. Review and comment on general contractor's construction schedule.				
4. Revise overall project schedule and budget as required.				
5. Establish time, day, and place for weekly construction meeting, and determine who shall attend.				
6. Obtain current insurance certificates from each subcontractor.				
7. Arrange for storage of materials.				
8. Start construction.				
9. Arrange for insurance on stored materials.				
10. Construction administration begins.				
11. Weekly construction meetings.				
12. Submittals and shop drawings.				

In-House Coordination

10 to 4 months before move-in:

Checklist Item	Start Date	Completion Date	Who Is Responsible?	Check Here When Complete
1. Assign offices.				
2. Determine if electrical or cabling changes are necessary due to office assignments.				
3. Arrange for refinishing or reupholstering of existing furniture.				
4. Develop change-of-address list.				
5. Order new stationery, business cards, and checks.				
6. Order new bank checks.				
7. Prequalify, interview, solicit quotes, and select movers.				
8. Prepare and send newsletters about the move to all personnel (personnel should not be allowed to visit the construction site).				
9. Make parking arrangements at new site.				
10. Schedule and coordinate with all utility providers.				
11. Determine any special new equipment such as high-density movable shelving or library shelving; bid or obtain quotes.				
12. If library is to be downsized, plan systematic removal or disposal of books.				
13. Continue systematic cleaning out and archiving of files.				

Checklist Item	Start Date	Completion Date	Who Is Responsible?	Check Here When Complete
14. Hire move coordinator, if one is to be used.				
15. Order new plants and plant containers.				
16. Select new art.				

Three months before move-in, send out change of address notices.

Trends in Law Firm Designs

5

[handwritten: •build flexibility into your plans to allow room for change
- esp w/ larger firms]

Law firms do not look or function much as they did a short time ago. The changes are reflected in and supported by their new office plans. Trends can change quickly and be reflected in law practice, so we emphasize the need for flexibility in your design and layout. Change always happens: in technology, in clientele, with new business opportunities, with changing regulatory frameworks and a host of other developing issues. The firm's physical needs cannot remain constant. Our chief bit of advice here is to build flexibility into your plans. As you support the newest iteration of your firm, build spaces that support multiple uses and changing technology. The reward for thoughtful building is an extended useful life for the firm's new quarters.

New developments in law firm design often appear first in larger firms. Since they do reflect the needs of the firm's clientele, as well as the economics of competition, smaller firms often find it important to remain aware of new developments that suggest means of maintaining their competitive positions. We often note that smaller firms produce some of the most innovative solutions. For this reason, we believe that mention of trends in law office design may tend to emphasize larger projects, but we see the issues they address as crucial to firms of all sizes.

As you build the conceptual framework for your new office, you may want to consider some of the trends we have observed in recent years. Most of these are occasioned by new requirements for providing services to clients, security concerns, cost savings, and space limitations. Here are some of the most important trends we have noticed.

Access

One Point of Entry

Almost without exception, we are seeing that all law firms want one point of entry and one reception area. Multiple-floor law firms are closing up their existing reception areas, and going with one or two centralized reception areas depending on how many conference floors they have. Visitors can only gain access to the firm through these portals. Keeping the visitors and clients on the conference floor also means that the firm can spend most of its money on that floor and cut back on the amount expended on the lawyer floors.

Vertical Transportation

Almost all multifloor law firms opt for an alternate means of vertical transportation to avoid waiting for the elevators. If they want to communicate within a floor or two, they typically take internal stairways. These internal stairways can be grand staircases. While these are very costly and take up considerable square footage, they also create a substantial architectural element and can be places of valuable social interaction among members of the firm. Fire codes limit the design of internal stairways. However, many firms find that fire stairs can be dressed up quite nicely, and security systems can be put on the doors so that only people with knowledge of the security systems have access into the space.

Offices

One-Size Offices for All Lawyers

In a growing number of firms, we see the establishment of one-size offices for all lawyers. This makes a lot of sense because it eliminates one of the main reasons for changing offices. Combined with the next trend on our list, this saves wear and tear on the office space from moving damage, and saves moving costs and downtime.

Smaller Office Sizes

Another trend is smaller office sizes. In recent years, we have seen a typical partner office size of 15×15 feet and associate office size of 10×15 feet. Rarely do we see (perhaps in only 1 percent of law firms) partner offices that are in the 15×20 foot category. In some cases, rectilinear floor plates mandate corner offices of 15×20 feet. (See the example in Exhibit 12.1.) The exception may be for a managing partner. The reason for smaller offices sizes is that lawyers are not meeting clients in their offices. Firms want client and opposing counsel out of the lawyer environment and into the sequestered conference room environment. We cannot emphasize this preference too much.

Interior Offices for Associates

In some parts of the country, large firms are putting first- and second-year associates into interior offices. However, these interior offices are normally augmented with some type of glazing to allow natural and artificial light to penetrate, even though they lack windows.

Standardized Furnishings

Standardized furnishings are becoming popular for lawyer offices. In a standard-furnishings environment, when people need to change offices for any reason, they simply pack up the contents of their desks and shelves. This cuts down tremendously on the amount of damage to the facility during the move, as well as cutting moving costs and downtime.

Small Visitor Offices

Something else we are seeing (in large firms, it occurs on conference floors) is small visitor offices, approximately eight feet square, with a work surface and electrical outlets, and data connections above the work surface. A visitor office is typically also provided with a small printer. In these spaces, a visiting lawyer can bring in a laptop and plug it in, connect to the Internet, or connect to the firm's network. This eliminates the problem that arises when a visiting lawyer shows up and says he needs an office for a day or so and the receptionist has to scramble to see where there is a vacant office. Visitor offices can also be used for summer clerks.

Food Service   · catering pantry for food staging

Also on conference floors, we see firms having the ability to manage food service. Many meetings continue through lunch, and to make them more productive, firms have caterers bring in food. This food needs to be staged in what we call a catering pantry. Depending on the size and number of people, these catering pantries can have facilities where the food can come in 75 percent complete, and only the presentation and plating of the food are done there. The food must be kept cool or warm as required.

Silent Serveries

Food service is made effective and unobtrusive by what we call silent serveries. This is a counter in a conference room that has some type of door on the front and back sides. If the conferees are in the front side of the conference room, the front doors are in the closed position. The caterer then comes into the room behind, opens the back set of doors, does the food service layout, and closes the doors. When the meeting is ready to break for lunch, the conferees open the doors (mechanically, electrically, or manually) and the food is presented buffet style. After the meal is completed, the meeting participants return their dirty plates and utensils to that same area, and the doors are then closed. The catering person comes in, opens the doors on the back side, clears away the dishes, lays out the afternoon beverages and snacks, and closes the doors. At break time, the conference-side doors are opened again and everything is set up for the conferees.

Preparing Food On Site

Many larger firms are even preparing food on site, providing three meals a day, seven days a week. The cost of the meals is typically offset in part by the firm. One caterer told us that it takes a firm of about one hundred thousand square feet to break even on this.

Conference Rooms

Clustering Conference Rooms

We see a new tendency in law firms to cluster conference rooms, meaning either that conference rooms are clustered around the reception area for a small firm or on an entire conference floor for large firms. We still see that there are approximately two conference rooms on typical lawyer floors. These conference rooms are likely to be nearest the elevator lobby in case a lawyer wants to take some people to the floor where his office is located. The conference floors that we have designed, however, tend to have support spaces for secretaries and for office machines and hardware. On conference floors we are also seeing several conference rooms set up as what we call "smart" conference rooms. A smart conference room has discreetly built into it a small copier, fax, small printer, and smart conference tables. The tables have electrical and voice/data lines wired into them to enable people to use their laptops during meetings and get online to their networks through hard-wired connections or wireless data points.

To determine the number of conference rooms a law firm needs, we know of two rules of thumb. The first is that you need one conference room seat for every lawyer. Conference room sizes can be staggered so that varying sizes of groups can be accommodated. This approach works for a large firm but probably falls short for a small firm. The second rule of thumb is to have one conference room for every six to nine lawyers.

In many low- to mid-rise buildings, conference complexes can be accommodated on the ground floor. This keeps all visitors off the lawyer floors.

Multipurpose Rooms

[handwritten: / w/ flexible partitions]

Some conference floors also have multipurpose rooms, which are large enough to accommodate all the partners. In a larger firm, these could be arranged either in classroom-style seating or theater-style seating. Some can be flexibly partitioned into two or more rooms. Technology has come a long way with the systems for physically dividing these rooms, so consider newer systems in your planning. Rather than the old clumsy partitions that came out of pockets in walls and required a five-hundred-pound gorilla to move, you can now push a button and a partition comes out of the ceiling to divide these rooms and provide an ample acoustical seal.

Lounge-Type Area

Something else that is cropping up on conference floors is a lounge-type area where visiting lawyers can go either before or after their meetings. A typical visiting lawyer lounge may have three or four small cubicles. It is akin to something you would see in an airline lounge area in an airport. It also has some soft seating. Visitors can check their e-mail and return voice mail messages. There may be a concierge or multitasking person who sits in this area to assist people with travel arrangements and reservations. This person may also be a backup receptionist or the person who escorts people to conference rooms.

Administrative Areas

Administrative Functions

[handwritten: cut cost on administrative func]

A trend for multiple-floor firms is to put administrative functions on an administrative floor where the build-out cost can be greatly reduced, or to design the administrative floor into a lower and less-expensive elevator bank. Some firms are even moving administrative functions off site to much less expensive space. They are also out-sourcing more administrative functions.

Office Services Area

Another trend is to keep the office services area out of the mix of typical lawyer floors, either putting it on an administrative floor, the ground floor, or into a basement area. This keeps all of the messengers, delivery people, and bike couriers out of the main reception area.

Policies, Technology, and Your Building Requirements

Firm policies of all sorts affect building requirements. Here are some sample policy issues where early decisions can save expenses or allow better use of the space.

- Institute policies about who washes office cups or glasses. Some firms make everyone responsible for his or her own. This only requires a sink and running water. Another approach is to have a dishwasher that runs at least once a day. Determine who is responsible for running, loading, and unloading it. *DW vs no DW*
- Encourage firm interaction at all levels. Some firms use a special multi-purpose room specifically for this beneficial activity. They consider the additional square footage to be well worth the cost.
- Establish meal and break policies. For example, are employees allowed to eat at their desks, in their offices, or in their workstations? This has a space impact. If the answer is no, provide space for them to eat. Not everyone can eat out every day, and there may be limited lunch facilities nearby. Remember, if employees have to leave the building to find a lunch place, chances are they will be gone longer than if they eat inside in a designated area. Will lawyers eat in a staff employee lounge, or will a separate one be provided? *Lounge or Breakroom or not?*
- Most facilities in the U.S. are now smoke-free environments inside; however, some law firms represent foreign clients who consider it insulting if they are not allowed to smoke while in a long meeting. If smoking is going to be allowed anywhere, make provisions to install a *ducted* exhaust fan. If the fan is not ducted to an outside source (for example, through the toilet exhaust system), it will merely be dumped into the plenum and dispersed throughout the floor. *smoking → ducted exhaust fan*

In all sizes of firms, technology plays a substantial role in trends toward greater security, communications, and information-handling systems, which have significant effects upon building requirements. Technology is covered in Chapter 9.

Determining Your Square Footage Requirements

6

The next three chapters are about gearing up for your decision making, finding a space that works, and getting a favorable lease in place. Planning any size of law firm relocation or existing space evaluation begins with drafting a program of the firm's requirements for every kind of space. The program or space requirements report guides your decisions about choosing and modifying space for a firm or office. And, of course, larger firms need more-sophisticated planning programs in order to keep from magnifying small mistakes or getting into unsuitable buildings and disadvantageous leases. In this chapter we talk about the following:

- Refining project goals and objectives as an element of executing, marketing, and financing the project
- Beginning the process: building and adding to the team
- Establishing project requirements in the program or space requirements report

Establish Your Goals

Our first objective is to refine and record goals of the project. Develop one or two sentences that define each of the goals we list here. Your carefully drafted statements are to be used in the space requirements report so that everyone is on the same page and in agreement. For your firm, explain your goals for:

- **Overall image.** See Chapter 1.
- **Tenancy.** Will the firm lease, own, or have an equity interest?

- **Location of building.** Will the firm be in the central business district, near courthouses, or in a suburban setting?
- **Type of building.** Will the building be Class A, Class B, old historic, or high rise?
- **Economics.** Will the firm pay expenses beyond the landlord's allowance. If so, how much?
- **Schedule.** When must the move be completed?
- **Technology.** Are new hardware or software systems planned? (See Chapter 3 for the implications of early planning for technology.) What new equipment is planned? What existing equipment will be reused? Develop an equipment inventory as this can affect space requirements. (Exhibit 6.1 is a sample an equipment inventory form.) Equipment and technology choices have significant effects on sizes and configurations of space in a building.
- **Furnishings.** Will existing furniture be reused or will new furniture be purchased? If existing will be reused, develop a furniture inventory (it could affect the size of work areas, conference rooms, and reception area). An example of a furniture inventory form is in Exhibit 6.2. You also need your furniture inventory for insurance purposes.

Building and Adding to the Team

It may be appropriate to add additional consultants to the team at this point.

MEP engineer. You may want to pay for the services of a mechanical, electrical, and plumbing engineer to review and evaluate the MEP systems of the buildings that are under final consideration to be sure that the buildings can accommodate the firm's requirements. For example: a large law firm decided to move their computer room to the basement of the large high rise they occupied. Upon further investigation, the MEP engineers determined that the base building lacked adequate power to accommodate the client's needs. The solution was to go directly to the local power company to see how and if additional electrical capacity could be brought into the existing building.

Structural engineer. A structural engineer may need to be hired to review and evaluate floor loading in buildings under final consideration, to be certain they can accommodate high-density loads such as libraries and file rooms.

For example, if moveable shelving will be used in those areas, it may be worthwhile to know if the building is a concrete structure, since the ramifications may be space constrictive. Concrete buildings usually must have steel beams placed on top of the existing slab, with a floor built on top of that. This can take a foot or more out of the slab-to-ceiling height. No furniture or equipment can be closer to the ceiling than eighteen inches. This means you could be forced to change from shelving with seven openings to shelving with six or even five openings. Plus, there is space required for an accessibility ramp.

Steel buildings typically can be reinforced with steel beams or plates below the beams so as not to interfere with ceiling heights. But be aware that you would have to get into the ceiling of the space below for such modifications; verify who and what is down there to be sure you can have access. (See the library section in Chapter 13 for an explanation of some serious issues in using compact or movable shelving and for using shelving in areas of restrictive ceiling clearance.)

Technology consultant. A firm may decide to hire a technology consultant to review and analyze existing hardware and software systems and communications systems. This is the time to review accounting, time and billing systems, and the firm's approach to knowledge management. Consider outsourcing these functions as appropriate, and consider your changing needs for staffing and staff space.

Security consultant. The firm may decide that security is a high-priority goal in their new or existing space, and may wish to hire a security consultant.

Food service consultant. If the firm decides that food service within their space is something they want to carry to higher limits, a food service consultant may be required.

The Program or Space Requirements Report

Establishing the amount and type of space that the firm needs is essential. Space requirements are associated with each of the above issues.

The data gathering process (programming) necessary for the production of a space requirements report is often, for the law firm, a soul-searching experience in which tough questions of growth and policy must be resolved. It is a period of concentrated effort requiring the expertise of the design professional and the firm. Your designer is prepared to raise the issues that affect your choice of building and control its design.

Although the goals of the project should provide direction for its duration, the program is never static. It will change during the course of the data gathering process and most likely change again as the design phases proceed.

The program establishes work space standards (square footage) for each of the firm's personnel positions, determines required square footage for ancillary functions, inserts an add-on factor for circulation, and comes up with the square footage required in the incremental years that correspond with the move-in date and lease-expansion date. Beyond square footage considerations, the program elicits the firm's needs for all of the characteristics of each space, such as its needs for filing, storage, power and communications, equipment, adjacencies, lighting, and finishes.

Begin a data-gathering process. Walk and review the law firm's existing space. Determine what works and what needs to be changed or improved upon. Solicit suggestions from other lawyers and staff members. They will appreciate being asked. Have them e-mail five things they like about the existing space and five things they do not like. Ask for constructive suggestions for the new space or for the existing space if remaining in place is an option.

Law firm tours, as described in Chapter 2, occur early in the process, and provide committee members an opportunity to refine their thoughts about features of similar firms. Chapter 2 includes a checklist to use on tours.

The design professional should distribute a version of a law firm planning questionnaire (see Exhibit 6.3 in this chapter) to members of the space planning committee, and explain how to complete the form. The committee needs to have key personnel present at that meeting (such as department heads) to complete their portions of the form. Give them a reasonable amount of time, perhaps two weeks, to complete the answers. Review their comments before forwarding them to the design professional.

The design professional meets with the committee or head of the committee after reviewing the completed law firm planning questionnaires, and meets with key staff personnel, such as department heads. Typically the person in charge of the space committee sits in on these meetings. A walk-through of each staff member's existing spaces should follow each interview, and particular attention should be paid to the filing and storage requirements for each department as well as existing and potential new equipment requirements. Make note of what equipment or files require special security (either electronic or manual). Department heads should be prepared to talk about work-flow processes within the department, adjacencies of personnel to each other and their managers, and adjacencies to communal equipment such as copiers, printers, and faxes. Filing requirements need to be identified in terms of linear feet or inches, not in quantity of file drawer units. One cabinet drawer may hold eighteen inches of files, while another might hold forty-two inches. This caveat also applies to shelving units.

The design professional and the committee work to establish typical work space standards. This means they establish the sizes of offices for lawyers (both partners and associates), paralegals, secretaries, and administrative support staff. Also established in this process are such standards as sizes and quantities of conference rooms, project workrooms, quantity of file drawers per lawyer, per paralegal, and per secretary.

The design professional needs to know the quantity of the following:

- Satellite copy areas
- High-speed printers, scanners, fax machines
- Typewriters (keep this to one per floor—any more than that is archaic!)
- Satellite coffee areas

Determine if administrative functions such as copying, collating, binding, faxing, messenger delivery and dispatch, incoming and outgoing mail, incoming and outgoing expressage, and supplies will be centralized under one department (which is definitely the trend).

See the law firm planning questionnaire (Exhibit 6.3) for additional questions that should be asked.

Preliminary Report

The design professional prepares a draft of the preliminary program or space requirements report. The preliminary report shows:

- Goals and objectives (see the beginning of this chapter).
- Work space standards diagrams for each personnel type.
- Summary report. This is an overview that shows current personnel and projected personnel over the life of the lease; current ancillary square footage and projected square footage; and total square footage requirement at move-in date, at first lease-expansion option, second lease-expansion option, and so on. It also shows square footage requirements for each ancillary department that will be located in less-expensive lease space. It is designed as a summary for someone who wants to look at the bottom line without having to review the detailed report.
- Detailed report that shows all required square footage.
- Ancillary spaces by function.

The report should have full written descriptions of what is required in each area, such as, how many tables and carrels will be in the library, how many linear feet of shelving the library will have at move-in and in the future, and a description of all the staff work areas in the library.

The design professional reviews the report with the space committee or the head of the space committee. Changes are made to the document based on the client's review and comments.

Blocking, Stacking, and Adjacencies

For a multifloor law firm, now that square footages have been agreed upon, the design professional prepares blocking, stacking, and adjacency studies. These diagrams provide an image of general space utilization throughout the project.

For example, it may be the firm's preference to have the transactional sections closer to the main reception area or reception floor. It may be desirable to have the litigation section near the library. The adjacency studies are included in the final program. See Exhibit 6.4 for a large firm stacking diagram.

Final Program or Space Requirements Report

The committee reviews and approves the final draft of the program or space requirements report. (See Exhibit 6.5 for typical excerpts from a program report.) One of the primary purposes of the report is to determine the required square footage needed to accommodate the firm's needs. The square footage determined in the program represents the *programmed area* required for planning, and not the rentable or useable square footage as defined by the building's landlord or BOMA under the current ANSI/BOMA Z65.1 standard. The programmed square footage may vary from building to building as well, and typically uses a 35 percent add-on factor for circulation. This factor can vary, depending on certain efficiency factors such as the geometry of a building, access to freight elevators, location of fire stairs, or other criteria.

Exhibit 6.1   **51**

Exhibit 6.1

EQUIPMENT INVENTORY FORM AND LETTER

ISD'S EQUIPMENT INVENTORY FORM

Item: _____   Code: _____
    (generic description)   (to be assigned by ISD)

Installation Code: _____   Manufacturer: _____
                                          Model Number: _____

(1) Provided and installed   Quantity: _____
    by General Contractor   Finish: _____

(2) Provided by Owner, installed by General Contractor

(3) Provided and installed by Owner (or Owner's Representative

---

Location(s): _____

Volts: _____   Amps (start-up): _____   Watts: _____

Hertz: _____   Amps (running): _____   Phase: _____

Dedicated   Shared/Common   Isolated Ground _____

Circuit: _____   Dedicated Circuit: _____   Required: _____

Dimensions of the Unit   Actual Space Required

(W × D × H): _____   by the unit (W × D × H): _____

Weight: _____   Receptacle: _____

Hours Operating: _____   Days Operating: _____

BTU/hr. Operating: _____   BTU/hr. Stand-by: _____

Required Temp. Range: _____   Required Humidity Range: _____

Cable Required: Yes / No   Cable Provided By: Contractor / Owner

Cable Specification: _____

Connector Spec.: _____

Cable Length Limitation: _____

Cable to what other termination point? _____

Cable labeling required: _____

Remarks: _____

_____

Exhibit 6.1 Equipment Inventory Form and Letter (continued)

SAMPLE LETTER EXPLAINING THE INVENTORY:

Date (allow one month lead time)

RE: Equipment Specifications

Dear ____:

We need specification information for all equipment which you anticipate using in your new offices. This information will allow us and the engineers to successfully plan and engineer the new space to prevent any problems concerning space, power, cabling or heat load.

Enclosed you will find an equipment inventory form. One sheet should be used for each piece of equipment. Please provide all requested data and attach a copy of the manufacturer's technical specification sheet(s) where this data was obtained from in case the engineers need to verify any information. If you have questions, typically you can contact the manufacturer's representative.

We will assign the equipment number (in the upper right-hand corner) as we group them by like types of equipment for easier reference. If you want, you many assign a numerical code now and reference that to the plans for the exact location of each piece of equipment.

The following is a list of equipment types we typically find in a project:

1. Computer related:	Personal computers, printers, scanners, File servers, modems, uninterrupted power source systems, surge protection systems
2. Copier equipment:	Copiers, facsimile machines, copier accounting systems
3. Food service equipment:	Refrigerators, dishwashers, ice makers,coffee makers, microwaves
4. Telephone equipment:	Switch, modems, etc.
5. Security system:	Personal computer, controller, printer
6. Library equipment:	Dedicated personal computers and printers, microfiche readers and printers
7. Mail Room Equipment:	Scale, postage machine, mail carts
8. Audio/visual:	TV's, VCR's
9. Miscellaneous:	Shredder

We need the information by __/__/____. Thank you for your assistance. Please do not hesitate to call should you have any questions.

Sincerely,

Suzette S. Schultz
Principal

Exhibit 6.2 **53**

Exhibit 6.2

FURNITURE INVENTORY FORM AND LETTER

FURNITURE INVENTORY FORM

Project: Date   Page #
                                  File

Photograph			
Item			
Manufacturer			
Model Number			
Dimensions	W	D	H
Top			
Body			
Hardware			
Return	L	R	
Frame/ Base			
Seat			
Back			
Arm			
Base			

Qty.	Existing Room #	New Location	Area/ Dept.	Condition			Color/ Finish	Remarks
				Re-use	Modify	Scrap		

Exhibit 6.2 Furniture Inventory Form and Letter (continued)

RE: Furniture Inventory

Dear xxxx,

Enclosed is an inventory form and instructions to assist you in completing an inventory of your existing furniture that is to be considered for re-use in your new facility.

In general, it is good for everyone in the firm to be aware of the inventory taking place and the importance of it so that 1) inventory tags, once applied, are not removed, 2) any relocations of furniture after inventory are reported, and 3) interruption of those performing the inventory are kept to a minimum.

The inventory works best when teams of two work together. A rolling cart will facilitate the process by carrying the materials necessary. These include:

1. Polaroid cameras with color film.
2. Tape dispenser
3. Blank inventory forms
4. Inventory tags, sticky-backed
5. Tape measure
6. Ring binders with sections for each major category:
   • Desks
   • Credenzas
   • Bookcases
   • Files
   • Storage cabinets/shelving
   • Tables
   • Seating
   • Systems/Panel/Component Furniture
   • Artwork, accessories
   • Miscellaneous
7. Existing floor plans with room numbers.

Specific directions are as follows:

1. Photograph one of each unique item of furniture. Fill out the descriptive section of the form for the first such item and list additional ones below with any minor variations such as different color upholstery noted in the Remarks columns. Attach photograph with tape to the designated spot on the form.

   a. Condition–The firm should establish a level of quality below which furniture will not be re-used. In the <u>Re-use</u> column, indicate whether item is "New," "Good," or "Fair" condition. If "Fair," indicate in the <u>Modify</u> column what needs to be done to make it useable or briefly describe what is wrong with it.
   b. Remarks - Indicate here any minor differences from the photographed item. For files, indicate if the format size or type of file is unique, i.e., letter or legal size, Pendaflex or compressor block style of filing.

2. Attach an inventory tag to each item in a discrete location. The tag should indicate the coded number which corresponds to the number on the inventory sheet. The employees should be advised not to remove these tags.

Exhibit 6.2   **55**

Exhibit 6.2 Furniture Inventory Form and Letter (continued)

Once your team gets familiar with the process, it will go very quickly. I suggest that you keep photocopies in binders for yourself so that as furniture is moved from place to place over the next year you can keep track of it by having inventory numbers reported.

We would like to have the inventory complete by 00/00/0000 (one month) so that we may have time to review and evaluate it prior the schematic design presentation.

If you have any questions, please call.

Sincerely,

Suzette S. Schultz
Principal

Exhibit 6.3

LAW FIRM PLANNING QUESTIONNAIRE

LAW FIRM PLANNING QUESTIONNAIRE

Page 1

Date: _____

Person or Group
   Responding: _____

Law Firm Name: _____

Current Address: _____
                                    _____
                                    _____

Desired Move-In Date: _____

Existing Lease Expiration Date _____

Current Space Occupied:
   (rentable square feet)

Personnel Projections

Please decide if your responses to the following questions concerning personnel will be for the total firm, or for Departmental/Specialty Practice Groups. If by Group, identify Group name:

1. Total Personnel:
   Now: __, at move-in: __, in 3 years: __, in 5 years: __, in 7 years: __, in 10 years__?

2. Total Senior Partners: (If your firm separates this category.)
   Now: __, at move-in: __, in 3 years: __, in 5 years: __, in 7 years: __, in 10 years__?

3. Total Partners:
   Now: __, at move-in: __, in 3 years: __, in 5 years: __, in 7 years: __, in 10 years__?

4. Total Of Counsel:
   Now: __, at move-in: __, in 3 years: __, in 5 years: __, in 7 years: __, in 10 years__?

5. Total Retired Partners:
   Now: __, at move-in: __, in 3 years: __, in 5 years: __, in 7 years: __, in 10 years__?

6. Total Senior Associates:
   Now: __, at move-in: __, in 3 years: __, in 5 years: __, in 7 years: __, in 10 years__?

7. Total Associates:
   Now: __, at move-in: __, in 3 years: __, in 5 years: __, in 7 years: __, in 10 years__?

8. Total Legal Secretaries:
   Now: __, at move-in: __, in 3 years: __, in 5 years: __, in 7 years: __, in 10 years__?

9. Total Paralegals:
   Now: __, at move-in: __, in 3 years: __, in 5 years: __, in 7 years: __, in 10 years__?

Exhibit 6.3 **57**

Exhibit 6.3 Law Firm Planning Questionnaire (continued)

10. Others:
    Now:__, at move-in:__, in 3 years:__, in 5 years:__, in 7 years:__, in 10 years__?

11. Do you desire to arrange the new offices by formal sections/departments and/or specialty practice groups? Yes:_____, No:_____, Undecided:_____.

12. If the new offices are to be allocated by sections/department or specialty practice group, please indicate all which would be required (R) or desirable (D) per group:

    ___ Dedicated Group Library adjacent to Group's area.
    ___ Dedicated Group Conference Room(s).
    ___ Dedicated Group War Room(s)/Project Workroom(s).

Personnel Projections (Continued)

    ___ Dedicated File/Storage Room(s).
    ___ Dedicated Paralegals in close proximity.
    ___ Dedicated Law Clerks in close proximity.

Attorney Offices

13. The most frequently encountered office sizes are multiples of a 5 foot grid and are generally 15 feet deep from door to window perimeter. If your new offices follow this example, select the office size from the left column which would be appropriate for the office types at the right. (Note: See examples of office sizes in Chapter 12.)

Office Sizes	Office Types
____' x ____'	Senior Partner
____' x ____'	Partner
____' x ____'	Of Counsel
____' x ____'	Associate

14. Do you wish Interior Space Design to consider a floor layout which uses common size offices? Yes:_____, No:_____.

15. If "Yes", what sizes would be adequate? _____', No:_____'.

16. Please indicate from the following list, those items for all attorney offices which you wish to be considered in the design. Use a "P" if consideration is for Partners' offices only; "A" if for Associates' offices only, and an "X" if for both.

    ___ Locks on doors
    ___ Primary surface work walls (in lieu of desks)
    ___ Primary work surface, desk:_____, or work wall:_____
    ___ Secondary work surface, credenza:_____, or work wall:_____
    ___ Secondary surface work walls (in lieu of credenzas)
    ___ Third work surface for PC
    ___ Office doors with glass (opaque)
    ___ Special acoustical consideration
    ___ Number of voice/data outlets
    ___ PC
    ___ Laptop
    ___ Docking station

Exhibit 6.3 Law Firm Planning Questionnaire (continued)

___ Fax machine
___ Printer
___ Special construction for drapery track at perimeter glazing
___ Individual thermostatic control
___ Guest phone outlet
___ Bookshelves; number of linear feet:_____
___ Standardized guest chairs
___ "Do Not Disturb" light
___ Outlet for TV
___ Cable
___ Desk accessories
___ Wastebasket
___ Office signage
___ Other; specify: _____

17. Does the firm intend to provide new furnishings for Associate offices? Yes_____, No_____.
    If "Yes," please indicate all which would be desired:

    ___ Primary work surface, desk:_____, or work wall:_____
    ___ Secondary work surface, credenza:_____, or work wall:_____
    ___ PC
    ___ Laptop
    ___ Docking station
    ___ Fax machine
    ___ Printer
    ___ Third work surface for PC
    ___ Guest chairs; quantity:_____
    ___ Desk chair
    ___ Number of voice/data outlets
    ___ Bookshelves; number of linear feet:_____
    ___ File cabinets; number of drawers:_____
    ___ Planter, plant
    ___ Desk accessories
    ___ Wastebasket
    ___ Office signage
    ___ Other; specify: _____

18. Please indicate your preliminary preference for how the firm might handle the furnishing of Partner offices:

    Partners are to have total freedom to decorate their offices, or;
    Some freedom within pre-established architectural constraints, or;
    Decor alternatives should be prepared by I.S.D. to show to Partners, or;
    The firm will sponsor individual design consultation with I.S.D. for each Partner, or;
    The firm wants to consider standardized furnishings in partner offices, or;
    Other:

Exhibit 6.3   **59**

Exhibit 6.3 Law Firm Planning Questionnaire (continued)

Legal Assistants

19. Please indicate your preliminary preference for how the firm might handle the furnishings of Legal Assistants' offices.

    Reuse existing furniture
    New furniture
    Work walls
    Standardized

20. Please indicate those items which should be considered in the design for Legal Assistant offices/work areas:

    Fully enclosed offices with doors
    Offices on building perimeter
    Interior offices
    Semi-private offices, partial height walls
    Unusual need for acoustical privacy
    Unusual need for visual privacy
    Special proximity need to: _____
    Equipment to be used in office: _____
    Guest chair(s)
    Bookshelves; number of linear feet: _____
    Filing; number of drawers: _____
    Other unusual storage need: _____

Legal Secretaries

21. What is the ratio of Legal Secretaries to Attorney _____; to timekeepers _____?

    Of the total number of Legal Secretaries listed in Question 7, how many support just attorneys?
    Now:_____, in 3 years:_____, in 5 years:_____, in 7 years:_____, in 10 years:_____?

    How many support just Legal Assistants?
    Now:_____, in 3 years:_____, in 5 years:_____, in 7 years:_____, in 10 years:_____?

22. Where would you prefer to have the Legal Secretaries located in the plan?

    Just outside the Attorney's door;
    ___   Directly across the corridor from Attorney offices;
    ___   In group proximity to other secretaries, but close to the Attorney;
    ___   Other (specify) _____

23. Please indicate all preliminary requirements for the design of Legal Secretaries' workstations:

    ___   Personal computer
    ___   Individual printer
    ___   Shared printer
    ___   Dictating transcriber
    ___   Plug in calculator
    ___   Lockable storage for personal effects
    ___   Bookshelves; number of linear feet
    ___   Filing; number of drawers per attorney
    ___   Desk accessories

Exhibit 6.3 Law Firm Planning Questionnaire (continued)

___ Electric typewriter
___ Other equipment _____

Reception Areas

24. If you anticipate having a single Reception Area, or a <u>Main</u> Reception Area (as opposed to equal reception areas on multiple floors), please indicate all required:

___ Single group of guest seating for_____, or
___ Two grouping of guest seats for:_____, and:_____
___ Receptionist within area, or
___ Receptionist semi-concealed from area
___ Does Receptionist perform secretarial duties
___ Private guest phone closet
___ What equipment will Receptionist have at desk
___ Messenger area with phone separate from guest area
___ After hours phone available to messengers and guest when space is secured
___ Beverage service to guests
___ Shielded or secondary waiting area apart from General Reception, or,
___ Small, adjacent, Conference Room to double for this function
___ Storage available for guest coats, luggage, etc.
___ Interconnecting stair

25. If you anticipate multiple (floor by floor) Reception Areas, please indicate all required:

___ Single group of guest seating for ____, or
___ Two groupings of guest seats for: ____,
___ Receptionist within area, or
___ Receptionist semi-concealed from area.
___ What equipment will receptionist have at the desk?
___ Does Receptionist perform secretarial duties?
___ Private guest phone closet
___ Messenger area with phone separate from guest area
___ After hours phone available to messengers and guest when space is secured
___ Beverage service to guests
___ Shielded or secondary waiting area apart from General Reception, or,
___ Small, adjacent, Conference Room to double for this function
___ Storage available for guest coats, luggage, etc.
___ Interconnecting stair

Conference Rooms

26. Aside from public (shared) Conference Rooms, indicate which from the following list would be desirable for your firm:

___ Semi-private (dedicated) Conference Rooms
___ Project Work Rooms (in-house "war" rooms)
___ Specialized Conference Rooms for:
    ___ Depositions
    ___ Mediations
    ___ Audio visual display
    ___ Video taping

Exhibit 6.3   **61**

Exhibit 6.3 Law Firm Planning Questionnaire (continued)

___ Catered lunches
___ Audio teleconferencing
___ Video teleconferencing
___ Television
___ Other: _____

27. Do you prefer:

___ Centralized Conference Rooms
___ Dispersed Conference Rooms
___ Mix of both

28. Please indicate seating capacities which you feel would be required and in what quantities:

6 persons	Quantity required:	_____
8 persons	Quantity required:	_____
10–12 persons	Quantity required:	_____
12–14 persons	Quantity required:	_____
16–18 persons	Quantity required:	_____
20 + persons	Quantity required:	_____
Multi-Purpose Room-Qty required		_____
(Seating _____ people theatre style)		
Caucus Room	Quantity required:	_____

29. Is the above response for the entire firm: Yes_____, No_____; or for a specific group:

_____ (specify group).

30. If you are answering for the specific group filled in above, please indicate if a dedicated Conference Room is desired: Yes_____, No_____.
If yes, how many should it seat:_____?
Any additional dedicated rooms required: Yes_____, No_____.
Please specify needs: _____

31. Please indicate what features you would like to have <u>common to all</u> Conference Rooms:

___ Special exhaust air
___ Individual thermostatic control
___ Unusual audio privacy
___ Unusual visual privacy
___ "Smart" conference tables (Pre-wired for voice/data/electrical outlets)
___ Beverage service
___ Food service (catered)
___ Conference call telephone
___ Perimeter layout space
___ Erasable pen marking surface
___ Tack-able surface
___ Audio-visual equipment
___ Special storage needs: _____
___ Additional air conditioning for after hours or weekends
___ "Do Not Disturb" light

Exhibit 6.3 Law Firm Planning Questionnaire (continued)

32. Are some of the above features desirable for one or more specialty rooms:

    Yes:_____, No:_____.
    Comments: _____

33. Project Workrooms (war rooms) not for client meetings

    ___ Quantity desired
    ___ Size desired

34. If War Rooms or Project Workrooms are desired, I.S.D. frequently recommends the following list of features - please check those which you <u>do not</u> desire:

    ___ Hard, resilient floor material
    ___ Inexpensive loop carpet
    ___ Locks on doors
    ___ Wall mounted phones
    ___ Folding tables
    ___ Stackable chairs
    ___ Movable File System
    ___ Shelving
    ___ Erasable pen marking surface

35. Comments: _____

Administration

36. Please indicate which of the following are required:

    ___ Telephone/Equipment Room
    ___ Computer/File Server Room
    ___ Locked doors, separately keyed
    ___ Accommodation for a safe
    ___ A vault room (fireproof room)
    ___ Special acoustical consideration
    ___ Other, (specify) _____

37. Staff requirements: (please list personnel and office sizes)

    Administrator:
    Now:__, at move-in:__, in 3 years:__, in 5 years:__, in 7 years:__, in 10 years:__?
    Assistant Administrator:
    Now:__, at move-in:__, in 3 years:__, in 5 years:__, in 7 years:__, in 10 years:__?
    Office Manager:
    Now:__, at move-in:__, in 3 years:__, in 5 years:__, in 7 years:__, in 10 years:__?
    Human Resources Manager:
    Now:__, at move-in:__, in 3 years:__, in 5 years:__, in 7 years:__, in 10 years:__?
    Human Resources Assistant:
    Now:__, at move-in:__, in 3 years:__, in 5 years:__, in 7 years:__, in 10 years:__?
    Benefits Manager:
    Now:__, at move-in:__, in 3 years:__, in 5 years:__, in 7 years:__, in 10 years:__?
    Benefits Assistant:
    Now:__, at move-in:__, in 3 years:__, in 5 years:__, in 7 years:__, in 10 years:__?
    Recruiting Coordinator:
    Now:__, at move-in:__, in 3 years:__, in 5 years:__, in 7 years:__, in 10 years:__?

Exhibit 6.3   **63**

Exhibit 6.3 Law Firm Planning Questionnaire (continued)

Recruiting Assistant:
Now:__, at move-in:__, in 3 years:__, in 5 years:__, in 7 years:__, in 10 years:__?
Marketing Director:
Now:__, at move-in:__, in 3 years:__, in 5 years:__, in 7 years:__, in 10 years:__?

38. Staff requirements: (please list personnel and office sizes) (Continued):

Marketing Assistant:
Now:__, at move-in:__, in 3 years:__, in 5 years:__, in 7 years:__, in 10 years:__?
Travel Coordinator:
Now:__, at move-in:__, in 3 years:__, in 5 years:__, in 7 years:__, in 10 years:__?
Conflicts Coordinator:
Now:__, at move-in:__, in 3 years:__, in 5 years:__, in 7 years:__, in 10 years:__?

39. Please check which of the following will be required in the Administrative area:

____ Separate waiting area
____ Dedicated conference room
____ Testing booth (for p.c./typing), qty
____ Dedicated copier
____ Unusual storage requirements
____ Locked storage area
____ Locked door, keyed separately
____ Other (specify) _____

40. Special needs:

Administration requires: _____
_____
_____
_____

Human Resources requires: _____
_____
_____
_____

Recruiting requires: _____
_____
_____
_____

Marketing requires: _____
_____
_____
_____

Other _____ requires: _____
_____
_____
_____

41. Comments: _____

Exhibit 6.3 Law Firm Planning Questionnaire (continued)

<u>Accounting</u>

42. Staff requirements (please list personnel and office sizes)

   Controller:
   Now:__, at move-in:__, in 3 years:__, in 5 years:__, in 7 years:__, in 10 years:__?
   Assistant Controller:
   Now:__, at move-in:__, in 3 years:__, in 5 years:__, in 7 years:__, in 10 years:__?
   Accounts Receivable:
   Now:__, at move-in:__, in 3 years:__, in 5 years:__, in 7 years:__, in 10 years:__?
   Accounts Payable:
   Now:__, at move-in:__, in 3 years:__, in 5 years:__, in 7 years:__, in 10 years:__?

43. Staff requirements (please list personnel and office sizes) (Continued):

   Payroll:
   Now:__, at move-in:__, in 3 years:__, in 5 years:__, in 7 years:__, in 10 years:__?
   Other (specify):_____
   Now:__, at move-in:__, in 3 years:__, in 5 years:__, in 7 years:__, in 10 years:__?

44. Accounting special needs:

   ___ Locked storage room _____ ' X _____ '.
   Accounts Receivable requires: _____
   _____
   _____
   _____

   Accounts Payable requires: _____
   _____
   _____
   _____

   Payroll requires: _____
   _____
   _____
   _____

   Offices that need to lock: _____
   _____
   _____
   _____

<u>Information Technology</u>

We are not going to try and list job descriptions in this department, as every law firm is very unique in how this department operates.

45. Staff requirements:

   Manager:
   Now:__, at move-in:__, in 3 years:__, in 5 years:__, in 7 years:__, in 10 years:__?
   Assistant Manager: _____
   Now:__, at move-in:__, in 3 years:__, in 5 years:__, in 7 years:__, in 10 years:__?
   Help Desk:_____
   Now:__, at move-in:__, in 3 years:__, in 5 years:__, in 7 years:__, in 10 years:__?
   Other Staff:_____
   Now:__, at move-in:__, in 3 years:__, in 5 years:__, in 7 years:__, in 10 years:__?
   Other Staff:_____

Exhibit 6.3   **65**

Exhibit 6.3 Law Firm Planning Questionnaire (continued)

Now:__, at move-in:__, in 3 years:__, in 5 years:__, in 7 years:__, in 10 years:__?
Other Staff:_____

Now:__, at move-in:__, in 3 years:__, in 5 years:__, in 7 years:__, in 10 years:__?
Other Staff:_____

Now:__, at move-in:__, in 3 years:__, in 5 years:__, in 7 years:__, in 10 years:__?
Other Staff:_____

Now:__, at move-in:__, in 3 years:__, in 5 years:__, in 7 years:__, in 10 years:__?
Other Staff:_____

46. Other Information Technology Requirements

		Qty	Size of Room
__	Computer room (This room also accommodates other equipment. See Chapter ___)	__	____' X ____'
__	Wiring closets (For multi-floor firms)	__	____' X ____'
__	PC furniture in room	__	____' X ____'
__	PC Repair room	__	____' X ____'
__	Equipment storage room	__	____' X ____'
__	Software storage room	__	____' X ____'
__	Training room	__	____' X ____'
__	Training room storage	__	____' X ____'
__	Other_____	__	____' X ____'
__	Other_____	__	____' X ____'

47. Information Technology special needs: _____
_____
_____

- We assume the computer room will require 24/7 air conditioning.
- Does your insurance carrier require the computer room to be fire rated: If yes, what rating? ____   Yes___; No___
- Are you comfortable with a regular sprinkler system in the computer room?   Yes___; No___
- Do you want the computer room to be wired to the firm's security system to sense for water leakage?   Yes___; No___
- Do you want to have the computer room monitored with a heat sensor and tied to the firm's security system so you can be notified immediately of a rise in temperature?   Yes___; No___
- Raised floor in computer room: Yes___; No___
- Cable tray in computer room above ceiling: Yes___; No___
- Ceiling in computer room: Yes___; No___
- Security system on door to computer room: Yes___; No___
- Other glass window in computer room: Yes___; No___

Exhibit 6.3 Law Firm Planning Questionnaire (continued)

Library

48. Please indicate as many of the following as possible:

    ___ Number of attorneys served by present Library
    ___ Square footage of present Library
    ___ Number of volumes in present Library (use 5 volumes per linear foot of shelf space.)
    ___ Number of reading spaces at tables in present Library
    ___ Number of study carrels in present Library
    ___ How many shelves high are the majority of your current stacks?

49. Please try to estimate:

    ___ How many linear feet of books at move in?
    ___ How many linear feet of books will the library ultimately accommodate?
    ___ Annual growth of collection by number of volumes
    ___ Number of reading spaces desired in new Library at move-in:
    ___ at carrels
    ___ at tables.

50. Check all which you feel might be desirable to incorporate into the design for a new Library:

    ___ Number of PC's for public use
    ___ Special depth shelves for oversized volumes,
    ___ Special stack arrangements for periodicals, reference material, newspapers;
    ___ Map, plot or chart storage
    ___ Soft seating area for "casual" reading
    ___ Special storage for: _____
    ___ Microfilm/microfiche readers
    ___ Microfilm/microfiche printers
    ___ Dictating booths or rooms
    ___ Copier
    ___ Number of printers

51. Check all which you feel might be desirable to incorporate into the design for the new library:

    ___ Lexis/Westlaw printer: _____
    ___ Dictionary stand
    ___ Newspaper/periodical stand
    ___ Personal Computers
    ___ Other workstations (specify): _____
    ___ Additional air conditioning for after hours or weekends
    ___ Dumbwaiter if Library has more than one floor
    ___ "Smart" reading tables (pre-wired with voice/data and electrical outlets)

52. Would you want to consider reusing your current bookshelves: Yes_____, No:_____.

53. If new bookshelves are required, would you prefer metal shelving with wood end panels or totally wood shelves? Metal and wood____, total wood____. Desired depth of shelves:___.

Exhibit 6.3   **67**

Exhibit 6.3 Law Firm Planning Questionnaire (continued)

Please indicate all of the following which might apply to the work area of the new Library:

___   Office for Librarian: private ____, semi-private ____.
___   Office for Assistant Librarian: private ____, semi-private ____.
___   Library staff work room
___   Control desk
___   On-line catalogue
___   Storage for ____ book trucks
___   Other (specify) _____

Records Management/Central File Room

54. Staff requirements:

    Supervisor:
    Now:__, at move-in:__, in 3 years:__, in 5 years:__, in 7 years:__, in 10 years:__?
    Assistant:
    Now:__, at move-in:__, in 3 years:__, in 5 years:__, in 7 years:__, in 10 years:__?
    Full-Time Clerk:
    Now:__, at move-in:__, in 3 years:__, in 5 years:__, in 7 years:__, in 10 years:__?
    Part-Time Clerk:
    Now:__, at move-in:__, in 3 years:__, in 5 years:__, in 7 years:__, in 10 years:__?
    Messenger:
    Now:__, at move-in:__, in 3 years:__, in 5 years:__, in 7 years:__, in 10 years:__?
    Other:
    Now:__, at move-in:__, in 3 years:__, in 5 years:__, in 7 years:__, in 10 years:__?

55. Equipment requirements of Central File area:

    ___   Linear feet of movable files now
    ___   Linear feet of fixed files now
    ___   Linear feet of lay out counter now
    ___   Percent of growth anticipated in 3 years from move in
    ___   Percent of growth anticipated in 5 years from move in
    ___   Percent of growth anticipated in 7 years from move in
    ___   Percent of growth anticipated in 10 years from move in

56. Comments: _____

    _____

57. Staff requirements:

    Operators:
    Now:__, at move-in:__, in 3 years:__, in 5 years:__, in 7 years:__, in 10 years:__?
    Supervisor:
    Now:__, at move-in:__, in 3 years:__, in 5 years:__, in 7 years:__, in 10 years:__?
    Assistant Supervisor:
    Now:__, at move-in:__, in 3 years:__, in 5 years:__, in 7 years:__, in 10 years:__?
    Other (specify):
    Now:__, at move-in:__, in 3 years:__, in 5 years:__, in 7 years:__, in 10 years:__?

Service Center

58. Would you consider combining Central Duplicating and Central Mail? Yes__;
    No__

Exhibit 6.3 Law Firm Planning Questionnaire (continued)

59. Please list below all existing equipment in the Central Duplicating area(s):

_____

_____

_____

Please comment on any changes or additions anticipated for Central Duplicating equipment:

_____

_____

_____

60. Staff requirements:

Now:__, at move-in:__, in 3 years:__, in 5 years:__, in 7 years:__, in 10 years:__?

61. Comments: _____

_____

_____

62. Do you prefer:

___ One central storage area, or
___ Several satellite storage areas, or
___ Combination of both?

63. If any personnel requiring workstations are located in a central supply area, please indicate:

Number of personnel: _____

Word Processing

64. Do you want to consider a centralized Word Processing department? Yes____; No____

Do you want to consider satellite Word Processing area(s)? Yes____; No____

Please check all of the following which will apply to the design of the Word Processing area(s):

___ Separate air handling equipment for 24-hour operation
___ Printers (high speed)
___ Collating room or extensive horizontal surfaces for collating
___ Drop off/pick-up counter
___ Proofreading booths
___ Special acoustical treatment
___ Hard surface floor
___ Dictating areas
___ Unusual storage requirements
___ Other, (specify) _____

Mail/Messenger

65. Please indicate your preference for:

___ Combined central mail/ central copy area
___ Central mail function, or,

Exhibit 6.3   **69**

Exhibit 6.3 Law Firm Planning Questionnaire (continued)

___ Central plus satellite centers, or,
___ Satellite centers only
___ Mail carts to deliver mail

66. What is the current size of your central mail area in square feet? _____S.F.

67. What size space do you feel would be adequate in a new facility? _____S.F.

68. General description of current mail pick up and delivery system:

Food Service Areas

69. Do you prefer:

___ One central pantry, or,
___ Several satellite pantries, or,
___ Combination of both
___ Catering Pantry
___ Employee Lounge (seating _____ people)
___ Attorney dining facility (seating _____ people)

70. Of the items on the following list, please indicate which would be desired in a central pantry (employee lounge) only (c), satellite pantry only (s), or both central and satellite (x).

___ Coffee maker
___ Commercial refrigerator
___ Commercial freezer
___ Commercial warming oven (hot box)
___ Double sink
___ Single sink
___ Full size refrigerator
___ Full size refrigerator with freezer
___ Full size refrigerator with ice-maker
___ Garbage disposal in sink
___ Instant hot water dispenser
___ Locked cabinets for storage
___ Microwave oven
___ Seating area for _____ people.
___ Soft drink dispensers
___ Under counter ice maker
___ Under counter trash compactor
___ Under counter refrigerator
___ Vending machines
___ Space for canned beverage storage
___ Warming oven
___ Toaster oven
___ Water cooler directly plumbed
___ Water cooler with bottled water
___ Space for bottled water storage
___ Water purification system
___ Other (specify): _____

Exhibit 6.3 Law Firm Planning Questionnaire (continued)

71. Is there a need for a catering type pantry adjacent to a Conference/Dining room?
    Yes_____, No_____.

72. If a catering pantry is required what type of meals are served?

    ___ Boxed lunches
    ___ Hot meals in caterer provided dishes
    ___ Hot meals in chafing dishes
    ___ Hot meals requiring steam table
    ___ Hot meals prepared on-site

73. Other: _____

    _____

General Questions

74. Please indicate which of the following you would like to consider in the design for
    your new space:

    ___ Private toilets
    ___ Shower facilities
    ___ First aid room
    ___ "Forty winks" room
    ___ Ladies lounge
    ___ Lactation room
    ___ Evidence room
    ___ Security system
    ___ Security officer station
    ___ Interconnecting private stair between all floors
    ___ Upgrading fire stairs to use as interconnecting stair
    ___ Other: _____

75. Are any of the following personnel types required who have not been already
    accounted for in this questionnaire?

    ___ Docket clerk; quantity: _____
    ___ Briefing clerk; quantity: _____
    ___ Summer clerk; quantity: _____
    ___ Investigators; quantity: _____
    ___ Other (_____); quantity: ____

76. Is there a budget established for your project? Yes_____, No_____?
    Comments: _____

    _____

77. Provide a list of all practice groups/sections: (Litigation, Tax, etc.)

Exhibit 6.4 **71**

Exhibit 6.4

STACKING DIAGRAM

STACKING DIAGRAM

Stacking BY PRACTICE GROUP, showing partners (P), associates (A) and paralegal spaces (PL)

FLOOR	SECTION	USED			VACANT	
46	LABOR	7P	5A	1PL	3P	2A
45	CONFERENCE					
44	LITIGATION	12P	10A	7PL		
44	ENVIRONMENTAL	1P	1A		8P	3A
43	TAX & EMPL. BEN.	6P	3A	2PL		
43	CORPORATE/COMM	9P	9A	1PL		
43	TRUSTS & ESTATES	3P	1A	2PL	3P	1A
42	HEALTH & INS.	2P	4A	1PL		
42	CORPORATE/SEC.	6P	3A	1PL		
42	REAL ESTATE & FIN	9P	5A	5PL	4P	2A
	TOTAL USED	55P	41A	20PL		
	TOTAL VACANT				18P	8A
	TOTAL AVAILABLE	73P	49A	24PL		

Exhibit 6.5

TYPICAL EXCERPTS FROM A PROGRAM REPORT

The Program Report and Analysis of Square Feet Per Attorney

After the preliminary draft of the program or space requirements report has been completed and the initial square footage requirement has been determined, the square footage per attorney can be analyzed. The term "square feet per attorney" has become a topic of very keen interest among law firms and their planning committees. Twenty years ago it was not uncommon to see square footages of 1000 to 750 sq ft. per attorney. In the 90's, law firms began to try a lean and mean approach. Secretary to attorney ratios have continued to fall from 1:1 to 1:3. Attorneys are opting for smaller sized offices.

Administrative functions such as mail, duplicating, messengers, fax and expressage are being combined into one area, and personnel are multitasking. Word processing departments are shrinking if not obsolete. As the concept of conference centers grows, the days when an attorney could take over a conference room as a private war room are diminishing. As we write this, the square footage per attorney can range from 575 sf to 800 sf.

Smaller law firms cannot expect to be as competitive as medium or larger firms in trying to lower their square foot per attorney ratios. A small law firm is a microcosm of a larger firm. It still requires the infrastructure or ancillary function spaces of a larger firm. For a medium or large firm it is easier to spread the ancillary functions over multiple floors, but for a small firm everything has to be accommodated on one floor. An opportune time to compare statistics and see how the firm is stacking up with other firms is when the preliminary program report is reviewed. It may provide some insight as to where the firm is fat and where it is lean. Once the lease has been signed, it is too late to tweak the square footage. The first example in this section illustrates the issues that determine square footage per attorney.

SAMPLE PROGRAM REPORT EXCERPT: SQUARE FOOTAGE REQUIREMENTS

	S.F.	2006	2007	S.F. 2007	2009	S.F. 2009	2010	S.F. 2010
Attorneys								
Partners	225	75	78	17,550	80	18,000	82	18,450
Of Counsel	150	8	8	1,200	8	1,200	8	1,200
Associates	150	44	47	7,050	51	7,650	55	8,250
Retired Partners	150							
Total Attorneys		127	133	25,800	139	26,850	145	27,900

Exhibit 6.5 Typical Excerpts From a Program Report (continued)

SAMPLE PROGRAM REPORT EXCERPT: SQUARE FOOTAGE REQUIREMENTS

	S.F.	2006	2007	S.F. 2007	2009	S.F. 2009	2010	S.F. 2010
Attorney Support Staff								
Paralegals	100	24	25	2,500	27	2,700	29	2,900
Total Timekeepers		151	158		166		174	
Legal Secretaries	144	66	66	9,504	66	9,504	68	9,792
Floaters	144	5	5	720	5	720	5	720
Special Projects	100	1	1	100	1	100	1	100
Subtotal Support				12,824		13,024		13,512
S.F. Total by Yr.				38,524		39,774		41,312
Circulation (40%)				15,410		15,910		16,525
Total Attorneys/ Support				**53,934**		**55,684**		**57,837**
Admin/ Support Summary	**S.F.**							
Reception Area		1	1	1250	1	1250	1	1250
Library		1	1	4500	1	4500	1	4500
Records Management		1	1	2700	1	2700	1	2700
Information Technology								
File Server Room		1	1	1230	1	1230	1	1230
Sys. Eng. Workroom		1	1	150	1	150	1	150
PC Workroom		1	1	225	1	225	1	225
Staff in offices	120	8	8	960	8	960	8	960
Staff in cubicles	50	12	12	600	12	600	12	600
15 Person Training		1	1	525	1	525	1	525

Exhibit 6.5 Typical Excerpts From a Program Report (continued)

SAMPLE PROGRAM REPORT EXCERPT: SQUARE FOOTAGE REQUIREMENTS

	S.F.	2006	2007	S.F. 2007	2009	S.F. 2009	2010	S.F. 2010
6 Person Training Room		1	1	200	1	200	1	200
Storage		1	1	100	1	100	1	100
Service Center		1	1	2500	1	2500	1	2500
Satellite Copy Areas		8	8	1400	8	1400	8	1400
Word Processing		2	2	225	2	225	2	225
Accounting								
Manager	120	1	1	120	1	120	1	120
Staff in offices	100	4	4	400	4	400	4	400
Staff in cubicles	50	5	5	250	5	250	5	250
Printer workroom		1	1	225	1	225	1	225
Equipment area		1	1	225	1	225	1	225
File Space		1	1	54	1	54	1	54
Office Administrator		1	1	150	1	150	1	150
Marketing								
Director	150	1	1	150	1	150	1	150
Staff in offices	120	4	4	480	4	480	4	480
Workroom		1	1	225	1	225	1	225
Storage		1	1	225	1	225	1	225
Human Resources								
Asst. Director		1	1	120	1	120	1	120
Message Center		1	1	225	1	225	1	225
Storage		1	1	100	1	100	1	100
Testing		1	1	80	1	80	1	80
Coffee areas		8	8	1280	8	1250	8	1250
Catering Pantry		1	1	1000	1	1000	1	1000
Employee Lounge		1	1	1200	1	1200	1	1200
First Aid Room		1	1	100	1	100	1	100
Audio Visual Storage		1	1	350	1	350	1	350

Exhibit 6.5 Typical Excerpts From a Program Report (continued)

SAMPLE PROGRAM REPORT EXCERPT: SQUARE FOOTAGE REQUIREMENTS

	S.F.	2006	2007	S.F. 2007	2009	S.F. 2009	2010	S.F. 2010
Furniture Storage		1	1	500	1	500	1	500
Project Workrooms	225	18	18	4050	18	4050	18	4050
Asbestos Case Workroom		1	1	1000	1	1000	1	1000
Legislative Workroom		1	1	225	1	225	1	225
Specific Case Workroom		1	1	900	1	900	1	900
Subtotal Admin/ Support				30,199		30,169		30,169
S.F. Total by Yr.				30,199		30,169		30,169
Circulation (40%)				12,080		12,068		12,068
Total Admin/ Support				**42,279**		**42,237**		**42,237**
Conference Rooms	**S.F.**							
Multi-purpose room	2300	1	1	2300	1	2300	1	2300
20 Person	750	2	2	1500	2	1500	2	1500
16–18 Person	650	2	2	1300	2	1300	2	1300
12–14 Person	550	6	6	3300	6	3300	6	3300
10–12 Person	450	6	6	2700	6	2700	6	2700
8 Person	350	6	6	2100	6	2100	6	2100
Admin Conference Rm	450	1	1	450	1	450	1	450
				13650		13650		13650
Subtotal Conference Rm		24	24	13,650	24	13,650	24	13,650
Circulation (40%)				5,460		5,460		5,460
Total Conference Rooms				**19,110**		**19,110**		**19,110**
GRAND TOTAL				**115,322**		**117,030**		**119,183**

Exhibit 6.5 Typical Excerpts From a Program Report (continued)

SAMPLE PROGRAM REPORT EXCERPT: SQUARE FOOTAGE REQUIREMENTS

Responses to the programming questionnaire produce reports for each area of the firm. The following example of a report is for a law library.

PROGRAM NOTES for the LIBRARY

1. Personnel:
   a. One supervisor in an office.
   b. Two and a half staff in one work area next to a storage area.
   c. Need additional space for staff growth.
2. They want to be able to accommodate 4,300 linear feet of shelving. (Please verify this.) The existing library can accommodate 3,500 LF of shelving.
3. They will continue to use existing Westlaw and Lexis printers. (Please verify this.)
4. Want to be able to see a staff person at the reference desk when entering the library.
5. There should be a non-networked PC in the library workroom.
6. Would like a catalog PC in a walk-up area. PC screen should be under glass.
7. Want a soft seating area with two comfortable chairs for reading the newspaper.
8. Want 18 LF of ready reference materials on tilted shelves.
9. Would like a book truck at the entrance to the library with a checkout area located above it.
10. Would like a small private phone room.
11. Would like 4 to 6 library carrels that are five feet wide. One or two carrels should have a built in PC. All carrels should be wired. They should have a tack-able panel above the work surface.
12. Would like 2 library tables.
13. Would like a walk-up PC and printer.
14. Would like 9″ deep shelves. Posting shelves are desirable.
15. Plan for four book trucks: 1 at return, 1 in the stacks and two in the workroom.
16. They are currently working on an automated checkout system. No details were available at this time.
17. Need a copier in the workroom. It should have a cabinet with doors.
18. They need an area where the copy center can pick up 20 to 30 books.
19. They need 18 LF of Pendaflex storage for newspapers. This should be in a closet to accommodate old papers.
20. Want a glare free work surface on the tables.
21. Want ergonomic chairs in the library.
22. Lighting needs to be good between the stacks.
23. Would like a place for step stools to be parked amongst the stacks.

Shopping for the Space

7

Once you have established your square footage requirements, you can begin analyzing and comparing buildings and building components.

Establishing a Building Criteria Report (Developing Your Shopping List)

To determine your desired base building and interior design criteria, the committee, the broker, and the design professional create a list of preferred features in the building (components, attributes, amenities, and financials) to produce a building criteria report. In short, the report is a wish list of what the firm would like to see in the building, its location, and how much it may cost. It gives the broker direction in what properties to consider. Exhibit 7.1 at the end of this chapter is an example of a building criteria report.

Shopping for Space

Based on the program square footages and the building criteria list, the broker begins the search for available space. This process can take anywhere from a week to several months depending on the size of the town or city and what is available on the market. It can also include searching for a developer willing to build if that is an option. We strongly urge that every option be explored.

Preliminary Building Analysis Study

For this first pass it is desirable to have at least ten viable options that can be explored in a cursory way. A few may be rejected because they do not meet the space planning criteria, such as having the wrong mullion spacing to make the office sizes work effectively, not having enough available core space, or not having enough contiguous expansion options. After all the buildings have been evaluated, the list should be shortened to four or five. These should be pursued further and in more depth.

Test Fits and Feasibility Studies

The broker should approach the prospective landlords and ask each one to pay for a test fit. A test fit is a quick space plan that tests the building's floor plate against the program. Each landlord probably has a space planner on board who can do these. However, it is more beneficial to the firm to have the landlord pay the design professional that the firm has hired. The law firm's designer is more familiar with the program and with the planning of law firms. Space planners typically are paid ten to twenty-two cents per rentable square foot for doing these test fits. If the project is to be a multiple-floor project, all floors should be test fit to study core area efficiencies. Also, during this process the building criteria questionnaire (see Exhibit 7.2) is distributed to all landlords for completion.

Preliminary Budget

Based on the test fits, the design professional prepares a preliminary budget for each building after it has been determined what each landlord is willing to contribute in the way of building-standard offerings or other concessions.

Final Building Analysis Study

This study should include the following from the design professional:

- Goals and objectives from the firm
- Final program
- Building criteria list (what was asked for)
- Test fits (space plans) for all the buildings
- A written analysis from the design professional setting forth the advantages and disadvantages of each building

- An analysis comparing building systems and components
- A statement of probable costs for each project
- An updated overall project schedule

See typical excerpts from a final building analysis study in Exhibit 7.3.

The broker should prepare a complete financial and legal summary that includes the costs and obligations associated with the lease, including:

- Initial length of lease
- Options to renew lease
- Initial useable and rentable square footage
- Any free rent
- Initial rent
- Matrix showing all rental costs over the life of the lease
- Rent increase schedule
- Operating costs
- Expansion options
- Contraction options
- Assignment or subletting rights
- Cancellation options
- Right of first refusal on other space in the building
- Length of other leases
- Availability of less-expensive space for administrative functions
- Landlord contributions towards tenant improvements or build-out costs
- Additional monetary incentives from landlord
- Landlord's willingness to finance build-out costs beyond the allowance

Exhibit 7.1
SAMPLE BUILDING CRITERIA REPORT

BUILDING CRITERIA REPORT (THE SHOPPING LIST)

INTRODUCTION

(Client law firm) has requested that (the design professional) prepare a description of the firm's requirements in terms of preferred planning features, financial criteria and projected occupancy and expansion. This information will provide the basis on which (Client) will evaluate the relocation options for their firm. It will also be used to evaluate their existing premises.

In order to establish the criteria to be used in this evaluation, (the design professional) has **also** prepared a **Program Requirements Report** which establishes (Client's) overall space requirements and expansion needs. This report is an integral step in a relocation evaluation and forms the basis for many of the decisions which will be required.

As a preface, it should be noted that the needs of a major law firm are different from many other organizations. The physical space that houses lawyers needs to reflect consistency in form and character, while allowing for individual expression. Further, the environment needs to accommodate the two major functional groups of (1) attorneys, paralegals, and their direct support, and (2) indirect support comprised of central as well as satellite services, in appropriate adjacency to one another. These factors, in conjunction with the need to occupy a building which reflects the dignity and character of the law firm, will result in certain relocation options being targeted to the exclusion of others.

This report is organized in three parts:

PART 1–INITIAL OCCUPANCY AND EXPANSION

The initial occupancy and expansion timetable is based on the Space Requirements Report prepared by the design professional specifically for the client. This will identify initial occupancy, square footage requirements and lease and renewal options within a specified time framework.

PART 2–OUTLINE SPECIFICATIONS OF PREFERRED BUILDING CHARACTERISTICS

The outline specifications for preferred building characteristics established the following criteria:

A. Building Identity
B. "Fit Factor" and Floor Plate Utilization
C. Vertical Factors
D. Architectural Base Building and Work Letter
E. Heating, Ventilation, and Air Conditioning (HVAC)
F. Electrical Distribution and Service
G. Riser / Shaft Space
H. Plumbing
I. Telecommunications
J. Fire Protection

Exhibit 7.1   **81**

Exhibit 7.1 Sample Building Criteria Report (continued)

PART 3–FINANCIAL LEASE TERM CRITERIA

The financial lease term criteria describe monetary considerations applicable for both existing and possible relocation sites.

INITIAL OCCUPANCY AND EXPANSION CRITERIA:

A. Initial occupancy is desired for (date).
B. Approximately 215,000 total square feet will be required at time of move-in. This total includes 35,000 to 40,000 square feet of support space which may be located on a low-rise floor. A portion of the total space may be sublet with no restrictions as required by (Client).
C. It is desired that renewal options be scheduled within the shortest time frame that is practical with the right of first refusal on all contiguous space, and no penalty imposed if renewal options are not exercised.
D. High-rise attorney floors to be approximately 20,000 square feet in size, with core to window wall dimensions as described in Part 2 of this report.
E. Centralized support floor to be approximately 35,000 to 40,000 square feet with a lower rent rate. This floor to have direct elevator access to attorney floors.
F. (Client) to be major tenant in building or to have major tenant privileges for expansion options.

OUTLINE SPECIFICATIONS OF PREFERRED BUILDING CHARACTERISTICS

A. BUILDING IDENTITY AND SITE LOCATION CRITERIA

   1. Involvement of a qualified developer, management company, and architect with a proven track record for similar projects;
   2. Prominent building in terms of image in the business community;
   3. A location west of (Location) in Central Business District is preferred;
   4. Appropriate mix of other targeted tenants (i.e., consider as a negative one major tenant with more than 30–50% of leased space in building);
   5. Access to adequate parking (within building preferred) and major roadways;
   6. Access to public transportation;
   7. Convenience to restaurants, hotels, shopping, located within busy, secure neighborhood;
   8. Retail services in building (bank with safe deposit box services, florist, newspaper stand, food facilities, etc.);
   9. Overall aesthetics to reflect Class A building in design, materials, and architectural detailing in all public areas.

"FIT FACTOR" AND FLOOR PLATE UTILIZATION CRITERIA–ATTORNEY FLOORS

   10. Regular 5'-0" building module for ability to house 10', 15', and 20' perimeter offices;
   11. 40' Clear window wall to core dimension for ability to accommodate 30' band of attorneys and secretaries, plus 10' for satellite interior support space. In selected areas a 30' wall to core dimensions would be acceptable.
   12. Interior column spacing, minimum number of interior columns for flexible planning concepts;

Exhibit 7.1 Sample Building Criteria Report (continued)

13. Regular perimeter column spacing, minimum size of perimeter columns (width and depth), minimum projection of convector enclosure, minimum soffit at perimeter window wall, minimum overall core dimensions;
14. Minimum number of core access points; grouped, if possible, near elevator bank, coordinated with tenants plans;
15. Minimum required circulation to access core openings;
16. Freight elevator entrance and vestibule shielded from major traffic area;
17. As determined by trail block layout, ability to house the programmed requirements. Aspects include functionality of overall floor shape and interior spaces, the percent of actual circulation space required, and the logical relationship of the parts to the whole;
18. A floor size of approximately 20,000 usable square feet, with the emphasis on maximizing perimeter offices and minimizing internal square footage;
19. Availability of high-rise floors with optimal views;
20. Direct elevator access (no crossover) to centralized support floor, and all attorney floors;
21. 40'-45' Minimum window wall to core dimension for ability to accommodate large departments on either the window wall or core wall;
22. 30' and 40' interior column spacing, minimum number of interior columns for flexible planning concepts;
23. Regular perimeter column spacing, minimum size of perimeter columns (width and depth), minimum depth of convector enclosure;
24. Minimum number of core access points, grouped if possible near elevator bank. Other locations require review on a case-by-case basis;
25. Location on low-rise floor with associated rental cost;
26. Distribution and size of interior spaces appropriate for use by large support services groups;
27. As determined by block layouts, ability to house the programmed requirements. Aspects include functionality of overall floor shape and interior spaces, the percent of actual circulation space required, and the logical relationship of the parts to the whole;
28. A floor size of between 35,000 and 40,000 usable square feet, with the emphasis on maximizing internal space and accessibility to freight and passenger elevators;
29. Availability of basement or low-floor on-site storage areas (and/or support service locations if Tenant desires);
30. Availability of area adjacent to loading dock for Receiving/Maintenance Department;
31. Direct elevator access (no crossover) to attorney floors.

VERTICAL FACTORS CRITERIA

1. Initial occupancy on high-rise floor(s) with optimum views, "best" views will be determined by building location and context;
2. Adequate expansion available on contiguous floors;
3. All high-rise floors (including expansion) to be served by single elevator bank; with transfer floor to access low-rise floors;
4. No elevator "crossover" floor within initial or expanded occupancy;

Exhibit 7.1 **83**

Exhibit 7.1 Sample Building Criteria Report (continued)

5. Elevator capacity and speed to provide an "up-peak" interval not to exceed 30 seconds, with the percent of population moved during an intense 5-minute "up-peak" period in excess of 12% of the population served;
6. Consideration should be given to whether building (or tenant occupancy) will have a cafeteria or service center, since elevator usage is significantly affected by these factors;
7. Separate elevator service to parking levels (from main lobby) for increased security of tenant floors;
8. Restricted access from building fire stairwell to tenant floors, for tenant security
9. Freight elevator and vestibules dedicated to tenant's use shall be provided at no additional charge to tenant;
10. Ability to add dumbwaiter to connect all floors including support floor, and interconnecting tenant stair.

B. <u>ARCHITECTURAL BASE BUILDING AND WORK LETTER CRITERIA</u>

Work letter items should be evaluated both for quality and quantity. It should be possible to take a cash allowance instead of accepting the work letter proposal from the landlord.

Exhibit 7.2
BUILDING CRITERIA QUESTIONNAIRE

BUILDING CRITERIA QUESTIONNAIRE

When reviewing and evaluating buildings during the preliminary building analysis study, these are criteria that need to be looked at for examples of the building components. You may want to give this to prospective landlords in the form of a questionnaire. It will become the basis of a building evaluation and comparison report.

1. Exterior glazing:
   - Is the glazing Insulated glass, dual pane glass, or non-insulated glass? Avoid the latter
   - What are the shading co-efficiencies?
   - Reflectivity rating–outdoors and indoors
   - Color of the glass
   - Height of the glass from the finished floor on a typical office floor
   - Height of the glass from the finished ceiling floor on a typical office floor.
   - In hurricane-prone coastal areas, does the glass meet applicable impact or windstorm codes?
2. Ground floor lobby walls:
   - What are the materials?
3. Ground floor lobby flooring:
   - What are the materials?
4. Ground floor lobby ceiling:
   - What are the materials?
5. Tenant Restrooms:
   - Walls—What are the materials?
   - Floors—What are the materials?
   - Lavatory Tops—What are the materials?
   - Lavatory—What are the materials?
   - Lavatory Trim and Accessories—What are the materials?
   - Toilet Partitions:
   - Ceiling Hung or Floor Mounted
   - Metal or Plastic Laminate or Stone
   - Finish Color or finish material
   - Quantity provided by landlord
   - Quantity provided by tenant
6. Tenant Standard Finish Materials:
   These are materials that the landlord is proposing to use within a typical standard build-out.
   - What are the structure and materials to be used?
   - Do they extend above the ceiling?
   - Do they break the ceiling grid?
   - Is it a pony wall that stops at the ceiling grid and then continues to the structure above?
7. Interior Partitions Within the Tenant Space:
   - Construction
   - Materials
   - Describe extent of partition; do they stop at the ceiling grid; do they continue to the structure above?

Exhibit 7.2   **85**

Exhibit 7.2 Building Criteria Questionnaire (continued)

8. Acoustical Ceiling Tile:
   - Manufacturer
   - Model Number
   - STC, NRC, CAC
   - Dimensions of the material
   - Quantity provided by landlord
   - Quantity provided by tenant
9. Acoustical Ceiling Grid:
   - Manufacturer
   - Model and Specification Numbers
   - Quantity provided by landlord
   - Quantity provided by tenant
10. Doors:
    - Height
    - Width
    - Thickness
    - Describe finish
    - Manufacturer
    - Flush panel or raised panel
    - Quantity provided by landlord
    - Quantity provided by tenant
11. Door Frames:
    - Describe material
    - Describe rating
    - Manufacturer
    - Model Number
    - Finish
    - Quantity provided by landlord
    - Quantity provided by tenant
12. Finish Hardware—Entrance Door:
    - Describe hardware set
    - Hinges
    - Lockset
    - Lock Trim
    - Closure
    - Door Stop
    - Security System, if available
    - Quantity provided by landlord
    - Quantity provided by tenant
13. Finish Hardware—Interior Passage Door:
    - Butt Hinge
    - Latch Set
    - Latch Trim
    - Door Stop
    - Quantity provided by landlord
    - Quantity provided by tenant
14. Carpeting:
    - Provide carpet specification
    - Installation method
    - Carpet cushion or pad

Exhibit 7.2 Building Criteria Questionnaire (continued)

- o Quantity provided by landlord
- o Quantity provided by tenant
15. Base:
    - o Describe typical base in carpeted areas
    - o Quantity provided by landlord
    - o Quantity provided by tenant
16. Resilient Surface Flooring:
    - o Describe VCT
    - o Manufacturer
    - o Model Number
    - o Colors available
    - o Associated Base
    - o Quantity provided by landlord
    - o Quantity provided by tenant
17. Window Covering Materials:
    - o Manufacturer
    - o Model Number
    - o Color finish
    - o Quantity provided by landlord
    - o Quantity provided by tenant
18. Light Fixtures:
    - o Describe building standard
    - o Light fixture size
    - o Number of fluorescent lamps
    - o Manufacturer
    - o Model Number
    - o Air supply or air return fixture
    - o Describe switching
    - o Indicate lamp temperature
    - o Indicate ballast
    - o Quantity provided by landlord
    - o Quantity provided by tenant
19. Electrical Outlets:
    - o Manufacturer
    - o Model Number
    - o Color of outlets and cover plates
    - o Quantity provided by landlord
    - o Quantity provided by tenant
20. Voice/Data Outlets:
    - o Wiring Description
    - o Cover plate and number of modular jacks under one face plate
    - o How wiring is pulled in the wall cavity; is it pulled through conduit?
    - o Quantity provided by landlord
    - o Quantity provided by tenant
21. Signage/Graphics and Identification Devices:
    - o Finish
    - o Size
    - o Location

Exhibit 7.2   **87**

Exhibit 7.2 Building Criteria Questionnaire (continued)

- o Manufacturer
- o Location of these items
- o Quantity provided by landlord
- o Quantity provided by tenant
22. Air Devices:
- o Describe how typical air handling is handled in the perimeter zone
- o Describe how typical air handling is handled in the interior zone
- o Number of exterior zone thermostats
- o Number of interior zone thermostats
- o Quantity provided by landlord
- o Quantity provided by tenant

Exhibit 7.3
BUILDING EVALUATION AND REPORT
(BUILDING ANALYSIS STUDY)

BUILDING EVALUATION AND COMPARISON REPORT

The Building Evaluation and Comparison Report is the product of your Building Criteria Questionnaire, the document illustrated by the previous exhibit sample. We present two sample reports. Remember that these reports reflect the very different needs of law firms and unique buildings, so you can expect them to be quite dissimilar.

BUILDING EVALUATION AND COMPARISON	Present Offices	Alternative 1	Alternative 2

I. Location—proximity to:

  A. Courts
  B. Key clients
  C. Transportation
    Access to public transportation
    Access to major freeways/ highways
  D. Parking
    Assigned spaces available
    Parking in the building- how many allotted spaces
    Visitor parking in building for clients
    Parking for non-attorney staff
  E. Security of neighborhood after business hours
  F. Proximity to lunch facilities
  G. Other (specify) _____

II. Rental rates

  A. Rates available
  B. Periods during which rates will be effective
  C. Escalation provisions
  D. Base year for escalation
  E. Rates for expansions options

III. Rentable / usable square feet

  A. Rentable square feet available
  B. Percentage of add-on factor (usable to rentable)

Exhibit 7.3 Building Evaluation and Report (continued)

	Present Offices	Alternative 1	Alternative 2
IV. Building Core			
A. Available square feet			
B. As percentage of building			
V. Satisfaction of firm's construction requirements (*Can the space be developed to meet the firm's requirements?*)			
VI. Satisfaction of firm's construction requirements (*Can the space be developed to meet the firm's expansion requirements?*)			
VII. Concessions			
A. Work letter allowances toward construction			
B. Other allowances or concessions			
VIII. Timing			
A. When the firm needs the space			
B. When the space is available			
IX. Lease term			
A. Firm's long-term wishes regarding lease commitment			
B. Lease terms available			
X. Contiguous space, option space, right of first refusal on space			
A. Is contiguous space available for future use? How many square feet? In what increments?			
B. When will such space be available?			
C. Will the firm be granted options on that space?			
D. Can the firm sublet space?			
E. Can the firm give back some of the initial space?			
F. What rental rates and escalation provisions will apply to space rented in the future?			
G. Are there "must takes"?			

Exhibit 7.3 Building Evaluation and Report (continued)

	Present Offices	Alternative 1	Alternative 2
XI. Building characteristics:			
A. Building core efficiency Are there large chunks of core space or is it small and broken up?			
B. Usable space efficiency			
C. Building planning module			
D. Heating, ventilation, air-conditioning, sprinkler systems, and life safety systems			
E. Curtain wall-mullion spacing, percentage of glass, height of sill, dual pane or un-insulated, mullion detail for acoustical			
F. Floor loading			
G. Height of header			
H. Lighting and ceiling			
I. Security system-parking garage, parking garage elevator, building entry, elevator access, access to tenant space			
J. Infrastructure			
K. Connecting stair link via fire stairs			
L. Bathroom, plumbing, and wet columns availability			
M. Elevators Dedicated freight elevators and freight elevator lobby			
N. Emergency power supply **Important**: Base building ability to provide emergency generator for lighting and life safety system backup			
O. Space planning			
P. Slab-to-slab height			
XII. Flexibility of firm			
A. Select its own architect or designer			
B. Select its contractors			
XIII. Other			
A. Cleaning schedule			

The following example of a test fit comparison has the additional virtue of listing the program requirements for comparison.

Exhibit 7.3 Building Evaluation and Report (continued)

SPACE ANALYSIS COMPARISON

	EXISTING	PROGRAM (Based on 2009 Projections)	BUILDING A	BUILDING B
Partners	15	29	24	32
Associates	34	70	36	36
Total Atty.	49	99	60	68
Legal Asst.	7	24	19	15
Total Billable Personnel	56	123	79	83
Legal Secretary	28	52	42	38
Ratio Secretary to Billable Personnel	1 to 2	1 to 2.37	1 to 1.88	1 to 2.18
Conference Rooms	6	10	8	10
Multi-purpose Room	0	1	1	1
Seating/Auditorium			63	48
Seating/Tables			30	18
Project Workrooms	2	3 to 4	3.5	2
Library Shelving	3123 L.F.	3333 L.F.	3429 L.F.	3297 L.F.
Library Seating	8	16 to 24	16	14
Central Files	1323 L.F.	2249 L.F.	3164 L.F.	1792 L.F.
Files behind secretary	93		144	168
Files elsewhere	35		95	42
Total file cabinets	128		239	210
File cab. per atty.	2.29		3.98	2.29
Employee Lounge	12	20	24	18
Auxiliary Coffee Areas	1		2	2
Central Mail/Copy/Fax	481 s.f.		982 s.f.	691 s.f.
Auxiliary Copy Rooms	2		3	3
Auxiliary Copy Rooms	384 s.f.		683 s.f.	340 s.f.
Word Processing Personnel	4	6	6	5
File Server/Tele. Equip.	96 s.f.		248 s.f.	170 s.f.

NOTES:

1. Building A has an abundant amount of perimeter in relationship to the core space. Therefore, you have more attorneys, however, the core space does not in many cases meet the program.
2. The building's geometry allows natural daylight to permeate the secretarial corridor. It also allows one to look outside to see what quadrant of the building they are in. (This can be disorienting in a square building unless you have some frame of reference to refer to such as outdoor landmarks.)
3. In the total number of associate offices deductions have not been made for office space for the Office Manager and Marketing Director.

Lease and Work Letter Analysis and Negotiations

8

When the prospective landlords' products have been compared, you will likely drop some of them from consideration and negotiate with the final one or two about exactly what you can get for your money. A critical part of your negotiation establishes the terms of the work letter, which is the part of your lease contract that establishes the rights and obligations of your landlord and your firm in building your offices.

If the word is out on the street that you have made your final selection, you lose some negotiating power, so avoid premature statements about your decisions. This chapter is about the issues that may be subject to negotiation, and we provide some suggestions for gearing up for the negotiation. Likewise, we suggest some important amenities and services to ask for, as well as some technical specifications to use in negotiating for them.

Building-Standard Features, Lease and Work Letter Negotiation

Most buildings have "building-standard" features—standard ceiling tiles, doors, frames and hardware, light fixtures, and partitions. For good reason, landlords generally want uniformity throughout their buildings. Repairs, moving tenants, supply costs, and labor costs all provide incentives for the landlord to limit changes to the building. In fact, most buildings maintain a supply of standard fixtures, doors, and other building components so that changes can be made quickly and economically in a way that provides continuity throughout the building. However, building-standard features may be inappropriate for your firm or for law firms in general, because law firms have special needs that often exceed the building standard. A law firm tenant may be able to negotiate allowances for improved features that exceed the building standard.

Law firms commonly confront unacceptable building standards in the form of inadequate soundproofing of partitions, and (occasionally) light fixtures with acrylic lenses, which cause fatigue and glare. But these are merely two examples. Building-standard features may be the beginning of numerous points in the negotiation of the work letter.

There are two general scenarios for work letter negotiation. First, you may be negotiating to have the landlord produce the space in its final turnkey form, so you negotiate features and prices on that basis. If the issue arises, your firm should argue that the landlord is not entitled to any fees or markup on the construction. Landlords sometimes insert this as a 3 to 10 percent add-on, saying that it pays for their time in the construction process. If a landlord inserts such a provision, you should ask the landlord to omit it as an inducement for you to move into their space. If the landlord builds out the space, remember whose interests he is going to protect first—his own. The landlord may take shortcuts in heating, ventilation, and air-conditioning (HVAC) that results in a space that is too hot or too cold, or acoustical details may be compromised by his subcontractors for their own ease.

The other approach is to use your own designer and your own contractor, and negotiate the contribution of the landlord to the project. As you might expect, the firm can control costs and quality more effectively by using its own designer and contractor.

The work letter describes the landlord's obligations regarding the build-out of the space and getting the tenant moved in. The more you can negotiate into the work letter, the more it will save you in out-of-pocket expenses. Ideally, you negotiate for the landlord to have your space built to your plans and specifications, paying all costs. In practice, this is probably not achievable unless your firm is large and has the requisite leverage ability.

Alternatively, you may negotiate a square-footage allowance. In some cases, for example, an allowance of $50 to $75 per square foot may be achievable. Another negotiating route is for the landlord to provide everything above the ceiling. This cost can be between $10 and $15 per square foot. It includes primary and secondary distribution ducts, the VAV boxes and other HVAC controls, one building-standard light fixture for every 70 square feet of rentable space, ceiling grid, ceiling tiles, and sprinkler installations per the tenant's final plans. The rationale behind negotiating everything above the ceiling is that these are all building-standard components and that everything that is above the ceiling stays in the space when you move elsewhere and the space is renovated to suit the incoming tenant.

As another example, some law firms have areas of highly concentrated floor loading such as in the central file room, the library, or fireproof filing systems. It may be desirable to negotiate for the landlord to pay for the additional floor loading support. If the building is being built, this can be placed into the landlord's specifications for those areas and the cost is substantially reduced. Initial upgrading of the size of a beam costs substantially less than adding additional beams at a later date.

Negotiating Approach

Recognizing that the work letter is the landlord's vehicle to provide further inducement for the tenant to enter into the lease agreement, it is paramount that the overall project requirements, both present and future, be established before entering into the negotiation. Therefore we recommend strongly that careful and thoughtful attention be devoted toward the space program, design concept, schedule, and budget.

Because the work letter principally establishes the tenant's and the landlord's responsibilities as they relate to preconstruction performance and construction cost issues, it is important that these agreements be established in conjunction with developing the lease provisions. A substantial amount of leverage and bargaining power can be lost if a commitment to a particular property is made before finalizing all aspects of the agreement.

Negotiating Team

The negotiating team should include the law firm's lawyer, broker, and design consultant. This coordinated effort provides the greatest opportunity for maximum benefits because each participant makes a unique and valuable contribution to the discussion. All members of the team should have substantial law firm experience, because the landlord will surely have a very experienced and seasoned team on his side of the table.

Work Letter Review and Subjects for Negotiation

Whether the terms of the work letter originate initially with the law firm as a request for proposal or as the landlord's standard offering, the following subjects should be addressed:

- Quality and quantity of building-standard products or monetary considerations
- Floor finishes and floor leveling tolerances

- Floor loading capacity
- Wall, column, and perimeter bulkhead construction
- Window treatment at exterior windows
- Partitioning (walls)
- Clear plenum space
- Sprinkler system
- Heating, ventilation, and air conditioning
- Core finishes
- Elevator lobby upgrade
- Lighting
- Doors, frames, and hardware
- Capacity and extent of electrical and mechanical service and distribution, as well as metering
- Schedule and building requirements
- Landlord's review and response time to the drawings
- Landlord's markups and administrative fees for construction supervision
- Use of landlord's contractor versus competitive bidding
- Preliminary pricing supplied by base-building contractor
- Overview time line project schedule
- Cost and payment of architectural and engineering services
- Responsibility for coordination of above-ceiling elements with reflected ceiling plan (guaranteeing clearances)
- Form of pricing response, lead times, and unit costs
- Change order process and response time
- Subcontractor selection
- Shop drawing review time
- Early issue of certain subcontracts and release of long-lead items
- Definition of landlord-tenant delays, date of substantial and final completion, late penalties
- Maintenance of added HVAC units
- Lamp (light bulb) and ballast replacement responsibility
- General conditions (if landlord's contractor performs the work)
- Accuracy of landlord-provided information (base building drawings)
- The ability to put your signage or graphics outside your suite or in the elevator lobby in the size and font selected by the firm

Other Negotiating Suggestions for Leases and Work Letters

While nothing is absolutely free, we encourage you to ask that certain landlord-provided features or amenities be provided at no cost. For example, negotiate for 24-7 free air-conditioning. Most buildings give free air-conditioning during normal business hours, perhaps 7 a.m. to 6 p.m., but law firms, because of their extended working hours, really need to negotiate for longer hours of air-conditioning. Many buildings these days are going with 24-hour air-conditioning. After-hours air-conditioning can run $50 to $150 per hour per air handler. Negotiate for the inside air temperature to be delivered at 73 degrees when the outside temperature is 100 degrees, and 72 degrees when the outside temperature is 20 degrees. These temperatures may need to be adjusted for your area of the country.

Negotiate for other utilities, such as free hot water and cold water. If at all possible, negotiate for free electrical service.

Negotiate for free use of a freight elevator. Some buildings charge for after-hours use or charge for an operator. Operators are not really necessary these days, and the charges can be substantial. For passenger elevators, negotiate for more operable elevators within your bank for after hours. Many buildings turn elevators off and operate only one after hours.

Negotiate for free replacement of (at least) building-standard light bulbs and ballasts, if not for all types of light bulbs. Negotiate for cleaning and janitorial services five days a week. Negotiate for 24-7 lobby security guards, and for day porter service.

Specifying Negotiated Work Letter Items

A frequent problem with negotiating with landlords is that without experience, few people know what to ask for or how to specify the conditions they prefer. There are many hidden issues that can make a space unusable or very expensive. For example, a floor slab that is not level or that does not support enough weight for its intended use is very expensive to upgrade. Given below are sample negotiating specifications to help you avoid some of the pitfalls. Of course, they must be tailored to your prospective building and local codes and conditions:

Floor finishes. Concrete slab cleaned and level to $\frac{1}{4}$-inch tolerance within a 10'0" × 10'0" given area (tolerances are not cumulative; elevator sills are to be established elevation 0'0"). Areas leveled subsequent to initial pouring of slab to be sealed after setting. Finished surfaces to be ready to receive carpet, ceramic tile, resilient tile, wood, or stone flooring without additional tenant preparation other than cleaning.

Floor loading. Floor loads shall be per applicable codes and base building standards throughout. Adequate supplemental bracing will be provided up to an additional six thousand square feet to accommodate tenant's heavy loading requirements where needed. Area to be so constructed will be identified on tenant's preliminary plans and will be engineered by landlord's structural engineer and installed by landlord's contractor, both at landlord's sole expense.

Wall, column, and perimeter bulkhead construction. All core walls, freestanding and engaged columns, and perimeter top and bottom bulkheads to be furred, dry walled, taped, floated, sanded, and ready to receive final tenant finishes.

Other perimeter finishes. Building perimeters will be fully finished as relates to waterproofing, caulking, glazing and metal finishing including all required glass replacement (in the event of defects or cracked or broken panes), glass cleaning on exterior, metal touch-up and cleaning, and any other actions required to render the perimeters to a tenant-ready condition. Building-standard window coverings will not be installed until just before tenant occupancy.

Other core finishes. Firefighting equipment enclosures, drinking fountains, janitor closets, electrical and mechanical rooms, toilets, fire exit enclosures, and related areas shown on the plans to be finished to base building standards except as subsequent deletions are mutually agreed, at which time full credits to the extent landlord is entitled thereto from its contractors shall be given to tenant allowance.

Ceilings. Completed and laser-leveled grid suspension system ($4'0'' \times 4'0''$) capable of receiving $1'0'' \times 1'0''$ concealed-spline acoustic tile installation.

Sprinkler system. Sprinkler piping shall be provided to include main runs with crosses to achieve a $10' \times 10'$ grid for future extensions and locations of branch piping, drops, and heads. Provide one fully recessed and concealed head per 100 square feet of floor area to be located, at landlord's expense, in the centers of suspended acoustical tiles per tenant's final space plans. Color of sprinkler head cover to be matte white.

Heating, ventilation, and air-conditioning. Landlord shall cause the appropriate mechanical and electrical engineers for the base-building work to prepare the plans for and install the HVAC primary distribution system, secondary distribution ducts, VAV boxes, and perimeter air slot for the leased premises, which plans shall meet the following criteria:

1. The plans shall provide a system of distribution ducts, supply registers and diffusers, return grilles, and associated fixtures and equipment designed and installed on each floor of the leased premises to provide individual control of cooling, dehumidification, ventilation, and heating in each division of the leased premises, as partitioned in accordance with tenant's plans.

2. The system shall be designed to conform to tenant's plans and to operate so that sound transmission levels do not exceed a Noise Criterion rating of NC35. Landlord shall diligently take appropriate cor-

rective measures to eliminate any disturbing noise or vibration of any mechanical equipment of system furnished and installed by landlord.

3. The design of the air-conditioning system shall take into account the following occupancy schedule:
   - General offices—1 person per 150 rentable square feet
   - Meeting and conference rooms—1 person per 15 rentable square feet
4. The occupancy schedule of particular areas shown on tenant's plans may vary between 1 person per 50 rentable square feet and 1 person per 200 rentable square feet, provided that the entire floor division of the leased premises does not exceed 1 person per 150 rentable square feet and that such variances are reasonably distributed. The heating, ventilation, and air conditioning system shall meet the following design conditions, at the stated outside design conditions:
   - Summer: 100 degrees F dry bulb outside, 73 degrees F dry bulb and 50 percent relative humidity inside
   - Winter: 32 degrees F dry bulb outside, 72 degrees F dry bulb inside
   - At all other times: 72 degrees F to 73 degrees F dry bulb inside

The air handling system shall be a variable volume system, and air-conditioning units shall be designed to deliver not less than 1.0 cubic foot per minute of air per rentable square foot of area.

All reception areas shall be air-conditioned to the same degree as office space. All interior areas shall be suitably zoned, with independent zone controls, in accordance with the working drawings and good practice.

Supply outlets shall be selected for minimum drafts and noiseless and good air distribution.

The type, size, and arrangement of the diffusers shall be determined by landlord after consultation with tenant's architect.

All supply and return ducts shall be equipped with fusible link dampers as prescribed by applicable laws, if any.

Existing ductwork to have insulation intact and be free of any leakage, pressure drop, mold, or mildew.

Thermostats calibrated and in good working order. The portions of the HVAC systems provided by landlord and included as part of base-building work shall be compatible with the above.

Electrical distribution and service. As part of the base building work, landlord shall provide an electrical distribution and service system as follows.

Electrical service shall be 277/480 volts, 3-phase, 4-wire, 60 cycles through a switchboard suitable for such service. Switchboard devices shall be selectively coordinated with a ground fault protection system.

Distribution voltages shall be 277/480 volts, 4-wire, 3-phase for fluorescent lighting and integral horsepower motors; 120/280 volts, 4-wire, 3-phase for receptacle circuits, small motors, and incandescent lighting.

The electrical service provided by the electric user system shall be 7.5 watts per rentable square foot for tenant's lighting and receptacles only, excluding HVAC equipment, special systems, miscellaneous electrical loads, and elevator equipment requirements.

Circuit breaker panel boards shall be located on each floor to serve electrical loads and the portion of the leased premises on the floor as follows:

- 480/277 volt panel boards shall be 20-amp circuit size and have at least 24 circuit breakers
- 120/480 volt panel boards shall be 20-amp circuit size and have at least 42 circuit breakers

Lighting. One 2' × 4', 2-lamp, T8 parabolic lens fluorescent light fixture in good working order per 70 rentable square feet (with air handling supply and return capacity). All light fixtures shall have adequate overhead clearance to provide flexibility in fixture placement.

Miscellaneous. Landlord shall provide one 4-inch diameter vertical sleeve (core drill) and one 4-inch diameter horizontal sleeve in the telephone closet for tenant's sole use for cabling access. *Note:* This may need to be doubled or tripled for medium- and larger-sized firms.

Additionally, the following shall be required:

- Ladies' and men's rooms complete and in compliance with Americans with Disabilities Act (ADA) requirements.
- Telephone closets complete.
- Janitor closets complete.
- Electrical closets complete with service and distribution panel boards and transformers, 480/227V and 208/110V.
- Core walls with finished drywall ready for paint.
- Drinking fountains (two per floor) and in compliance with ADA requirements.
- Fire hose cabinets finished and complete with hoses and extinguishers, or as required by code.
- Exit signs (eight per floor).
- Lobby elevator doors primed and ready to receive tenant's finish or elevator lobby complete with building-standard finishes approved by the tenant and in compliance with ADA requirements.
- Core area corridor doors primed and ready to receive tenant's finish.
- Stairwell doors primed and ready to receive tenant's finish.
- Locking devices and closers for all exits, stairwell, and mechanical, electrical, and telephone room doors, and ladies' and men's toilets.
- All hardware used in public areas or core area doors shall meet ADA requirements.

- Finish paint exit corridor walls.
- Space clear of all pipes, conduits, ductwork, etc., for maximum ceiling height in accordance with the plans and to accommodate building-standard fluorescent fixtures without modification. It is also understood that all building-standard fluorescent light fixtures will fit properly under any structural beams or joists.
- All pipe sleeves in beams, walls, and slabs to be packed airtight with required fireproofing material.
- Fire and life safety requirements per city, county, state, and ADA codes.
- Ground level complete (elevator lobbies, landscaping, truck dock, fan rooms, etc.)
- All mechanical, electrical, elevator, escalator, etc. base-building systems complete and operational.
- All general exhaust requirements complete and operational.
- Certificate of Occupancy.

Exhibit 8.1
BASIC NEGOTIATION GOALS

The exhibit below illustrates issues that need to be negotiated in the work letter where the law firm assumes control of the project.

The following describes the condition of a tenant's leased premises and provisions in the base building prior to commencement of tenant construction. This would be for a <u>very low to mid-range cost build-out</u>. High-end build-outs require more allowances.

Negotiation Goals: Base Building Shell Conditions of Tenant Space

a. Completed elevator lobby including millwork paneling on walls, marble base and border floor tile, inset carpet, painted drywall ceiling, and ceiling mounted incandescent lighting fixtures. (This can be modified to describe any level of design finish and detail. The object is to get the landlord to pay for something he would benefit from later.)

b. Completed ADA compliant men's and women's restrooms; ceiling hung metal toilet partitions, gypsum board ceiling, granite counter tops at lavatories, wall-mounted toilets and urinals, porcelain tile on floors and all walls. (This is a typical definition of restroom finishes in a Class A building.)

c. Lease space must be broom clean and free of debris. Floor slabs smooth and level to $\frac{1}{4}''$ in 10' non-accumulative, per American Concrete Institute Standards.

d. Completed perimeter drywall column covers and soffits taped, floated, sanded and ready to paint.

e. Completed core drywall taped, floated, sanded and ready to paint or to receive wall covering.

f. Building standard 4' × 4' fine-line Tegular ceiling grid installed at 9'0" above floor slab except at floors with higher ceilings.

g. Building standard 2' × 2' ceiling tile stocked in boxes on the floor.

h. Building standard 2' × 4' 18-cell parabolic fluorescent lighting fixtures lamped and stocked on the floor per allowance as stated in the lease.

i. Building standard 277 V lighting grid installed above ceiling grid.

j. Building standard 110 V power grid installed above ceiling grid.

k. Building standard HVAC distribution trunks installed above ceiling grid.

l. Heating units and air slots installed at perimeter drywall soffits.

m. Building standard sprinkler grid installed at ceiling height on a 15' × 15' distribution grid with temporary heads in upturned position.

n. Sleeved openings in the floors of base building telephone closets to chase your voice/data lines so you do not bear the costs.

Technology and Law Firm Design

9

Every firm needs a technology plan, if for no other reason than to adapt to the obsolescence of its infrastructure and to keep its software licenses in order. The existing and projected technologies employed by a firm have a major effect on the suitability and choice of buildings, so technology systems deserve careful analysis early in the planning process. In fact, we consider lead time so important that we include the technology discussion near the front of this book, rather than letting it appear to be an afterthought.

This is the first of two chapters about finding technological solutions to design problems and about housing technology. Technological support for the firm merits two chapters because it is vital to support the practice, it enables design solutions, and it can be very expensive. Large domestic and international law firms have grown and developed right along with higher technology, and law firms now demonstrate an unprecedented level of technological sophistication. Technology costs for law firms can exceed 25 percent of the cost of construction. Investments in technological solutions must be cost effective.

One of the most striking and tangible examples of cost-effective technological solutions is that modern law firms are now able to use spaces that would once have been considered inconceivable as law firm real estate. Inventive approaches to security, access, and communication issues have made these spaces work. Communication technology may make it possible to avoid moving the firm by (a) permitting expansion of selected functions into remote buildings, (b) allowing the firm to move some functions to noncontiguous parts of the original building, or (c) letting the firm use less-expensive space in the same building.

Today's technology will never again be considered as valuable as it is right at this moment. Equipment, security needs, and communications will undergo significant changes during the time it takes to build your law office. If we are to be at all helpful, our advice about building for technology needs to be in generalities, and we must also advise you to be ready for changes. In the Technology Checklist we include information for pointing your building design in the right direction.

Sidebar: Technology Checklist

- Build flexibly, so that you accommodate technology that is current on your moving day, as well as your best estimate of technology you will adopt later. Carefully consider your specific needs for technology infrastructure, mobility, comfort, security, and connectivity, and be certain that your building and ancillary spaces can accommodate specific requirements.

- Consider using technologies from industry leaders. Moving or reworking your office provides a fine opportunity to review systems needs, and whatever drives your move is likely to change your technology needs. Presuming that the leading systems are stable and backward compatible, minimizing future changes to your technological infrastructure tends to produce a corresponding stability in your longer-range building needs. In any case, scalable systems that can grow or change with the firm should be preferred because they minimize changes to your infrastructure and your building. The longer a system remains useful and supported by the seller, the less likely it is that your space needs will change in response to system changes. Although the biggest-selling systems are not necessarily the best for a given application, you may find some comfort in determining which are the most popular with peer law firms. To find out which systems the bigger firms use to support their services, check the annual AmLaw Tech Survey, which appears as a supplement to *The American Lawyer.*

- Allow for changing work styles in a new technological environment. When electronic legal research was very young, we designed a big rolling cart to hold the bulky new Westlaw equipment and an acoustic modem, so that a single system could be rolled into any

---

office and used by plugging the telephone handset into the machine. Later, the little red Ubiq terminal made it possible to put Lexis on everyone's desk and use a centralized printer. Not too many years later, the availability of these systems on handheld machines serves as a reminder that work styles and workplaces change. Technology companies are working to develop products that are less dependent on building configurations. Make the most of their products. Wireless technologies, if secure, can save infrastructure costs. At relatively low costs, the storage capacity of our computers and other appliances is growing by leaps and bounds, increasing the efficiency and independence of our machinery. As we write this, some especially noteworthy improvements are becoming available: inexpensive large-capacity hard drives, improved video monitor technology, and radio frequency identification gear.

- Consider space outsourcing. If technologies make it possible, move functions to cheaper space. Space costs are part of document handling, and automation of document handling can save on the cost of building space, as well as providing improved information management, retrieval, and storage. Technology solutions expand the usability of law firm conference rooms and multipurpose rooms, and this chapter presents some of the technologies that add value to a new office or a renovation project.

Conference Room Technology

At a minimum, all conference rooms should allow audio teleconferencing. The least expensive way to accomplish this is by speaker phone. A speaker phone typically sits in the middle of the conference table. It is wise to provide power and voice/data outlets under conference tables so that cords do not have to stretch from a wall outlet and become a tripping hazard. More sophisticated systems have microphones built into the tabletop, table edge, or in the ceiling, and have speakers recessed-mounted in the ceiling.

Conference room technology has rapidly changed in the last decade to support the needs of people who travel with laptop computers. For all-day meetings, people whose laptop batteries are not going to last all day require external power sources to keep their computers going. Attendees often do not want to use their batteries in the conference room because they may be getting on a plane right after the meeting and need to save their battery resources.

The firm's answer to this is smart conference tables. Smart conference tables have electrical wiring and voice/data connections. This can provide everyone in the room with the ability to contact his or her own server, and retrieve, share, and edit documents during the meeting. The key is that the table needs to have multiple types of phone and data outlets. Outlets should be color-coded so that it is readily apparent which is for voice, data, or analog. The connectors should also be standard jack types such as RJ-45 (typically used for voice) and RJ-11 (typically used for data).

It is common practice to install the telecom or audio teleconferencing devices within the conference table so that wires do not have to be stretched across to a wall outlet. Various methods of concealing equipment in the table top makes it unobtrusive. For example, one manufacturer features a square cutout in the tabletop that can be the same material as the table. Pushing on one corner of this fifteen-inch square causes the telecommunications outlets to appear, and pushing it again causes it to return to the flat tabletop surface. This device can also be used to hide speaker phones when not in use.

Electrical power outlets may be done in the same fashion, or concealed in a trough down the center of the table with small, concealed-hinge doors with plug outlets a few inches below the tabletop. With the doors closed, brush sweeps allow the cords for the PCs or other devices to come up unobtrusively through the table.

Very small microphones may be mounted under conference tables, around the edge or in the center. They may be very discreet, approximately one-half inch in diameter. They need to be placed and designed carefully so that they do not pick up the rustle of papers on a table.

Within the same smart conference table, you can have controls for the audiovisual system. In a typical large conference room or boardroom, all the cables go back to a rack, usually wall-mounted in a control room behind the conference room. Technicians can work on the system in this room while a meeting is taking place. In essence, all of the technology is in the control room, although it integrates seamlessly with activities in the conference room.

Another phenomenon that we have observed in smart conference rooms is an armoire or breakfront unit that is built to conceal a flat plasma screen. This unit can also house a printer so conferees can immediately print out changes to a document. The armoire might also have a fax machine and scanner, becoming a minioffice in a single piece of furniture. The equipment can be discreetly hidden behind the armoire doors not in use.

Speakers are typically mounted eight to ten feet apart in conference rooms. They should be directly behind the people seated at the conference table. Skillful implementation of the system insures that when a person is speaking on the microphone at the front of the room, he or she can be heard at the same voice level throughout the room.

As the cost of plasma screens drops, we anticipate that they will be common features in smart conference rooms and smart reception areas. Some firms have installed them in reception room walls to deliver programmed content. In some areas of the country, especially where news media provide critical legislative or administrative news, we also see smart credenzas, where the push of a button raises a television or flat-screen monitor from the top of the unit.

These technology devices in conference rooms come at a high cost, so firms are not wiring every conference room in this manner. However, basic smart-table equipment can be found at reasonable cost, so we now see a majority of conference rooms being built with support for laptops and other equipment.

Videoconferencing

Videoconferencing has recently seen major changes, both in technology and affordability. The cost of video technology has dropped, permitting multiple permanent installations as upgrades from portable units. In video projection systems, images are projected either through front screen or rear screen projection technology. Rear screen projection produces less distortion and a better quality image than front screen projection, and seems to be regaining popularity with law firms. Front screen projection requires careful selection of the mounting location, which is normally recessed in the ceiling. Most people prefer not to see the projector mounted to the ceiling where it is always visible, and the automatic lifts are expensive.

Modern rear screen projection uses Plexiglas screens instead of the very costly glass screens used in the past, and the Plexiglas produces the same high-quality image. In a typical installation, a technology room eight to ten feet deep is located behind the screen, adjacent to the conference room. The equipment in this room is rack-mounted and everything is controlled from a smart podium in the conference room. All the surfaces (walls, ceiling, and floor) in the rear screen projection room must be black. An interior room is best, but if the room is on the exterior, it needs blackout shades.

Smart Podium

A smart podium is not portable within a room because of the myriad of cables coming up from the floor below. A decision on a permanent location for the podium needs to be made early in the process. Typically, a flat screen is mounted at a slight angle in the podium work surface. This is a touch screen that allows the speaker (for example, a managing partner who is not familiar with all the bells and whistles of the smart podium) to operate the controls by touching icons on the screen with a finger. These icons control such things as the beginning and end of the presentation, as well as making preprogrammed connections with other locations. For example, if there are offices in five or six other cities, the person at the podium can automatically connect to those locations by touching the screen.

A smart podium can also control the lighting within the room. The lighting typically has five or six preset scenes—the lights could be all illuminated for one type of presentation, and selectively dimmed for other types of presentations. The touch screen can also control a projection screen that rolls down from the ceiling, or blackout shades for the windows. The touch screen can also be used to automatically raise a set of doors that conceals a food service setup. (For more on this, see the conference room section in Chapter 5.

The infrastructure for these smart conference or multipurpose rooms needs to be built along with the other construction, so planning for them must occur very early in the design process. This is another decision that the firm must make at the very beginning, when setting goals and deciding about the kind of leading technology they want to see in their public areas.

Multipurpose Rooms

Larger firms often have multipurpose rooms from 1,200 to 4,500 square feet in size, big enough to accommodate all the partners or all the lawyers in the firm. The rooms may become so large that screens at the front of the room may not provide images large enough for the people in the back of the room to see. Rooms this big need screens mounted on the side walls, halfway down the length of the room. This is typically a plasma screen on an arm or bracket that pulls out from the wall so that people from the middle to the back of the room can see detailed images.

When planning the wiring for multipurpose rooms, do not forget to consider flush floor outlets for power, voice, and data lines. These rooms may be set up in multiple configurations, either with tables in small classroom-type groups, in a large U-shaped configuration, or other arrangements. There should always be power and data available for people (such as vendors) coming from outside the firm to plug in equipment for video presentations, power their laptops and access data, or set up other types of demonstrations like mock arguments or continuing legal education presentations.

Web Conferencing

Until recently, videoconferencing has been almost exclusively used by larger law firms. Web conferencing, however, is a fast-growing business phenomenon used by firms of all sizes. As we write this, more and more videoconferencing is being done over the Internet. Web conferencing is developing quickly, making giant steps in the quality and security of video applications for business. We expect that improving video applications using common, inexpensive cameras and high-speed Internet connections will be suitable for less formal applications than is the typical video-equipped conference room. In addition to being less expensive, newer applications run with minimal requirements for space. When doing technology planning, your firm should develop a position on the informal teleconferencing your technology needs to support, and what your clients require.

It is useful to find out what firms similar to yours do to support networking technology and applications. *The American Lawyer* magazine, in addition to its regular features, publishes the AmLaw Tech Survey, an annual survey of technology use in larger firms.

The Association of Legal Administrators' Web site, **http://www .alanet.org**, provides a search system that directs members to topics of interest, and articles on specific technologies and building design issues are included there.

Utilities, Lighting, and Security

10

Technology planning, as we treat it in this chapter, includes not only computer technology and its related security and information management aspects, but also communications, lighting, electrical, mechanical, and the building technology of heating, ventilation, and air-conditioning.

Electrical Power

Suggested power and communication locations in lawyer offices are shown in Exhibit 10.1.

A partner office typically has at least one duplex electrical outlet on each wall. The wall behind the desk or credenza normally has a fourplex outlet. This is four simplex (single) outlets rather than two duplex outlets. Two of the outlets in the fourplex are typically wired in what is called a daisy chain to identical outlets in other offices. These outlets are used only for computers, printers, and other peripheral devices. This avoids having a dedicated run back to the panel for each office, and allows three or four offices to be linked. These outlets are color-coded, perhaps gray rather than white, and everyone in the firm is instructed to use only the gray outlets for computer equipment. The other two outlets in the fourplex are called general convenience outlets. They are there for plugging in a radio, pencil sharpener, or (heaven forbid!) a space heater. The idea is to keep "clean" power just for computers, because isolated equipment can be better protected from voltage spikes and can avoid getting "dirty" power from such things as paper shredders and electric pencil sharpeners.

An associate office typically has one fourplex outlet and one or two duplex outlets, one for the credenza and one for the desk. An associate usually has two voice and two data outlets (one set) mounted under one faceplate. Partner offices typically receive two sets of voice/data outlets, each under one faceplate. The main reason for the distinction is simply that partner offices are generally larger and allow more flexibility of furniture arrangement. Technicians typically pull at least two Category 5 or Category 6 cables. These outlets can be split for either voice or data, but it is inexpensive to pull a second cable along with the first, and it provides valuable flexibility for adapting to changing technology. Networking technology no longer requires dedicated Ethernet cabling. Voice and data lines are interchangeable, depending on how and where they are terminated. Typically there are different-sized jacks for voice and data, RJ-45 and RJ-11. To install a fax machine in an office, one of these lines can easily be converted to an analog line. To bring in a network printer, one can be changed to a data line, depending on where and how lines are terminated at the end user and back at the termination or punch-down blocks. See examples of typical power and communication device locations within the typical workstations. To decipher the symbols, the triangle represents a voice/data box location. A duplex electrical outlet is shown as a circle with two lines through it, and a fourplex outlet is the circle with four lines through it in a crosshatch pattern. A more complete table of architectural symbols is shown on page 267.

It cannot be stated too strongly or too often how important it is that a law firm think about technology from the very beginning of the planning stage—where technology will be in the new space, and how power and data will be connected to it. For that reason, an equipment inventory should be done as soon as you start the project. See an example of an equipment inventory form in Chapter 6, Exhibit 6.1. An inventory form should be completed for each item of equipment that the firm anticipates using. Note that dimensions and *servicing* dimensions are very important. You should also request technical cut sheets from all vendors for each piece of equipment. If you have different models of equipment, you need a cut sheet for each model. The cut sheet should indicate all of the environmental requirements for the equipment. The environmental requirements include the electrical power, amperage, voltage, BTU output when running and idling, special outlets, and space needed. Space requirements are typically larger than the piece of equipment itself to allow for technicians to access the back and sides of the equipment. Space requirements include, for example, access for changing toner, cartridges, or other consumables, and for clearing paper jams. The location of the on-off switch should be considered in the planning.

Lighting

In any office, lighting plays a significant role in physical fatigue and eye strain, which can affect efficiency and profits. For people who spend long hours at their desks, the effect is magnified. The most noticeable way that good lighting can reduce eyestrain and fatigue is by minimizing or eliminating glare on a computer screen, but the same is true for eliminating glare on books and papers on the work surface.

The best type of lighting is indirect or ambient lighting, where the light source is suspended from the ceiling and bounces off the ceiling and downward to the task plane (the desktop). A new generation of lights recessed in the ceiling can accomplish the same goal. Ambient lighting can be augmented by task lighting, which is an additional direct light source for reading fine print and doing detailed work. This light source should be below the user's eye level when seated so as not to direct light into the eyes. This can be accomplished with an adjustable-arm task light or a linear strip under an overhead cabinet.

Fluorescent lighting is most frequently used in office space for several reasons:

- Low operating cost
- More lumens (amount of light) for the money
- Long lamp life (20,000 hours versus 2,000 hours for a typical incandescent lamp)
- Low heat output (so it is easier to air-condition the space)

Most buildings come equipped with building-standard lighting. These are typically 2′ × 4′ or 2′ × 2′ fluorescent light fixtures. A landlord generally wants uniformity in lighting so the building looks the same from the exterior, as well as for ease in changing burned-out bulbs. The 2′ × 4′ fixtures usually accommodate two or three four-foot fluorescent tubes. This is the most economical type of lamp. In our opinion, the best type of 2′ × 4′ fixture is an indirect-direct fixture. This fixture allows light to bounce off the light fixture housing and down to the user plane (desktop). The perforated basket allows some filtered direct light as well. These fixtures are recessed into the ceiling.

The next-best type of 2′ × 4′ light fixture is a parabolic. This typically has an eighteen-cell reflector. These fixtures are fairly effective for eliminating glare on computer screens. The deeper the height of the reflector, the better the glare cutoff. Ideally, the reflector is about four inches deep. In some buildings where the height of the plenum (space above the ceiling) is limited due to ductwork, sprinkler lines, and so on, reflectors may be two inches deep. The glare cutoff is not nearly as good as with the deeper cell.

One of the worst types of 2′ × 4′ fluorescent fixtures has an almost opaque acrylic lens. We urge you to avoid these because of the high degree of glare they cast on your screen.

The worst possible type of fluorescent light fixture is the type that is surface mounted to the ceiling. They tend to give the room a cave-like appearance as the top portion of the walls goes into shadow.

Private Office Switching

Among the best new developments in 2′ × 4′ fixtures are those that have two ballasts. With this feature and two light switches in an office, you can have one lamp, two lamps, or three lamps operating. Not everyone has the same preference in the amount of light they use for work. This gives the office user a choice. It is a good feature for conference rooms, and a very good feature for multipurpose rooms.

Placement of Lighting Fixtures

The placement of lighting fixtures is important to combat eye fatigue. The best position is to the left and right of your shoulders. This position allows the light to spread evenly over the work surface. Try to avoid having light fixtures in front and behind you. If a light is in front, the glare can bounce off your desk and back up into your eyes. Fixtures behind your head can mean you will be working in your own shadow. Both of these things cause eyestrain and fatigue.

Color

Although fluorescent lighting is the most effective for reasons stated earlier, it has its deficiencies. In your office, color is as you light it. The lighting spectrum for most offices goes from 1900K to 4200K (K stands for Kelvin–the standard color temperature measurement system). A typical A lamp has a color rendering of 1900K. An A lamp is what you probably have in a living room tableside lamp. It gives off a yellowish light. "Cool white" fluorescent begins at about 4200K. This kills most of the warm tones of the color spectrum and gives off a very cold, blue light. It is very unfriendly, because it takes away warm skin tones and makes people appear washed out. Avoid this type of light. You may find it as building standard in cheaper office buildings. If this is the case in a building you have selected, negotiate into your lease a provision for SP3200 or SP3500 lamps in your fluorescent light fixtures for the life of your lease. These lamps fall near the midpoint of the Kelvin scale, meaning that they are friendly to all colors of the light spectrum.

Another type of fluorescent lamp to avoid is "warm white." Although this used to be considered a high grade of industry standard; it is passé because it emits a pink-yellow coloration.

For public areas such as conference rooms and reception areas, lighting can vary from the normal fluorescent. Incandescent lighting in public areas can be very warm and inviting, and some combinations of fluorescent and incandescent lights can be quite effective.

The trend in lighting is to emit a whiter type of light. This is true in both incandescent and fluorescent light sources. The next time you are in a high-end boutique or jewelry store, observe the type of lighting that is used. (For that matter, look at a Gap store.) It is basically a quartz type of lighting that is color friendly to the whole color spectrum, from reds to blues to yellows (the three basic colors from which all other colors are made).

If you rent an existing space as-is, re-lamping the existing light fixtures (changing the light bulbs to more current technology) can have a very dramatic effect on the space for very little money. For example, if there are down lights or wall washers in the space, re-lamping them to a quartz type lamp source can turn a dark, dull reception area or conference room into a vibrant, new-feeling space. Typically, the landlord has a maintenance person who can do this for you. If not, get on a ladder, take out the existing lamp, measure the diameter of the reflector (the opening) and the height from the socket to the bottom of the light fixture. See if you can read any information as to the manufacturer's product number or the maximum wattage of the fixture. (*Do not ever* exceed the recommended wattage; you could cause a fire or overload the circuit and trip a breaker.) Then take the information to a lighting store and ask them to suggest a replacement in a quartz or halogen type of lamp. Try one or two at first, until you are pleased with the result. Then re-lamp the remaining fixtures.

Because incandescent lamps can be costly, here are a few tips:

- Using 130V lamps rather than 120V lamps can prolong the life of a lamp, because the 130V lamps can handle voltage spikes better (a common cause of lamps burning out).
- Installing a dimmer on incandescent lamps and dimming them to 80 percent of the maximum can prolong lamp life.
- Turn off the lights when leaving. The whole floor does not need to be lighted just because one or two lawyers are working late. Lamps are not designed to be constantly on—they need a rest. Having said that, we should clarify that in commercial space, codes require enough light to find the fire exit in the event of a power failure. This can either be done through the base-building emergency generator or through battery backup systems. Therefore, it is wise to use a fluorescent light source for emergency lighting due to its longer lamp life.

Cabling and Fiber Optics

Twenty years ago, we heard that fiber optics would be the cable of the future. This has not proven to be the case because of the expense involved. Though the price of fiber optics has gone down greatly, the technology is not being implemented for much other than network backbones. A backbone is a cabling run that covers a great distance. For example, a law firm might be located on the thirtieth floor and above, with their computer room in a lower elevator bank on the eighth floor. To run many, many lines that distance would be space prohibitive in terms of the number of core drills that would have to go down through all of the floors. Therefore, a fiber optic backbone is typically installed for the building, and each floor has a wiring closet where the wires can terminate and pick up the fiber optics. The fiber optic cable becomes the backbone and runs to a computer room to be broken down and distributed into wiring panels.

The industry standard for cabling today (though it will probably change again in a few years) is moving from Category 5 and Category 5e cabling systems to Category 6. Advancing technology and the increasing speed of data transmission require new capabilities in wiring standards. Category 6 wiring is designed for the Gigabit Ethernet standard, and because it uses a changed wiring scheme, a temporary current limitation with Category 6 is finding qualified people who can properly terminate Category 6.

Another determination that needs to be made (typically by your computer system vendor) is whether cable should be shielded or unshielded. Cable is typically run in the plenum. In most instances, the plenum is fire rated; therefore the cabling has to be fire rated as well, or it has to be run in conduit. Conduit is expensive, cumbersome, and quickly outdated, so the best choice is fire-rated cable. All cable needs to be tied in bundles and supported by metal wires attached to the structure above. The cable vendor should not be allowed to use the ceiling grid support wires to support cable. An even better solution is a cable trough to carry the cables above the ceiling, but cost issues often make this the first item to go from the cable budget.

In the case of an older building with a gypsum board ceiling rather than an accessible ceiling, it may be advisable to install one or more four-inch conduits and run cable in them. If that cable needs to be changed, there will be a chaseway for the new cable and you will not need to tear up hard ceilings for access.

Ideally, cables in the walls should be in conduits. The alternative is "ring and string," where cables are pulled through walls without conduits. Be aware, however, that if you pull wires without conduits before both sides of the wall are covered with drywall, you run the risk of skewering the unprotected wires with drywall screws.

Ergonomics in the Workplace

Ergonomics are very important in law firms because of the number of long, continuous hours people work. This is true for all staff levels. The last two decades has seen a rise in musculoskeletal disorders (MSD). Carpal tunnel syndrome is probably the most notorious of these. Many legal secretaries are experiencing these problems due to long hours spent on a computer keyboard. The U.S. Department of Labor is now saying that MSD cases are on the decline, probably because of steps that have been taken to design work areas with more flexibility. People do not come in the same sizes and shapes, but typically workstations are designed alike for economic reasons. Some important improvements can be made to workstations to make them more user-friendly. Since not everyone is the same height, adjustable chairs are important, along with adjustable ergonomic keyboards. Before we go any farther, we need to insert a word about expectations. One cannot expect user-friendly furniture alone to eliminate fatigue and stiffness. Even with the best of furniture, people should occasionally get up and move, such as walking rather than rolling a chair to the printer. Even if it is only a matter of getting up for a minute or two to stretch your spine and legs, this gets the circulation going.

Work surface heights have also changed with the use of computers. A secretarial station used to have two desk heights: one about thirty inches for the major work surface and one about twenty-six inches for a typewriter. Typewriter depths were several inches.

The important thing has always been to keep the forearm and thigh parallel to the floor. The guideline from the Occupational Safety and Health Administration (OSHA) recommends a lower desk height. The new standard is twenty-eight and one-half inches.

Now, with more shallow keyboards, work surfaces can be one height, thus eliminating the step-down. We also can have adjustable keyboards. Keyboards can be as simple as those that pull out from below a work surface, or can be models that may be raised or lowered, and permit adjustment of the forward and backward tilt. Some have padded wrist rests. It is good to vary the keyboard position to avoid keeping the hands and arms in the same position.

Secretarial chairs no longer need to be armless. Nowadays, many have small arms, since it is good to support the tip of the elbows on a partial-depth arm to help support the weight of the shoulders and neck.

Another practice that proved injurious to secretaries was raising the height of their computer screens. Computer screens diminished in size after LCD screens were first introduced (though now they are getting larger), and one of the mistakes that secretaries made for many years was putting a phone book, CPU, or surge protector under a monitor to elevate the height of the screens. The thought was "the higher, the better," but this is not the case. The top of the screen (not the monitor case) should be equal to the user's eyes. In effect, your eyes should be at the same angle as if you had a newspaper in front of you and were holding it with both hands reading it.

Another way to demonstrate a natural eye level is to close your eyes for fifteen seconds while in a seated position, and then open your eyes and remember the position your eyes were in when they opened. This is the natural reading position to eliminate back-of-the-neck and shoulder strain. Again, properly fitted equipment does not insure that people will avoid ergonomic problems. For example, many computer users who wear bifocals or trifocals have to tip their heads back in order to read through the bottom section of their lenses. A remedy is to purchase a pair of reading glasses and avoid tipping your head back constantly, which creates neck and back strain.

For basic comfort and productivity, the most important piece of furniture is the adjustable chair. Nowadays, task seating is more universal. Many firms are standardizing on the same type of seating for partners, associates, paralegals, and secretaries. Since the range of human body shapes is so great, some furniture makers offer work chairs in small, medium, and large sizes. Some firms keep an assortment of chair sizes to handle individual needs.

An office chair typically is equipped with a pneumatic gas lift that raises or lowers the height of the seat for the user. Arms can be moved outward for wider body styles or inward for narrower body styles. The tilt of the chair can be either in a rocking position, in a tilt position, or it can even be tilted slightly forward. Some people find it more comfortable to type in a slightly forward position. But you can still have the lower back support follow you as you lean forward if a chair has lumbar support.

Lumbar (lower back) support is very important, and the backs of some chairs are built to support the lumbar area. All chairs need to swivel so that the user can switch from one work surface to the other without exerting much effort. Workstations are typically designed these days so that you can work to the left or to the right, creating either a C-shaped work surface or an L-shaped work surface. Users can choose to put a computer on the desk, on the side, or at the rear. In many offices where glare comes in from an outside source, being able to position the screen out of the glare is extremely important.

Eyestrain from computer glare can cut productivity dramatically. Eyes become very tired and people become physically fatigued if they are constantly looking into a screen that has glare sources. (The section above on lighting discusses how to eliminate glare sources on a computer screen.) Also to avoid eyestrain and fatigue, when shopping for monitors, buy the best resolution you can afford.

Anyone who has seen the diminishing returns of a long meeting has seen good evidence that ergonomics should also be considered in designing a conference room. The height of work surfaces has lowered over the years; so has the height of conference tables. Conference tables should never exceed twenty-nine inches. Adjustable-height chairs can be used in conference rooms to accommodate different body sizes. (A problem with using adjustable chairs in conference rooms is that the chair arms may hit the underside of the table. When this happens, the arms wear out. One solution to this is that the "conference room police"—the people cleaning up after a conference—go in and lower all of the chairs to the same height, which is easy to do with pneumatic gas lifts. It is also aesthetically displeasing to walk into a conference room and see chairs around a table where each has a different back height.)

Ergonomic issues translate into economic and human-resource issues. Our understanding of productivity, fatigue, and job-related injuries tells us that the bottom line looks better if we mind the lighting and the work spaces to make them better places to work. New work styles in law firms are making it more important to consider ergonomics, especially in the growing number of situations where a workstation or a desk is used by more than one person. The trend toward standardization of offices provides flexibility to move lawyers from one office to another with a minimum of trouble or expense. However, since lawyers come in all shapes and sizes, adjustable furniture is critical to the success of the arrangement. The same is true of shared work spaces, such as offices for visiting lawyers and support functions that operate 24-7.

Because your choice of furniture is important to the firm, asking furniture dealers for sample chairs to try in your office is a good practice. The office furniture business is very competitive, and dealers often lend chairs from their stock. Mock-ups are worth their weight in gold! A mock-up is an unfinished or finished full-sized vignette of a secretarial station, a lawyer office, or a paralegal workstation that can be tested for space dimensions, height, functionality, convenience, and acoustical integrity. It can be modified and fine-tuned before many multiples of the real thing are built.

Acoustics

Acoustics are extremely important in a law firm for obvious client confidentiality reasons. Mass is what stops sound. Sound travels in one direction until it hits an object that causes it to refract. When touring other law firms before beginning your planning process, it is important to see demonstrations of different levels of acoustic privacy. For example, check privacy between lawyer offices. Have one person go into an office, and another person go into an adjacent office. One of them should make a conference call with raised and lowered voice levels. Let the person in the other office determine what level (we call it a threshold of pain) he or she is willing to live with. Most people do not want to hear intelligible speech, while the muffled sound of unintelligible speech may be acceptable. Some people do not even want to be able to hear any type of noise between offices.

There is obviously a price tag for silence. Because mass stops sound, the more layers of wallboard you put on the studs between the offices, the more sound will be stopped. The best way to achieve good sound integrity is to take the partitions from the floor (or slab) to the underside of the structure above. This requires cutting the ceiling grid. If you extend the partition above the ceiling to the floor structure above, that also stops sound. There are various ways to do this. One way is to build what is called a pony wall above the office walls, which are normally supported by the ceiling grid. The pony wall is a studded wall on top of the ceiling that reaches to the structure above. It may have only insulation within the studs, which are still typically on sixteen-inch centers. It can have wallboard on top of the studs as well as insulation, or it can be covered with rigid fiberboard. The least-expensive way to create a pony wall is to attach rigid fiberboard to the structure above and not use studs above the ceiling.

Your builder can also lay batting insulation over the top of the partitions above the ceilings. The insulation, especially if you use two layers and stagger the joints, helps muffle sound. Remember that the plenum space is used for air return back to the mechanical room. It is typically not a ducted exhaust. This means that the whole airflow is pulled back to the mechanical room through this four-foot plenum space; therefore, sound and odors also travel there above the ceilings.

Blanketing the entire ceiling with three-inch insulation batting is another way of cutting down on sound without taking partitions to the deck above, but your builder must remember not to cover any light fixtures with the batting, as it then becomes a combustion hazard.

Another way to neutralize sound is with a sound-masking system. These are also called white-noise or pink-noise systems. They were developed back in the 1960s and early 1970s when the open-office concept was very popular. These systems consist mainly of speakers mounted in the plenum above the ceiling that generate noise to muffle intelligible speech. The system distributes background noise into the space. Occasionally, when these systems are shut off (such as on a weekend) and a lawyer goes into his office when another lawyer is a few offices away, they both suddenly become very aware of hearing each other. Without the sound-masking system on, a very intelligible level of speech can be heard. Hard construction (taking partitions to the deck above) and sound-masking systems cost approximately the same. We prefer hard construction because we know it is always going to work, while sound masking only works if it is turned on. Sound-masking systems tend to be inadequate if they are not professionally designed. We have seen an instance where a two-gallon paint can was installed in the ceiling with a speaker in it to produce noise!

Acoustic privacy in law firm conference rooms is extremely important and you should never rely on sound masking alone to achieve it. At a minimum, conference rooms need to have at least two layers of wallboard continuously going to the structure. In this construction, the wallboard does not stop at the ceiling, but continues up through the ceiling level to the deck above. The ceiling is then installed around the partitions. We also recommend doubling the number of layers of wallboard on the studs below the ceiling.

To be very certain about sound transference, there really should be four layers going to structure; two on each side of the stud. We have even installed six layers on these studs; four of which continue to the structure above and two that stop just a few inches above the ceiling. Also, it is extremely important in law firms that partitions be insulated. This is typically in a 2½-inch stud, which is the most common means of construction. A 2½-inch metal stud needs a 2½-inch sound blanket in it. This should run vertically between the studs for the distance of the stud. If the stud continues to structure above, then the sound batting should continue to structure.

Other areas of acoustical leaks are through air return grilles. Air is supplied into an office and has to be returned out of the office to a plenum. In Class A buildings these air returns are typically done through perimeter air slots that are also used for supplying air. Depending on the quantity of air being returned, the task can also be accomplished through return air openings in light fixtures or through an air grille of appropriate size (often 2′ × 2′ or 1′ × 1′). Along with the air, sound is transferred back into the plenum and carried throughout the offices.

Electrical and voice/data outlets are mounted in a metal junction box that is a source of sound transfer. Never mount the junction boxes for two different offices in the same stud cavity. (See the diagram in Exhibit 10.2.) Between lawyer offices, you should typically have a pliable, acoustical outlet pad applied to the back of those boxes. This should be done in every conference room as well, and also in demising walls (walls that separate a tenant's suite from another tenant's suite, or from building common areas). We are not as concerned about the transfer of noise from a lawyer's office into the corridor because typically that is where the doors are, and if the doors are not shut, you have acoustical transfer anyway through the door opening. Also, that is often where the secretaries are, and they usually are not right next to lawyer offices but are located at a distance from them, separated by a corridor that is used for transportation around the floor. People typically do not stop and listen outside a lawyer office because people may be watching. Therefore, the wall between a lawyer office and the corridor can have a lesser sound rating.

When it comes to a demonstration of the various acoustics when doing law firm tours, a space planning professional is of great value. He or she can show you different levels of acoustics, and give you an idea of the costs of the various solutions.

Also, at a minimum, junction boxes need to be caulked because they are another source of sound transfer. Any openings in partitions above the structure need to be caulked (for example, after the cabling is pulled there will be holes in the partitions which need to be filled). Every partition to structure also should have the wallboard joints floated and taped above the ceiling. This does not have to be final float quality, but they do need to have tape and float compound to stop sound transfer. Sound transfer also occurs around ducts that are penetrating partitions to structure, and these need to be filled with insulation or backer rod and caulked as well.

A serious acoustical breach also occurs where a partition meets a window mullion. This would be in a demising partition between lawyer offices. Be sure that your space planner adequately details an acoustical sound condition at such locations. Because floors are not level, another acoustical breach is under the wall partitions. Likewise, sound slips through two parallel planes. It is necessary to caulk under the wallboard on each side of the partition. If a contractor caulks only under the floor runner, this is not enough.

Security Systems

Sidebar

One special note seems appropriate here, and that concerns administering the security system installation. This might appear to be a vendor that you could administer yourself. However, due to the nature of the multiple interfaces that affect obtaining the all-critical certificate of occupancy (CO), we recommend that this contract be put under the general contractor. The security system has to be tested with the life safety system, the door hardware, and possibly the millwork, door, and frame manufacturer. Additionally, consider the required coordination of the base building's elevators and entrance devices, the tenant's security cameras, and the other installations that fall within the responsibility of the general construction contract.

Every law office or law firm needs some type of security system to control entrance into their space. This can be as simple as a manual keypad on the front door lock or as sophisticated as biotech devices. Security system locations are typically found at every entrance off the elevator lobby and freight elevator lobby, fire stairwell doors (when fire stairs are used as means of internal vertical transportation for the firm), and computer rooms. The software for the security system is provided by the security vendor. It is typically installed on one of the firm's personal computers that resides in the computer room.

A duress button is usually mounted on the underside of the receptionist's desk. The receptionist can discreetly hit this button is there is a disgruntled person in the reception area. The duress button can be programmed to send a signal to the security desk of the building (which is typically on the ground floor) or to the local police department. Whoever receives the alarm knows that they need to dispatch someone immediately.

If the law firm is in a smaller building and has windows on the ground floor, they should also install contacts that alarm if the windows are opened after hours.

Security systems can be programmed so they are activated only after office hours. Local building codes often affect elevator lobby security. In an elevator lobby, the security system is tied into the base-building life support system. If a fire alarm is activated within a floor or on contiguous floors, the typical system automatically shunts electricity to the door contacts, thereby allowing free entrance into the space so that people can find the fire stairs. Some cities require that unless there is a direct means of exit to fire stairs from the elevator lobby, no security systems are allowed in elevator lobbies. Likewise, some cities or municipalities do not allow locked doors. Some cities allow you to install a panic button, typically about three inches in diameter and in close proximity to the door that says something like "In case of emergency press button and door will release within 15 seconds." This sometimes defeats the purpose of a security system, since anyone can walk up at any time, hit the button, and gain access to the space. If this happens, however, an audible alarm goes off and the security vendor is notified.

Most full-floor law firms also install discreet security cameras in the elevator lobbies and freight elevator lobbies to monitor after-hours entrance and exit. Security cameras these days can be very small—about the size of a nickel and a quarter-inch thick—and can be mounted just about anywhere.

Security systems are equipped with motion detectors that shunt power to the security device so that exit out of the space can occur without an alarm sounding.

Almost all base buildings are equipped with some type of security system for after-hours exit and entrance. Also, the parking garage within the building is typically controlled by some type of security system. Avoid having multiple security cards or systems requiring more than one card or security device. Negotiate with the landlord to have the parking garage, building door, and tenant space security all controlled by the same card. This does not mean the law firm cannot control their own security system; most firms prefer to have immediate control of their system for programming purposes.

Some of the more sophisticated security systems have an audit trail so the firm can track who has entered the space and at what time. You can also have the ability to program employees out of the security system when their employment is terminated.

The base building also has varying levels of security systems to gain after-hours entrance to the space. Many elevators now require a security card inserted in the elevator to gain entrance to floors after normal business hours. Many law firms with a single reception floor have elevators programmed so that a card is required to make an elevator stop at any lawyer floor during the day.

Law firms should also be mindful that their demising walls should extend to the structure of the floor above. The reason for this is that in a typical office building with accessible ceiling tile, someone could conceivably, after hours, use a ladder, pop up the ceiling tile, climb over the partition, and enter into the law firm space. All demising partitions should go to structure if you are on a multitenant floor. If you occupy the entire floor, the demising walls at the elevator lobby should go to structure.

The reason for security-access devices such as a card reader for entry from fire stairs is to enable people in multifloor firms to use the fire stairs as a means of vertical transportation, rather than waiting in the lobby for the elevator. Card readers and other security devices are used in freight elevator lobbies so that staff of the firm can use them as means of entry into their space, while the general public cannot.

Security cameras are typically used in freight elevator lobbies so that a receptionist or someone watching the monitor can see, for example, when a messenger arrives and wants to enter the space. This person can see the person's face on the monitor and with a push of a button release the door contact.

Keys and Initial Security

Law firms and other businesses are most susceptible to burglaries immediately after they have moved their offices. It is very important to have your system tested and operating before your move. Consider the cost of a break-in or a security breach. Aside from the loss of information or physical property, the loss of confidence in your firm could devastate your practice.

You need a combination of access systems that ensures high security, and keys are a part of it. Keys may be combined with other systems, such as keys that incorporate an electronic chip, or used together with cards or biometric identification systems. Retrofitting all of your locks is usually possible, even if the locks are made by different manufacturers. Replacing the lock cylinders with cylinders from your new key company can update all types of locks.

Proliferation of keys produces more security breaches. Limiting duplication of keys extends the useful life of your keying system as well as improving security. Various levels of security are possible with mechanical keys. Preventing duplication of keys is most effectively handled by using a system with unique keys that are not generally available. Duplicates can be made only through affiliated locksmiths with various requirements for identification or authorization, or for the highest level of security, they can be made only at the vendor's factory.

Departing employees pose another major risk of misused keys. Before you decide on a system, determine how your system will recover and deactivate keys, cards, or ID badges as soon as an employee leaves.

Masters and submasters help avoid a proliferation of keys, but their distribution must be severely limited. In most buildings, the grand master key is reserved for the building engineer and the head of security. This should unlock everything in the building. At the next level, all the locks in the firm can be keyed to one master key. Typically, the executive director, administrator, or office manager has these. The next level is submasters, which are typically for the head of a single department. Other sub-sub level keys can allow a person access to a certain group of rooms, such as an office and a project workroom, and the lowest level in the key hierarchy is for single rooms. With new hardware, keying and lock assignments are usually made in consultation with the vendor's representative, someone certified as an architectural hardware consultant (AHC) by the Door and Hardware Institute. If you do not have an AHC available, check to see if your building engineer is qualified to advise you, or hire an outside locksmith. Lock cylinders are usually keyed shortly after the lock hardware arrives. Be sure that you have an adequately large, locking key cabinet.

Biotechnology

Moving a law office provides opportunities for upgrading existing office systems. Systems for accountability and access control for copiers and network printers, mailing and shipping systems, and multifunction office machines are common upgrades, especially when new equipment can be delivered to the new office for installation before move-in.

New technology applications for physical access control and logical access control (access to information) are responding to escalating needs. Concerns about security issues have been fueled by terrorism, hacking, cost control, employee theft, confidentiality issues, and a host of related management issues. In addition, upgrades of older applications include such things as recognition of a person's signature and fingerprint-controlled time and attendance systems.

The security industry has developed new products with varying degrees of effectiveness, but the resulting trend is that we can buy better security for less money. Newer technologies, even though they may be effective, may not be appropriate for most situations, as we have seen with retinal scanning systems. These have fallen out of favor because they seem too invasive for many users. Fingerprint recognition, on the other hand, can be relatively inexpensive, unobtrusive, and effective.

Biometric security includes these types of systems:

- Fingerprint scans, which identify the characteristics of an index finger
- Retinal scans, which identify the patterns of blood vessels on the retina with laser technology
- Iris scans, which use the unique external patterns of the eye
- Hand scans, identifying the unique shape and bone structure of a hand
- Face scans, using the unique bone structure of the face, especially the relative distances between key features such as the eyes, nose, and cheekbones

Some of the newer systems are less reliable than others; however, as you investigate available products, you can expect to see different technologies used in tandem to produce better results. For example, identification cards can be set up with both magnetic strips and bar codes to activate and operate fingerprint identification or face recognition. In addition to the single-function biometric systems mentioned above, we see frequent use of keypad systems with fingerprint identifications and the use of proximity cards or devices with biometric systems.

Law firms generally have the following requirements for security:

- Easy management—not necessarily a simple system, but one the firm can control, given staff turnover, occasional hardware problems, and software or data source failure
- The ability to record the history of access by user and time
- The ability to make changes readily without compromising the security of the system

Remember that biometric security can usually be added to existing systems as an upgrade. Newer systems of all types may suffer from insufficient memory to handle the volume of new activity you contemplate, so be sure that you are acquiring a system that will not be rendered obsolete by an increase in volume. Both hardware and software should be carefully tested, preferably on site, with the key users of the system and the actual software to be used.

Networking

Because sharing and protecting the firm's work product must be a high priority matter for new offices, and since technology upgrades occur most readily with office moves or with other major changes to the building, your technology advisors need to be involved early in the process.

As we write this, servers and their client machines are more frequently being connected by wireless networks. Wi-Fi wireless technology, at this point, has been adopted more frequently in small and medium-sized firms than in larger firms. For those who have decided against installing wireless networks, security of data and standardization of systems have been the leading reasons for hard wiring the machinery. Like many other technologies, we expect improvements that address these concerns. In major installations of wireless connectivity, the materials and configuration of your building affect the placement of wireless units on the ceilings or walls. Investigate newer wireless technologies, and expect increasing wireless applications, such as storage options that require no physical connection between the data source and the storage medium.

Security advisors or consultants should work to establish the networking needs of your security systems.

Firewalls and extranets, while requiring relatively minor adjustments in the building, still have electrical needs and other technical requirements that need to be part of the plan from the beginning.

Heating, Ventilation, and Air-Conditioning

HVAC heats, cools, and supplies air circulation and humidity control within the office space. In a typical office building, there are exterior zones and interior zones. Exterior zones, because they are subject to the exposure of the glass window wall, have the ability to heat and cool as required. Interior zones are typically only cooling zones. They have no exposure to the outside, so they only circulate air and provide constant air temperature.

A typical building has chillers located either on the roof or in an adjacent structure. The chillers manufacture cold water. The cold water is pumped to the floors, where the air handler unit for that floor conditions the air. The conditioned air is then pumped out onto the floor through a primary duct distribution system. From primary ducts, it is then taken to a variable air control volume box or similar appliance. The VAV box has one thermostat that controls it. That thermostat tells the VAV box whether it requires cool or warm air. Typically, there are about twenty-two VAVs on a 20,000 square foot floor plate. Approximately fourteen of these are in exterior zones with the remainder in interior zones. Not all sides of the building require the same degree of cooling. Cooling requirements are affected by solar swing. Solar swing occurs because as the sun rises in the east it puts heat on the east side of the building, but not on the west side. As the sun moves around the building to the south during the middle of the day, that side requires most of the cooling. Then the sun goes to the west side of the building, typically the highest demand zone at that time of day. Therefore, the east does not require the same heating or cooling as the west. Likewise the north, because it is fairly passive, does not require the same cooling energy as the south.

Now, who controls the temperatures? Some people are hot-natured; some are cold-natured. Whoever has the thermostat controls the temperature. Typically, partners have priority over associates for thermostats. Also, conference rooms have priority.

In the interior zones, thermostats should be located where people are, not necessarily in storage or file rooms or project workrooms. Most buildings are now smart buildings; a building engineer can sit in his office and monitor the HVAC systems. He can then adjust thermostats from his computer. In response to a telephone call, the engineer can automatically adjust the thermostat controlling a particular person's office. Obviously, this is something he would not want to do continually, but in an emergency it can be done. Other building control systems also monitor HVAC. Remote control of temperature is a feature of small buildings as well as larger ones.

A law firm needs some type of auxiliary air system for the computer room. This should be independent of the building's system, and be capable of operating 24-7. It will probably manufacture its own chilled water for cooling.

Be aware that computers and leaking water do not mix. Have your engineers suggest monitoring and water-containment devices in case something leaks over the weekend, and install a device that immediately notifies your IT staff if there is a problem. It should also provide immediate notification if the temperature increases and approaches levels that could damage the system.

Exhibit 10.1A
PARTNER OFFICES

EXAMPLES OF TYPICAL FURNITURE
LAYOUTS FOR PARTNER OFFICES.
ALSO SHOWN ARE TYPICAL ELECTRICAL
POWER AND COMMUNICATION OUTLET
LOCATIONS. NOTE THAT THE SAME
OUTLET LOCATIONS WORK FOR ALL
FURNITURE ARRANGEMENTS.

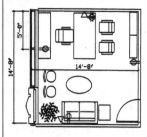

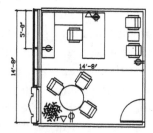

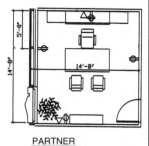

PARTNER
OFFICE 'A'

Traditional desk and credenza, bookcases, guest chairs and loveseat. This is giving way to the more modern layout shown in Partner Office B.

PARTNER
OFFICE 'B'

"C" or "U" shaped worksurface with guest chairs, small conference table. Additional storage can be made by shelves or cabinets on the wall above the worksurface.

PARTNER
OFFICE 'C'

Desk, workwall which includes computer area, files, closet, shelves and storage in a vertical unit.

Exhibit 10.1B
ASSOCIATE OFFICES

EXAMPLES OF TYPICAL FURNITURE AND ELECTRICAL
POWER AND VOICE/DATA OUTLETS IN ASSOCIATE OFFICES

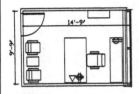

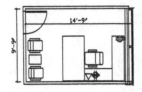

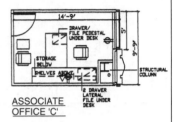

ASSOCIATE
OFFICE 'A'

ASSOCIATE
OFFICE 'B'

ASSOCIATE
OFFICE 'C'

Example of typical 10' x 15' associate office with a traditional desk and credenza arrangement, 2 guest chairs with side table, and a bookcase.

Example of typical 10' x 15' associate office with a 'C' or 'U' shaped furniture arrangement. This is very work friendly for P.C. usage. It could also have shelving mounted on the wall above the work surface.

Example of typical 10' x 15' associate office with a structural column in it and the use of a workwall. A 'T' shaped workwall works well when a credenza cannot be placed immediately behind the desk.

Exhibit 10.1C
PARALEGAL OFFICES

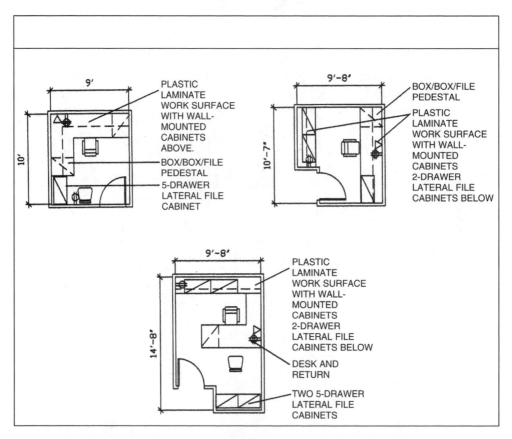

Exhibit 10.2
MOUNTING OUTLETS FOR ACOUSTICAL PRIVACY

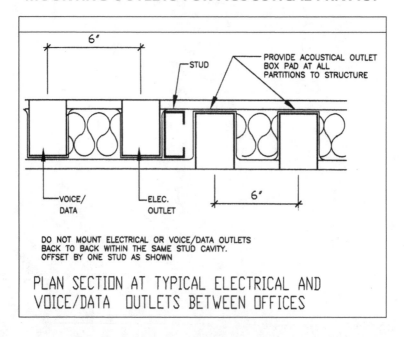

Design Standards and Decisions

11

Initial decisions for planning work areas include establishing design standards for the project and other benchmarks that control the design. This chapter suggests some generally accepted principles that help with decisions on such things as office sizes, office layouts, and traffic flow.

Offices and Work Spaces

On a typical lawyer floor, a rule of thumb is that one-third of the office space is taken up by lawyer offices. The remaining two-thirds of the space is for support facilities and ancillary functions such as secretarial and paralegal work areas, core functions such as copying, coffee service, filing, project workrooms, administrative staff and functions, and the circulation area (corridors).

High-traffic corridors, like those immediately outside the lawyer offices or those leading to and from reception and conference rooms, should be at least five feet wide. Optimally, corridors should be between 5'6" and 5'10". This allows two people to walk together and still pass another person or mail cart. Five feet is also a minimum corridor width for accessibility under ADA, unless other five-foot turning radius areas are located so wheelchairs can turn around. A minimum corridor width is 44 inches per most fire codes, except in certain areas like library stacks, where 36 inches is permissible. Always check with local code authorities for accessibility requirements. There should be a minimum of 36 inches between desks. The circulation space for corridors and aisle ways typically consumes 30 to 35 percent of the floor plate.

131

In private offices it is best to locate doors so that people cannot see from one office into another. One reason is that it is distracting to see someone else at a desk, and another reason is sound transmission. Sound travels in a straight line until it hits something. See Exhibit 11.1.

If possible, have demising walls between offices intersect structural columns that are sheathed in wallboard, rather than at mullions. Window mullions are hollow and made of metal, both of which create bad sound transmission conditions. See Exhibit 11.2.

These exhibits show sound transmission information, which is critical to acoustical integrity in law offices. There are many ways to detail these very important conditions, should they occur. Consult with your design professional, as technical aspects of sound detailing are beyond the scope of this book.

To control visual clutter, it is always best to pair doors together. See Exhibit 11.3.

If possible, avoid having a large structural column in an office. It destroys the exterior view and makes furniture arrangement difficult.

A desk typically faces a door so that visitors can be seen as they enter. The door should be placed on the wall opposite the desk. See Exhibit 10.1.

For two reasons, the typical depth of a lawyer office is fifteen feet from the perimeter glass to the corridor immediately outside the office. First, given the typical five-foot building module, there is generally a corresponding mullion for the perimeter wall to tie into at the fifteen-foot point on the opposing window wall. Second, around the perimeter of the building, a fifteen-foot HVAC zone (for heating and cooling) controlling the perimeter offices (the exterior zone) is handled differently from the HVAC in the interior offices (the interior zone).

In laying out perimeter offices for multiple-floor firms, it may be advantageous to have identical perimeter office layouts on all floors. As the firm grows and office moves occur, it is more efficient and less confusing to deal with one typical floor plate layout when assigning offices. Identical perimeter layouts tend to democratize the office floors, lessening conflicts over preferred office space. Furthermore, it is less confusing for everyone, from the managing partner to the mail clerk, if all floors are typical. Identical perimeter layouts also make sense for office numbering and telephone extensions. Firms find it very advantageous to use floor and office number designations as phone extensions. For example, phone extension 4735 is for office number 35 on the 47th floor.

Accessibility Standards

Places of public accommodation (like law firms) need to comply with the accessibility requirements of the Americans with Disabilities Act and its state and local counterparts. The ADA and its predecessor, the Architectural

Barriers Act of 1968 (ABA) that applies primarily to federal facilities, are interpreted by guidelines of the federal government's Access Board, and the 2004 revisions of the guidelines are expected to make the requirements of the two acts more consistent. The Access Board's guidelines serve as the baseline for standards maintained by the federal agencies that enforce the ADA and ABA, namely the Departments of Justice and Transportation. As we write this, the Department of Justice has announced its intention to revise its ADA standards according to the Access Board's new guidelines.

As you might expect, there are numerous books and guides to help ensure compliance with the provisions. There seem to be dozens of books with the title *Americans with Disabilities Act Handbook*, but we mention only one. The classic is the original version with over 750 pages, published in 1992 by the U.S. Government Printing Office. It is listed as out of stock, but reprints abound, some with additional materials. The book has drawings and advice for compliance, and while it is somewhat outdated, it is very valuable. The major online booksellers seem to have plenty of these at reasonable prices.

State regulation frequently calls for stricter enforcement, and examples of state-specific compliance books are found in a series by James E. Jordan of Jordan Publishing, also widely available from the major online book suppliers. The second edition of the *ADA Compliance Pricing Guide,* from R.S. Means, provides localized pricing and information about compliance, including new ADA guidelines that apply to new construction and remodeling.

Exhibit 11.1
DOOR PLACEMENT FOR VISUAL AND ACOUSTIC PRIVACY

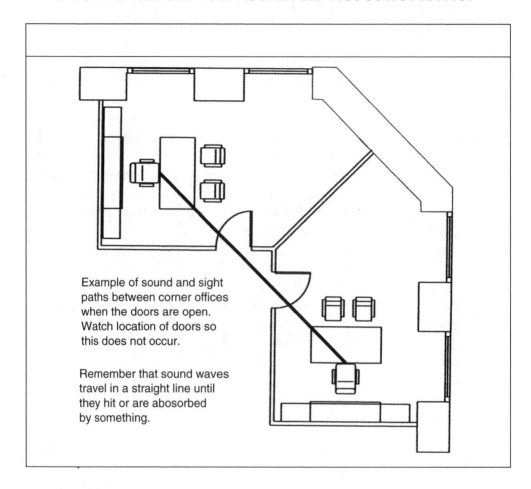

Example of sound and sight paths between corner offices when the doors are open. Watch location of doors so this does not occur.

Remember that sound waves travel in a straight line until they hit or are abosorbed by something.

Exhibit 11.2A
PARTITIONS TERMINATING INTO SHEETROCK

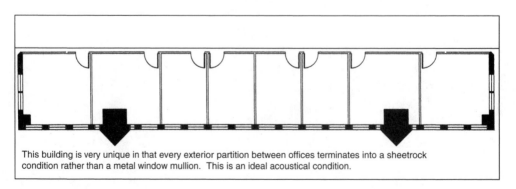

This building is very unique in that every exterior partition between offices terminates into a sheetrock condition rather than a metal window mullion. This is an ideal acoustical condition.

Exhibit 11.2B
PARTITIONS TERMINATING INTO METAL MULLIONS

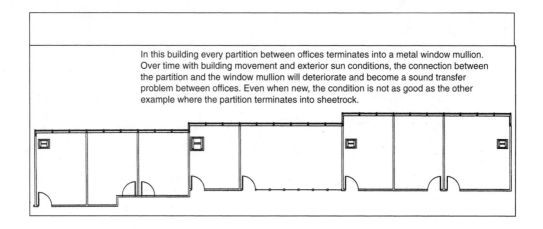

In this building every partition between offices terminates into a metal window mullion. Over time with building movement and exterior sun conditions, the connection between the partition and the window mullion will deteriorate and become a sound transfer problem between offices. Even when new, the condition is not as good as the other example where the partition terminates into sheetrock.

Exhibit 11.3
PAIRING DOORS TO ELIMINATE VISUAL CLUTTER

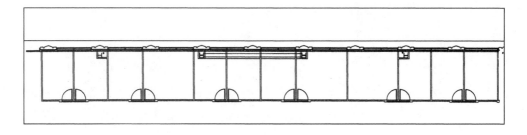

Designing Offices and Workstations | 12

This chapter covers design of the work areas for lawyers, paralegals and secretaries. For most work areas we discuss the following topics:

- Location
- Sizes and layouts
- Technology, including
  - Cabling (voice, data, TV, flexible layouts)
  - Electrical
  - Lighting
  - HVAC (thermostats, supply and return)
  - Acoustics and privacy
  - Equipment in the work area
  - Security
- Ergonomics
- Special storage needs
- Finishes
- Furnishings
- Sample layouts

Lawyer Offices

Lawyer Office Location

Partner offices and associate offices make up the perimeter window wall offices. They are typically as evenly interspersed as possible. Usually practice groups or sections are located together and adjacent to other practice groups with which they commonly interact. The more senior partners typically occupy corner offices and offices with the best views. When planning smaller firms, the most expeditious way to start the planning is to lay out the perimeter offices according to the number of partners.

Lawyer Office Sizes

Partners, of course, should garner the most attention when planning their offices. If you are thinking about a move, now is the time to start thinking outside the box: Office sizes affect profitability, and a 15′ × 20′ partner office is becoming a thing of the past. Almost no law firm being built today has 15′ × 20′ offices. Most partner offices are nominally 15′ × 15′, which could mean 14′ 6″ × 14′ 6″ or 15′ × 14′, depending on the mullion or column spacing, the building shape, and the depth from the core to the window wall. Occasionally a managing partner may be in a 15′ × 20′ office, but many managing partners are leading by example and opting for the nominal 15′ × 15′ offices. In some rectilinear buildings the corner offices become 15′ × 20′ by default to allow for door placement.

There are five primary reasons why partner offices are shrinking or becoming standardized:

1. For security reasons, lawyers are not meeting with clients or opposing counsel in their offices. Also, privacy legislation and regulations have reinforced the practice of keeping visitors away from the lawyer environment and sequestered in the conference room area. As a result, lawyers require less guest seating in their offices.

2. As computer usage grows among partners, more ergonomically friendly work areas are being used, typically adding a "return" or third work surface that was not there in the past.

3. Smaller offices allow for more timekeepers per floor. Reducing the square footage per lawyer, and therefore the corresponding rent and utilities, means greater take-home profit for the partners.

4. As baby boomers become the typical partner, younger partners want to give up that old "couch" look for a younger, more interactive image, thus opting for a small conference table for in-house meetings.

5. As senior partners retire, many firms face the dilemma of what to do with their offices. Many retired partners still like to keep an office to receive mail, have secretarial services, or meet friends for lunch. However, to keep a 15′ × 20′ office vacant is expensive. Ideally the firm has a policy where the partner occupies a smaller office of 10′ × 15′, but even a 15′ × 15′ office is an improvement over the cost of a 15′ × 20′ office.

See Exhibit 12.1 for examples of these offices.

One Size Fits All

There is an emerging tendency toward uniformly sized offices for all partners, associates, and of counsel. One advantage of this is that people do not have to be constantly moving because of promotions or new hires, or when someone leaves the firm. Another advantage is that if a firm has a practice group (such as litigation) with a high ratio of associates to partners as well as another group (such as transactional) with a lower ratio, the different ratios do not matter. The only hierarchy in offices is who has the best view. Reducing the number of office moves saves a lot of wear and tear. It means less nonbillable time, lower moving expenses, fewer disruptions, less damage to the offices, and fewer misplaced items.

Uniformly sized offices can add between six and ten additional offices per floor, depending on the floor plate size and mullion spacing. If the building is built on a five-foot window mullion grid, the size of the offices could be from $10' \times 15'$ to $10' \times 18'$. If the building is on a six-foot or four-foot grid the size could be from $12' \times 13'$ to $12' \times 15'$.

Associate offices are typically $10' \times 15'$ if the building is built on a five-foot grid. Size may vary slightly depending on the building grid, but the average is 150 square feet. Associate offices are typically located on the perimeter window wall. In larger cities with higher rents, it is not unusual to see first- and second-year associates or staff lawyers in interior offices. These offices are typically across the hall from perimeter lawyer offices. Some firms give lawyers special incentives for occupying the interior offices, such as all new furniture or slightly bigger offices. These interior offices are typically designed with some type of glass to allow more light into the offices. The glass can either be in the door, a transom over the door, or a glass clerestory.

Lawyer Office Technology

Cabling

Cabling for voice, data, and TV requires some flexibility in layouts; partner offices, however, typically have voice and data connections on two walls to facilitate various furniture layouts. Associates typically have voice and data connections on just one wall. In Washington, D.C., and some other cities, it is common to find TV cable outlets in some partner offices for C-SPAN or other cable-based information services.

Electrical

For detailed information on electrical services, see Chapter 10.

Lighting

Lighting is typically recessed fluorescent light fixtures with dual switching. See Chapter 10 for more discussion on lighting.

HVAC

All perimeter offices have heating and cooling, but there are a limited number of thermostats. Usually three to five offices share one VAV box, meaning that there is only one thermostat available for these offices. Typically the thermostat goes to a partner rather than an associate office. This is another reason to intersperse partner and associate offices. Class A office buildings in most large cities have a perimeter linear slot diffuser that both supplies and returns air. Good-quality fluorescent light fixtures in most parts of the country have the ability to supply and return air as well. A combination of slots and light fixtures is usually adequate, and no additional supply and return grilles are necessary in the ceiling. If supply grilles are required, position them carefully to insure that air does not blow down someone's neck.

Acoustics and Privacy

Acoustical privacy, or the assurance that speech is unintelligible from one space to the next, is paramount to every law firm. These requirements become somewhat more relaxed if clients are not meeting in lawyer offices. The biggest offender to acoustical integrity is the speaker phone. Speaker phones seem to encourage raised voices. No client wants to sit in a lawyer office and overhear the speaker phone conversation in the next office. Beside concerns for clients, it may not be in the best interest of the firm for a partner or associate to hear the conversation. There are four basic levels of acoustics that can be achieved through partition or wall construction. It is extremely important when doing your law firm tours that your design professional demonstrates these levels of acoustical integrity, and that the design committee decides which level they are comfortable with.

Equipment in the Work Area

Almost without exception, lawyer offices have personal computers or laptops. Occasionally they have printers or fax machines, but typically a lawyer prints to a secretary's printer or a remote high-speed printer. With fax software on computers, fax machines in offices are a thing of the past except in service centers or satellite copy areas.

Security

Security for partner offices may include a lock on the door. The lock should be master keyed to the grand master or submaster. Associate offices typically do not lock.

Lawyer Office Finishes

Typical standard finishes in partner and associate offices may be summarized as follows:

Low Budget	Med Budget	High Budget	Very High Budget
Flooring			
Carpet glued	Carpet glued	Carpet w/ attached cushion, direct glued	Carpet w/ attached cushion, direct glued
Base			
2½" rubber	2½" rubber	Partner: wood; Assoc: rubber	Partner: wood; Assoc: rubber
Walls			
Painted	Painted	Painted	Painted

As the chart indicates, finishes in partner offices are becoming increasingly simplified; we very seldom see wall coverings and crown molding.

Lawyer Office Furnishings

It is presumed that when an associate just out of law school joins a firm, the office furnishings are provided for his or her office. When an associate makes partner there are several typical ways of furnishing the office:

- Partners provide all the furniture at their expense. If a partner leaves the firm, the partner takes the furniture. This approach can become a nightmare for some administrators. Partners should not be allowed to have custom built-in furniture such as credenzas and bookcases, because it can make the partners territorial. When the day comes to move offices, moving the pieces is a nightmare and they never fit correctly in the new office, to say nothing of the moving and modification costs and the repairs to the original office.
- Partners are given cash allowances by the firm and may select whatever furniture they desire. One problem here is that a partner might select something that is not compatible with the firm's taste. A further problem with partners buying their own furniture is that when they leave the firm they may want the firm to buy their furniture if they do not need it.
- Another option is that the firm provides a standardized desk, credenza, computer stand, desk chair, guest chairs, and perhaps a bookcase. If a partner wants to personalize the office with other guest seating or a small conference table, he or she pays for it and is allowed to take those self-purchased items when leaving the firm.
- The fourth option is that the firm purchases all the furniture, and it is standardized among offices so that if a partner changes offices, only the contents of the desk, credenza, and bookcase need to be packed. Every-

thing else stays in the office for the next occupant. This method is much heralded by executive directors and legal administrators because it saves on the wear and tear of all the architectural elements in the space, such as doors, frames, carpet, and wall finishes that are bound to get marred during moves. Also, when a big move must occur, only boxes are being moved, not furniture. Standard furniture saves on downtime, non-billable time, damage to moved furniture, and moving cost. It also promotes a feeling of equality among offices. Many of the country's largest and most successful firms take this approach. (Lawyers can personalize their offices with their own art and accessories.) In this scenario no one has to cringe when they walk by the office of a partner who just *had* to have a pink marble desk with matching lamps.

Another option for partner furniture includes work walls. A work wall is a piece of furniture that acts as a credenza, personal computer surface, bookcase, closet, file cabinet, pedestal (drawer unit), and shelving display unit, all in one piece of furniture. Work walls take advantage of vertical space. They are free-standing pieces of furniture and are not attached to the walls, so they depreciate at the same rate as furniture. Work walls are typically built of components; and lawyers can opt for storage, shelves, and files in a variety of configurations. Work walls are more flexible than traditional desks and credenzas, so they may be appropriate for offices with interfering columns. This is especially true in associate offices. There may be more than one style to choose from, making them even more adaptable to the size and column configuration within the office. Work walls are typically provided by the firm for partners and associates. Some partners elect to purchase these themselves if the firm does not provide them. Typically, these are designed by the firm's design professional and made by a custom millwork house. Many standard furniture manufacturers have copied them and have them in their standard product lines.

It goes without saying that the firm needs to have a clear policy regarding each of these options and the partners need to agree to the policy from the beginning.

Samples of Typical Partner Offices

A size of 15′ × 15′ (nominal) is typical (see the discussion earlier in the chapter).

Partner Office A (Exhibit 10.1A)
- Traditional desk and credenza
- Two guest chairs at the desk
- Small sofa with side tables
- Two bookcases

Partner Office B (Exhibit 10.1A)

- C-shaped desk-credenza
- Computer work surface
- Two guest chairs at the desk
- Small table with chairs for in-house meetings

Associate Office A (Exhibit 10.1B)

- Typical desk and credenza
- Two guest chairs and side table
- One bookcase

Associate Office B (Exhibit 10.1B)

- C-shaped desk-credenza
- Computer work surface
- Wall-mounted shelving
- Two guest chairs and side table

Note: Any time there is wall-hung shelving it is best to support it with wood blocking inside the wall. In the absence of wood blocking, use Z-clips screwed to the studs.

Associate Office C (Exhibit 10.1C)

- T-shaped work surface unit (a good solution when a structural column occurs in offices)
- Shelves either mounted on the wall or integral to the furniture unit
- Guest chair

Paralegal Offices

Paralegal Office Location

In the vast majority of law firms, paralegal offices are located in the interior core area or just off the secretarial corridor outside the lawyer offices. There is an unwritten adage with law firms: "If you want a perimeter office—go to law school." An exception to this may be if there is a litigation support floor and paralegals are assigned to be near case documents. If there is perimeter space in that case, it might as well be occupied by humans rather than files. Also, the majority of paralegal offices are enclosed (with a door) rather than being in cubicles or systems-type furniture. The exception to this is if they are located in a project workroom or case room. Paralegals should be in close proximity, if possible, to the lawyers to whom they are assigned.

Paralegal Office Sizes and Layouts

Sizes of paralegal offices are generally about $9' \times 9'$, $10' \times 10'$, or $8' \times 12'$. They should include at least three work surfaces: primary, secondary, and computer. Paralegals need as much filing and storage space as possible. Too often the vertical areas (walls) are not adequately used. At least one wall, and in some cases two or three walls, should be used for shelves or cabinets.

See Exhibit 10.1C for typical layouts.

Paralegal Office Technology

Cabling

See Chapter 10 for typical layouts.

Electrical

See Chapter 10 for typical layouts.

Lighting

Lighting in paralegal offices is important because of the time paralegals spend on the computer and reading documents, and because of the smaller size of the offices. Optimally it is best to use a task-ambient lighting solution. This eliminates glare and shadows, and makes the room appear larger in size. It results in less fatigue and eyestrain. If recessed parabolics are used, beware of light cutoff angles, and position lights so that people are not working in their own shadows.

HVAC

Since paralegals are located in the interior, the air for their offices comes off the interior mechanical zone. Therefore, it is better to locate thermostats in their offices rather than in unoccupied areas such as project workrooms.

Acoustics and Privacy

Years ago, some paralegal offices were accommodated in systems furniture or partial-height partitions. Today, paralegals are typically in offices with full-height partitions and doors. The amount of phone work or confidential telephoning that a paralegal does requires acoustical privacy. The partitions around paralegal offices should have sound insulation batts within the walls. It is preferable to have four-foot sound batts over the tops of the partitions above the ceiling as well.

Equipment in the Work Area

All offices should be designed to accommodate a computer. Printers are discouraged due to the heat they dissipate in a small area and the valuable work surface space they occupy. It is a rare exception to see a printer in a paralegal office.

Security

Paralegal offices do not typically lock, but their files should be lockable.

Paralegal Office Special Storage Needs

Paralegals can use as much filing space as possible in their offices. A minimum is a five-drawer lateral file cabinet and at least two box drawers and a file drawer in a pedestal (known as a box-box-file pedestal) for supplies and personal effects.

Cabinets or shelving should occupy at least two or three walls. Closed cabinets with adjustable shelving keep the files out of sight and make the office appear neater. Open shelving can be used; it is less expensive but can be unsightly if not well organized.

Paralegal Office Finishes

Finishes are similar to associate offices: carpet, rubber base, and painted walls.

Paralegal Office Furnishings

The least expensive furniture option is built-in plastic laminate case goods. This consists of horizontal work surfaces and overhead cabinets or shelves. The pedestals and file cabinets are best done in metal units for durability and effective cost savings. Systems furniture can be used, but is more expensive.

Secretarial Work Areas

Secretarial Work Area Location

In most cases, two secretaries share a workstation or work area. Careful planning can ensure each secretary adequate privacy. Two secretaries to a work station generally works well because they can share a printer and can cover for each other in the event one leaves the area. The secretaries are typically located outside the lawyer offices for the convenience of both parties. An additional planning decision is whether the secretarial station backs up to the lawyer office or is located across the corridor, facing the lawyer office. See Exhibits 12.2A and 12.2B for examples.

Secretarial Work Area Size

A typical secretarial station occupies approximately sixty to seventy square feet. This produces a footprint of about 7' × 9'. The height of secretarial stations should conceal the contents on the work surface. Most lawyers like being able to see the top of a secretary's head to tell whether he or she is at the desk. Eye level when seated is about four feet for most people. This is a good height for a station because it offers the secretary enough visual and acoustical privacy without the feeling of being walled or penned in. Anything higher can make a small space feel claustrophobic. The four-foot height allows visual supervision of secretaries. It also allows secretaries to look up and see someone trying to get their attention—a taller station would require a visitor to enter the space and possibly startle the secretary.

Secretarial Work Area Layouts

Secretarial work areas are typically configured in a C shape so there is a main work surface with an adjacent work surface for a computer, plus a work surface behind for collating or other tasks. Vertical space should be used as well, taking advantage of vertical storage for notebooks and other items.

Because the majority of law firms have two secretaries sharing one printer, it makes sense to combine a double secretarial station with an area for the printer between them. Many secretaries prefer to put their computers in a corner so that they can easily reach the phone and have the copy they are typing next to them. However, with thin-profile LCD monitors becoming popular and less expensive, the need to put the computers and monitors in corners may soon be a thing of the past.

Secretarial Work Area Technology

Cabling

Beside the necessary voice and data cable, secretarial stations should have additional cable for a printer so that it can be networked.

Electrical

Secretaries need to have at least two separate electrical circuits at their stations. These can be on circuits shared with other stations. A secretary needs one circuit with clean power for computers only, and another for dirty power for a pencil sharpener, dictation equipment, radio, calculator, or space heater. Some equipment manufacturers do not recommend having a printer on the same circuit as a computer. Also, printers can be big power consumers and many require a separate circuit to handle the amperage. Verify power requirements with the equipments manufacturers.

Lighting

Lighting is extremely critical in the secretarial work areas because secretaries spend long hours working on the computer screen, and lighting can become a source of glare, diminishing their productivity. It is best to use an indirect lighting source that bounces light off the ceiling and eliminates most of the glare. In an indirect or ambient lighting situation, this can give people the sensation of not having enough light. Task lighting is very useful here, and can be used at the work surface that is used for reading small print. The secretary should have the option of switching the task lights on or off at the work station.

Acoustics and Privacy

Secretaries need some degree of acoustical privacy even though they are in an open work station. This can be accommodated by putting mass between adjacent secretaries (see Exhibit 12.3). Another feature that absorbs and reduces sound is fabric-covered tack panels located directly above the work surface. These panels can absorb sound from a telephone conversation.

Security

Secretaries need lockable drawers to secure their personal belongings. This can be in a pedestal (box-box-file drawer). Be sure to have the locks master-keyed when ordering them so that if the secretary is ill or absent, you do not need a locksmith to open the desk or pedestal.

Floaters and Special Projects Secretaries

Floaters are secretaries who relieve or fill in for legal secretaries who are on vacation or out for other reasons. Special projects secretaries are those who are called in when there is a unique situation such as a special report. These workers have really taken the place of a word processing group. They go where needed and work on the team for the duration of the project. Both types of secretaries can be accommodated in a regular secretarial station. Therefore, when planning quantities of secretarial stations, it is helpful to add an extra one or two. The extra stations can also be used for collating special documents or for housing the typewriter that seemingly will never be eliminated.

Ergonomics

OSHA recommends that a secretarial work surface height should be 28½ inches. Most furniture manufacturers still make their furniture at 29 or 29½ inches, really too tall for ergonomic comfort. The lowered machine work surface at 26 or 26½ inches, meant to accommodate typewriters, is a thing of the past. One thing to remember is that when typing on a keyboard, the forearm should be parallel to the floor. We know secretaries come in all different sizes and shapes. Two ergonomic solutions accommodate this difference. The first is to provide task seating that is easily adjustable in height, width, depth, and lumbar support; the second is to provide pull-out articulating, adjustable keyboards. A wide variety of these keyboards on the market can be adjusted for tilt, height, and width, and have room for a mouse on the keyboard tray.

Secretarial Work Area Special Storage Needs

Filing in the secretarial stations area–there is just never enough. Typically, lawyers are given about twelve file drawers per lawyer in the secretarial corridor outside their offices. Partners may have a little more; associates a little less. The filing (in cabinets or file walls) is typically done near a secretarial station, since the secretary or the paralegal is responsible for maintaining the files. In our designs, we have not used traditional vertical file cabinets for three decades. Lateral metal file cabinets are also being phased out because they are very limited—they cannot accommodate Bankers Boxes and bulging red rope files. In order to accommodate more varied files, we use something called a file wall, which consists of a bank of tall wooden cabinets, usually thirty-two to thirty-six inches wide with two doors. Each unit houses adjustable shelving that is typically about six shelves high. (Anything taller than that is out of the human reach range.) File walls allow for a multitude of file types. They can accommodate Bankers Boxes, red ropes, accordion files, or Pendaflex files. Pendaflex files, however, are typically side-tabbed, and are somewhat awkward to access on higher shelves.

Secretarial Work Area Finishes

Finishes at the secretarial station can be stained wood veneer, painted lacquer, painted wallboard, fabric panels, or whatever fits the budget and desired image. The secretarial station should be on carpet for acoustical reasons. This means that a plastic chair mat should be installed—no carpet can withstand up to ten years of constant chair movement.

Secretarial Work Area Furnishings

Should secretaries have systems furniture or custom millwork? This question has long been debated by facility managers and designers. In our opinion, custom millwork is less expensive and holds up better over the long haul. Why? Systems furniture is made of standard parts and components. Every ten years or so, when manufacturers introduce new designs and phase out older ones, replacement parts become impossible to find. Frequently, systems furniture manufacturers attempt to sell their product based on reconfiguration flexibility, but secretarial stations really do not need to be reconfigured. Systems furniture is built in modules and does not offer much flexibility.

Custom secretarial stations can be made to fit the space and take advantage of every inch. A well-designed custom secretarial station will have that well-designed feeling, as opposed to something that looks (and is) mass produced. However, before deciding on a custom-designed station, we strongly urge you to build a mock-up so the staff can try it out and "kick the tires." The mock-up can be made out of painted particle board to save money. The purpose is to see how the station functions.

When designing a station, remember these key things:

- Try to keep as many items as possible off the work surface to avoid clutter and maximize the work area.
- Provide an area for the secretary to discreetly display personal photos or mementos where they are not visible to everyone else.
- Take advantage of storage space beneath the work surface.
- Make good use of vertical storage space.

Exhibit 12.1
LARGER CORNER PARTNER OFFICES

In both of these examples, corner offices may need to be 15'x20' to allow for door placement. Typical partner offies are 15'x15'.

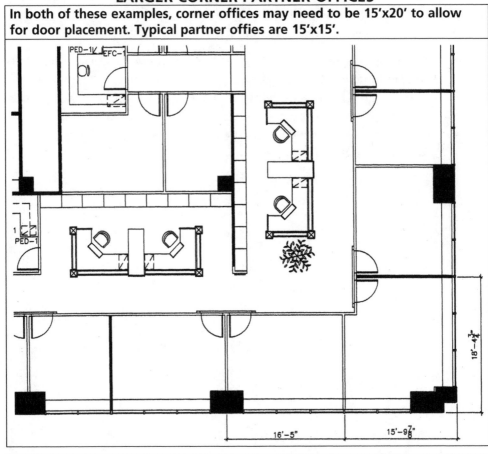

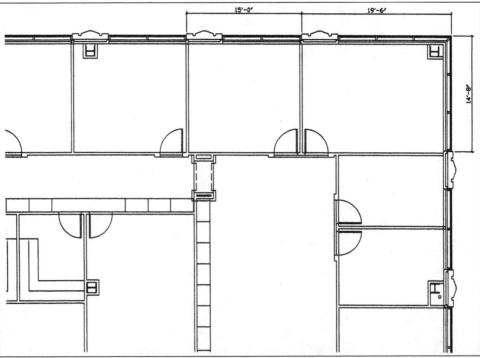

Exhibit 12.2A
SECRETARIAL STATIONS

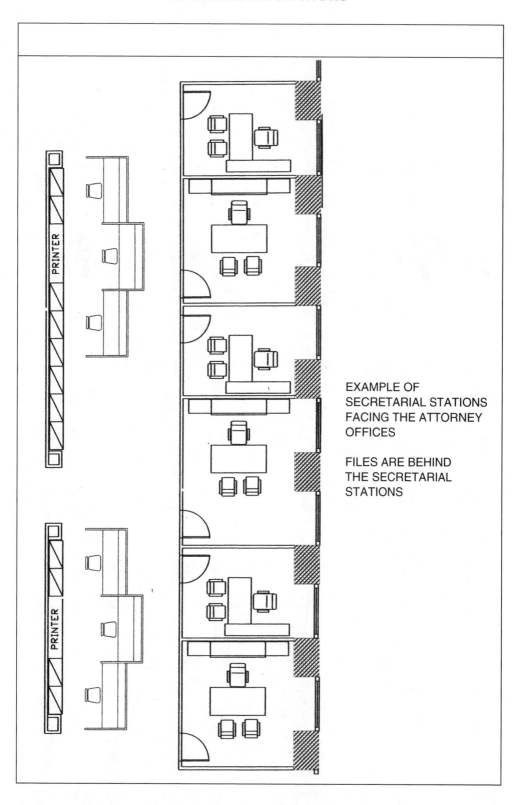

EXAMPLE OF
SECRETARIAL STATIONS
FACING THE ATTORNEY
OFFICES

FILES ARE BEHIND
THE SECRETARIAL
STATIONS

Exhibit 12.2B
SECRETARIAL STATIONS

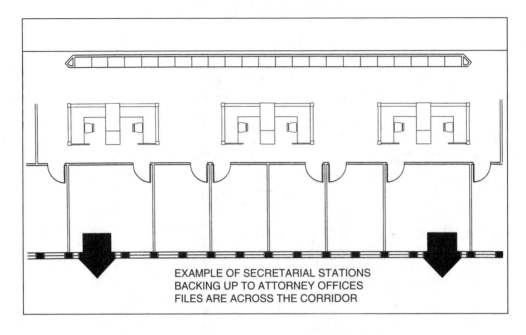

EXAMPLE OF SECRETARIAL STATIONS
BACKING UP TO ATTORNEY OFFICES
FILES ARE ACROSS THE CORRIDOR

Exhibit 12.3
SECRETARIAL ACOUSTICS AND PRIVACY

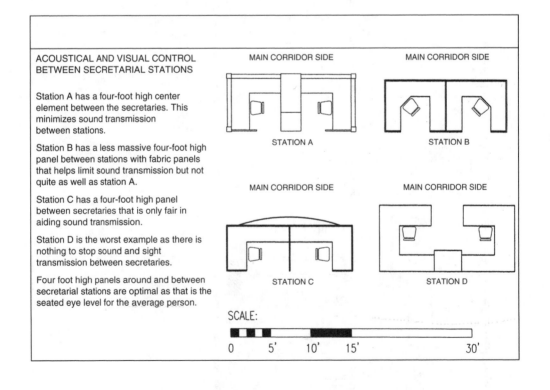

ACOUSTICAL AND VISUAL CONTROL BETWEEN SECRETARIAL STATIONS

Station A has a four-foot high center element between the secretaries. This minimizes sound transmission between stations.

Station B has a less massive four-foot high panel between stations with fabric panels that helps limit sound transmission but not quite as well as station A.

Station C has a four-foot high panel between secretaries that is only fair in aiding sound transmission.

Station D is the worst example as there is nothing to stop sound and sight transmission between secretaries.

Four foot high panels around and between secretarial stations are optimal as that is the seated eye level for the average person.

MAIN CORRIDOR SIDE

MAIN CORRIDOR SIDE

STATION A

STATION B

MAIN CORRIDOR SIDE

MAIN CORRIDOR SIDE

STATION C

STATION D

SCALE:

0   5'   10'   15'   30'

Administrative and Support Areas   13

Legal Administrator, Office Manager, or Executive Director

Executive directors typically have a partner-sized office on the perimeter of the building. Legal administrators usually have an associate-sized office on the perimeter of the building. Office managers are typically in an interior office. (All of this, of course, is up to the managing partner or committee.) These offices typically lock because confidential information is stored there. They would be located fairly close to the reception area because of the number of exterior visitors their occupants see. Other administrative personnel are placed in offices or in cubicles.

Generally, managers who deal with staff and personnel issues are housed in private offices within the core area. Their office size can vary from $10' \times 15'$ to $10' \times 12'$. Some administrative personnel need offices (rooms with doors versus open cubicles) because they may need to discuss personnel issues on the phone or have confidential salary data in their files. See the example in Exhibit 13.1.

Other administrative personnel are generally housed in cubicles. The size of these cubicles is about 50 to 60 square feet. See the example in Exhibit 13.2.

The cubicles can be systems furniture from a furniture manufacturer or they can be made of plastic laminate. Built-to-suit plastic laminate is usually the least expensive alternative. If properly designed, it can also depreciate at the same rate as furniture even though it appears to be built in. Plastic laminate can also maximize the available square footage, since systems furniture is available in only certain modular dimensions. For example, within a given area you may be able to accommodate six plastic laminate workstations, but only five systems-furniture cubicles can be placed in the same space because their dimensions are not as flexible.

Filing for administrative areas can be at individual workstations or centralized within the specific department, depending on who needs access to the files.

In newer law firm construction, there is a definite trend toward administrative functions being moved to another space in the building that has lower rental rates. From a cost standpoint, the level of finish for administrative areas does not need to be as high as a typical lawyer floor. In some cases, administrative functions are being moved off site to less expensive buildings. Some law firms are experimenting with outsourcing administrative functions overseas, and we noted that at least one large firm recently outsourced its word processing function to an offshore company.

Human Resources

The human resources department is typically located in the core area. The suite or offices should lock because confidential material is stored there. Many human resource managers like to have a discreet entrance or exit for people who come to discuss problems or issues and do not want to be seen coming or going from the area. The department should also have a small testing room with a computer and printer for evaluating candidates' computer skills. Files for this department are either secured in locked offices or a locked file room, depending on the size of the firm. In small firms, the administrator usually handles personnel duties.

Training

Every firm needs to train employees at some time or another. This can be when new computer software or hardware is implemented, to discuss and explain new insurance coverage, or to offer in-house continuing legal education (CLE) for lawyers. The size of the firm dictates how training is accomplished. For a very small firm, it may be in a conference room or employee lunch room. For a medium-sized firm, training needs a dedicated room (in the core area) where computers and a printer are permanently set up. The training area needs adequate electrical, voice/data, and television cable connections.

Audiovisual systems may be incorporated so that video teleconferencing can be used. More often than not the design of this room includes easily moved or reconfigured tables with concealed electrical and computer cabling. Another nicety to have at these tables is a modesty panel that blocks views from the knees up and conceals the electrical wires and cables.

The electrical outlets should be fully flush, floor mounted, and located to accommodate different furniture layouts. The room typically has a white board on at least one wall for the trainer to draw on. Lighting needs to be versatile to allow for different level requirements. Many trainers like to teach in low-light conditions so as not to detract from computer monitors and a screen used for a presentation. The room should have a projection screen of some type. The cost of flat plasma screens is coming down, and the quality of the image far exceeds that of a standard projection screen. Adjustable ergonomic seating is important to accommodate the many different body sizes that occupy this room. Consider a podium for the trainer. Also, the trainer needs to be able to stand in a spot that allows a view of each trainee's screen. Flat screens work best in this situation, since they minimize work-surface space. Trainees need work space adjacent to computers for note taking and material layout. The room also needs storage for handouts and brochures.

Information Technology

This broad category encompasses the technology infrastructure—software and hardware—as well as technical and user support for the law firm. Every firm has its preferred way of structuring the IT department.

The computer room contains hardware such as the file servers for the computer systems (word processing, data processing, accounting, timekeeping), telephone system, and security system. The room typically contains the termination blocks, mounted on plywood backboards, for both the computer and telephone systems. The IT manager or director probably has his or her own thoughts about how the room should be laid out and how it should function. The manufacturers of the equipment can also provide advice. Alternatively, a technology consultant can be engaged. Planning for IT needs to happen in Phase I of the project so that the program can accurately reflect the correct square footage.

Chapter 10 addresses network issues to be considered for this area. Currently, people are opting for overhead cabling racks rather than a raised accessible floor system to handle the huge bundles of cables that come into the room. Overhead racks allow easy visibility of the cables, compared with having them concealed below the floor. This room must also be ADA accessible, so if you have a raised flooring system, you need an accessible ramp that takes up an inordinate amount of floor space. Since all computer rooms require some type of supplementary air-conditioning system, there is always the possibility that the water from these systems could leak below a raised floor and not be detected for a while even with water-sensor systems in place. For similar environmental control reasons, we caution that under no circumstances should this room be located on the perimeter window wall or next to an elevator shaft.

The ceilings in computer rooms are usually eliminated to provide for more room and flexible access to the cable racks. To keep the overhead area from being unsightly, usually everything above a typical ceiling height level (approximately nine feet) is sprayed flat black so it "disappears." This includes the walls above nine feet, cable rack, ductwork, piping systems, and electrical systems. Painting the overhead area black adds an element of visual control, so that the spaghetti mess up there does not appear to jump out at you.

This room also needs a sealed concrete floor or a floor covered in a dust-free material such as vinyl composition tile (VCT). Be sure that the contractor cleans and thoroughly waxes the floor before moving in any equipment.

This is a room that you want the contractor to have ready before move-in. It is not unusual for this room to be done two or three weeks before the occupancy date. The vendors who install or relocate equipment need the room in advance to test all punch-downs and install the hardware. The best of all worlds is that you opt for new computer system hardware both in the computer room and at the end users' stations or offices, as well as a new telephone system. That way everything can be burned in (tested) before the move.

The other vital element in the computer room is the security system. Every computer room needs to be secured. This can be as simple as a lock on the door with the keyway being restricted to a few select people, or via a security system that is part of the firm's overall security system. In any case, access is limited to a select few, with an audit trail to see and record who enters and at what time. Walls around the room should extend all the way to the floor structure above.

If you are relocating existing equipment, be sure the punch-downs (or terminations) have been thoroughly tested and numbered at each end of the cable before move in.

Most IT managers prefer a visible connection between the IT staff area and the computer room itself. There should be some type of glass or a non-operable window in the wall or the door that allows the IT staff to have visual control of the computer room without being in it. Computer room temperatures may be kept so cold that most people are not comfortable being in there for any length of time. The glass should not be in an area where other staff or visitors can see into the room. In a small firm, the glass may be between the IT manager's office and the computer room.

In addition to the computer room, firms typically provide cubicles for IT personnel. Also, firms need an area for a burn-in room or computer setup space. This is a room where the IT staff sets up computers, installs and tests software, or customizes software to the firm's needs and requirements. IT personnel may be working on multiple systems at a time, so specify sit-down counters that provide contiguous layout space. There must be adequate electrical service, voice/data connections, noninvasive lighting, and storage for tools and parts. Electric and voice/data lines should be especially plentiful, and should be mounted above the counter.

A locked storage area is needed to accommodate extra computer hardware, equipment, parts, and accessories. A few extra monitors, keyboards, or laptops are always in demand. An extra fax machine or printer may be needed when someone has to go out of town for a trial. Almost every IT operation needs space to house shelf spares, and the extra hard drives, power supplies, and other backup hardware that allow quick response to hardware crises in the servers or the desktop machines. Additionally, storage is required for software—a locked cabinet. Computer storage is a very real need.

Determine where and how cables are to be terminated. It is typical for a floor of cables to be terminated in a wiring closet on each floor. Then a smaller number of cables are run back to the computer room. On multifloor projects it is not unusual to see the backbone of the system done in fiber optics for speed and for space savings. The wiring closet is sometimes shared with the base building voice/data closet. (This is something that needs to be negotiated with the landlord before the lease is signed. Some landlords allow you to share this closet; others will not.) This is the closet in the core where the main trunk lines run vertically to service the entire building.

Records Management

Law firms probably struggle with filing and the space it consumes more than with any other space issue. One day a firm takes on a new case, and suddenly five hundred Bankers Boxes appear in their offices. It is not unusual for files to be kept on site years beyond their need because someone is too busy to deal with closing them out or too stubborn to let them be archived.

One of the first questions to answer is a philosophical one: will the files be centralized, noncentralized, or both? For centralized files, will they be centralized by practice section or department?

Law firm files are housed in several places:

- In lawyer offices
- In open areas near lawyer offices

- In paralegal offices
- In project workrooms
- In central file rooms on site
- In central file rooms off site

Also, files may be converted to digital form, archived, or destroyed.

Most lawyers prefer to keep active files near their offices. However, since lawyers do not do their own filing, the files must be easily accessible to those who do. Generally, filing is done by legal secretaries, paralegals, file clerks, or a combination of all three. Therefore, it is fairly impractical to keep case files in one lawyer's office, when other lawyers are probably working on the case. This is not to say that lawyers do not need filing in their offices. Lawyers will usually take as much filing space as they can get their hands on. A rule of thumb is to have ten to fifteen file drawers in close proximity to each lawyer's office. In addition, we suggest four file drawers within each partner office, two file drawers within each associate office, seven file drawers per paralegal, and the equivalent of ninety file drawers per project workroom. Space in the central on-site file room is usually determined by the available core area square footage. Often there are large active cases that require their own dedicated file rooms. Obviously the size requirements of these areas are determined on an individual basis.

Filing Options

Not every law firm, section, practice group, or lawyer within those broader categories manages files in the same manner.

Common filing systems include red rope or redwell files, Bankers Boxes, file folders (top indexed or side indexed), notebooks, Pendaflex hanging files, and combinations of these. In the secretarial filing section above, we mentioned two ways of housing files within the immediate lawyer environment: a file wall cabinet custom-made of wood with doors, and the conventional lateral steel file cabinets that are available from many manufacturers. For a firm that utilizes a combination of filing methods, we have found a file wall cabinet to be the most versatile. These file walls can be price competitive with good-quality steel lateral files, and typically provide more capacity per square foot. They save the space required by steel file cabinet drawer glides, and file walls can typically accommodate six openings rather than five. There is typically one metal posting shelf installed in each file wall cabinet at about waist height so that a user can remove a file, open it, and briefly read it to see if it is the correct file before taking it.

For many applications, we prefer file walls because of their simplicity and flexibility. With fewer moving parts, they avoid the problems that sometimes plague drawer suspensions in steel filing cabinets. They avoid the leveling problems of steel cabinets and since they are built-in millwork, file walls do not require you to build a level base on an uneven floor. They have a better appearance, avoiding the "pizza oven" look, and they are much quieter than metal file cabinets.

If you elect to use steel file cabinets, do not buy the least expensive or even the next-least expensive. Buy middle to high grade and the suspension systems will cause far fewer problems over the long run. If five-drawer metal lateral files are used, specify the three bottom drawers with fixed drawer fronts and the upper two drawers with pull-out shelves and retractable drawer fronts. You may configure files within the drawers in steel cabinets by varying both the internal hardware accessories that you use and the width of files.

If you use steel lateral file cabinets contiguous to one another (where two or more cabinets are ganged together with no space between them), your designer needs to specify that these cabinets be bolted together side to side and leveled as a continuous unit. If the cabinets are not secured together, with use and doors closing over time, the cabinets will "walk" so that they are not flush with one another. File cabinets must be level in order to operate properly. A fully loaded file cabinet may need to be adjusted after it is loaded. The suspension systems can twist and fall if they are not properly adjusted.

Steel lateral file cabinets come with adjustable levelers under the cabinets. These can be extended to compensate for an uneven floor. There are limitations, however, which increase dramatically with a sloping floor. The levelers that typically come with a lateral file are nominally 1-inch levelers. However, their maximum leveling capability is only ¾ inches. Manufacturers can provide longer levelers of perhaps 1½ inches, but who wants to look at a run of file cabinets that is tight to the floor on one end and sticking up 1¼ inches at the other end? One way to deal with this is to construct a wood platform base for the lateral files. In Chapter 8, in the discussion of work letter negotiation specifications, we suggested that your lease negotiations contain limitations on how much the floor may be out of level. The filing system provides a fine example of why level floors are important.

Also, if you are using steel lateral files, be sure to order the type of cabinets that allow only one drawer to be open at a time to prevent a cabinet from tipping over. This does not happen with the file wall cabinet because it is bolted to the wall.

Filing in paralegal offices typically consists of one five-drawer lateral file and one two-drawer lateral file. Filing in project workrooms is usually on open metal shelving with either five or six shelf openings. The standard industrial gray metal shelving is the least expensive. If floor loading allows, a bi- or tri-metal filing system can also be used. With these systems, the front one or two units are moved sideways to access the back unit. Small moveable shelving units can also be used, but floor loading must be considered with these as well.

Litigation Support Filing

Because of the voluminous nature of litigation filing, many firms opt for litigation support centers. In some cities these centers are moved off site to less expensive space or to space within the building's basement. (Slab on grade foundations typically can support more weight than typical office floors.) The concept behind a litigation support center is that it provides a space for cases with a high volume of documents. One or two paralegals might have a work area within a large room that does nothing but support this case. It can be an area where digital imaging is taking place. It can be several workrooms clustered around a movable file system. As cases go on hold for appeals or other reasons, the files can be moved to this nearby movable file system so that they do not completely tie up the workroom and render it unusable for a considerable period of time. A litigation support center should have the ability to accommodate 24-7 shifts. It may contain a restroom equipped with a shower and a "40 winks" room. It obviously needs a large document copy center and other necessary electronic support. One design firm we interviewed said they were taking first-floor retail space that had been unleaseable and turning it into litigation centers. The people staffing this center loved the fact that they actually had natural daylight and street activity to look at.

High density or moveable shelving is by far the most space-economical way to file. It has more linear filing inches than any other type of system. The drawbacks are the weight per square foot, and the need to convert filing to side tabs. It is not unusual for the weight of media and shelving to be 200 pounds per square foot. Most buildings are built for about 70 pounds a square foot. A steel building is reinforced by adding steel beams or adding plates to existing beams under the floor, and this can usually be done with minimal loss of space. A concrete building, on the other hand, tends to present more obstacles and requires more space to increase floor loading. It is always far cheaper to add the reinforcement when the building is initially built. In a new steel building, reinforcing the floors for a system that accommodates ten thousand linear filing inches costs about $20,000, and the filing system itself is about $35,000. Construction costs vary, and as libraries move away from storing paper, you may be able to find pre-owned movable systems at reasonable prices. Be sure to specify safety stops for the system so that a user cannot accidentally close an aisle with someone in it. Be wary of pre-owned electrically-assisted mobile shelving systems. Manually operated systems are generally more reliable.

One final point here: when sizing any filing or shelving system, remember that in a sprinkled building, nothing can be closer than eighteen inches to the ceiling, and check codes to verify clearance requirements and limitations.

Off-Site Options

Some firms elect to move their central file operation off site to a facility that they operate. This works particularly well when a law firm has several locations within the same city. This facility might be located in a light industrial area that is fifteen minutes from any of their offices. A firm could operate a van and have files to a lawyer within thirty minutes of a request if necessary. Having this system also lets the firm manage their own archives rather than outsourcing the responsibility.

Library

Most of the traditional law firm library is brought to lawyers' desks by electronic research systems like Lexis and Westlaw and a multitude of Internet services. While we know that law firm libraries are generally shrinking in terms of their total space requirements, the shift in most firms is toward less space for books and more space for research and information staff. Generally speaking, libraries need fewer carrels, less shelving, and less total space, but they do require more librarian and staff space. With some exceptions, libraries are less frequently becoming a showpiece for the firm. Clients, increasingly aware of overhead costs, may balk at the prospect of funding a showpiece. While libraries need fewer books, those books that remain have survived through a process of natural selection. They are critical for their users. Accordingly, law firm librarians' offices should be near the books, especially the ready reference books. Law librarians, in their capacities as information managers, are increasingly assigned responsibility for indexing and retrieval of the firm's work product, as well as for conflicts management and the general knowledge-management effort of the firm. Proximity to these functions should be considered. The librarian should have a separate office with shelving, a desk, and work surfaces, and a full complement of communications and computer hardware. The office should have a door and guest seating for conversations with library staff and lawyers. Library work areas for technical services should have ample space and work stations for handling serial publications, invoices, loose-leaf filing, and mail processing. Areas for library supplies, storage, trash, and processing equipment should be planned in consultation with the librarian, as should power and communications availability and locations for printing, scanning, and fax equipment. Library work areas should be separated by walls from the library seating area. The most common failures in law library design are evidenced by inadequate spaces for technical services operations, storage, and equipment such as book trucks.

Books, microfilm, and paper records are very heavy, so be sure that your building's floor can hold the weight of your collection. Because widely differing shelving configurations can be used to limit the live load on a floor, the commonly accepted requirement for a floor load capacity of 125 to 150 pounds per square foot may need to be adjusted up or down. This is especially critical for compact mobile shelving and storage systems. Your structural engineer can determine whether floors need to be reinforced. If you need to avoid paying for structural modifications to support heavy loads, one option is to increase the aisle spacing between stacks. Increasing the spacing from three feet to four feet may keep the floor loading within the existing slab's design parameters, and reducing the shelving from seven openings to six or five can have a similar effect. Consult with your structural engineer.

As you plan for shelving, expect to put from sixteen to nineteen regular-sized law books in each three-foot shelf. Some reporter volumes and periodicals take more space. As you squeeze shelving into your plan, try to stick with the standard shelving sizes that are approximately three feet wide and use the manufacturer's measurements for your planning, because variations in size are magnified as shelving units are placed end to end. Carefully select the depth of your shelves, because large amounts of space can be lost by using deep shelves all throughout the library just to accommodate the small number of large, deeper books or binders the firm owns. Most law books are smaller than eight inches in depth, so shelves that measure a nominal ten inches are adequate for most applications. Nevertheless, some deeper shelves should be provided for big loose-leaf binders. Allow for enough growth space to accommodate new books through the period of your lease.

Bookshelves, especially law bookshelves, need to be sturdy. Shelves tend to sag or deflect under the weight of law books. Particle board shelves will not support the weight. Solid wood shelves need to be no less than one inch thick. In comparing metal library shelves, consider the gauge of metal, the supporting mechanism, the system of bending the edges of the shelves to increase load bearing support, and the durability of the finish. If you might need to adjust the shelves to accommodate taller books or to hold more shelves of shorter books, consider the adjustment features. In general, the cantilever-style shelf systems that support shelves from the center posts of double-faced shelf units are more readily adjustable than the four-poster styles. Unlike many fixed-shelf units, the cantilever style allows shelves to be mounted at different heights on opposite sides of a double-facing unit.

If your building can support the weight, compact movable shelving may give you more room or increase shelving capacity. Compact shelves economize on aisle space. Shelving ranges are moved manually or by electric motors. The electrically operated systems have long been criticized because of their high rates of failure. In general, librarians prefer the reliability of the manually operated units, but improved technology has made the motorized units dependable, and electronic monitoring and notification features keep the newer systems running reliably.

Most shelving configurations for law books use tall shelf units that are seven shelves high, and counter-height shelves, usually forty-two inches high, that provide a work space on the top with three shelves below. The height of the shelves is an important consideration for several reasons. The number of shelves in each shelf unit affects the load on your floors, so carefully consider how tall to make your shelving units. Fire codes require shelves to be a minimum distance from sprinkler heads, and more than one law firm has had to endure the expense and loss of space caused by replacing or altering shelves that were too tall. Taller shelves tend to restrict the amount of light that gets to the shelves, especially the lower ones, so be sure that you have enough lights. Lighting needs to penetrate from above to the bottom shelves. Fluorescent tubes provide better light coverage (especially for lower shelves) if they run perpendicular to the rows of shelves. This is especially necessary with compact mobile shelving, since the light angles change as shelves are moved. For the most flexibility in a library area, banks of fluorescent lights should be run in rows diagonally, at 45-degree angles to the walls, so that they provide light throughout the shelving, no matter how it is arranged or changed.

For code compliance in earthquake-prone areas, library shelves need to be attached to the structure above by way of seismic bracing.

Library seating should be varied, from open tables to carrels to lounge seating, to accommodate different working styles. Network access should be available at library seats, whether by wired connections or wireless data access points, and electrical power should be available as well. Carrels should be no less than forty-two inches wide, and should have shelving above the work surface. Open library tables tend to have more chairs than occupants. A 4′ × 6′ table seldom handles more than two people, even though more chairs can be arranged around it. Work surfaces should be glare free.

Accounting

Depending on the size of the firm, accounting departments are usually structured under one chief financial officer for larger firms, or under an administrator for small firms. Some people within the accounting department may need a 10′ x 12′ private office, depending on the confidentiality of their work. Most others are in cubicles that average about fifty square feet. In addition, the department needs room for line printers and a collating area. Accounting departments may be located off site or elsewhere in the building.

Office Services Center

It is accepted practice to combine all office services into one multifunctional area so that people can multitask and cover for one another. These services include:

- Reproduction
- Central mail, in and out
- Faxes in and out, desktop fax
- Supplies
- Satellite copy, mail, fax, supplies
- Binding, collating
- Expressage in and out
- Messengers

Both clients and delivery trucks visit the firm, and the office services area handles trucks, messengers, and mailing and shipping visitors, while the receptionist handles clients and people who meet with the lawyers. For security reasons, work-flow reasons, and for the convenience of everyone, it is important to separate the two types of visitors. Offices services, if at all possible, should have a separate entrance to handle messengers and deliveries. Multifloor firms never put their offices services on the reception floor, and most do not put them on lawyer floors.

It is often preferable to have all of these support functions in a large open area so staff can see when an area needs help or backup. A supervisor should be able to see the whole area. Functional areas may have their own territory within the office services space. The central supply room can be a convenient, lockable room within the area.

It is preferable not to have lawyers, secretaries, and other staff wandering around the services area; a control counter to stop traffic avoids this situation. It also keeps messengers out of the area. It is ideal if the entrance can be located directly off the elevator lobby to control messenger traffic. A secondary entrance should have an oversized (four-foot) door or double doors so that large deliveries can be accommodated. These doors need to have a protective finish material so they hold up against damage from two-wheeler and cart traffic.

Mail carts need soft rubber disks (bumpers) around their legs that are larger than the diameter of the wheel so that when a mail cart hits an elevator door or secretarial station, it is the rubber bumper that makes contact first and not the metal of the cart. Some law firms have even done away with mail carts and have the mail hand delivered. If a mail runner spends fifteen more minutes delivering mail, it is much less expensive than repairing the daily damage from a mail cart.

The work areas need adequate layout space for collating and binding large projects. They should have built-in counters with storage above and below. Remember to have space for large two-wheel dollies and other moving equipment. Each copier needs counter space next to it. Sometimes it is useful to have this be a small cabinet on wheels that can be moved or positioned to the operator's preference. A rolling cabinet also allows easy access to a copier when it needs servicing. Allow for space for a newly arrived pallet of copy paper.

Employees in this area often need to be all over the firm and need a se-cured small locker where they can keep their personal effects. The heat load in this room can build up, especially in the afternoon when deadlines are ap-proaching. Ceiling fans can help, especially if the building's cooling systems are being stretched.

You may decide to outsource the office services function to a repro-graphics company. For continuity, that company could hire the firm's employees who have been running the center. Some advantages are that the other company can own and be responsible for all the equipment, and they can send in extra staff on short notice for a big project or if work-ers are absent. They also can take projects to their own facilities, so the firm needs less equipment and less space. The firm may not need to keep a manager-level position in that department and can deal directly with the outsourcing firm.

Example: See Exhibit 13.3 on page 171.

Satellite Copy Areas

In addition to a service center where the bulk of copying is done, the firm needs approximately one copier for every 10,000 square feet of space, or one for each twenty to twenty-five lawyers. These copiers are typically located on the lawyer floors in unmanned satellite copy areas. These are in the core area, typically located near a corridor that accesses both sides of the build-ing. On a typical floor (18,000 to 20,000 square feet) there are two satellite copy areas. Unfortunately, a smaller firm with about 10,000 square feet prob-ably still needs two copiers, one in a central service area and a smaller one elsewhere.

Example: See Exhibit 13.4 on page 172.

The satellite copy areas may also accommodate a high-speed printer, scan-ner, fax machine, a typewriter for forms, and an outgoing mail drop. In these ar-eas, built-ins should accommodate layout work surfaces and storage for copier paper, some office supplies, and packaging for overnight expressage.

Litigation Support Centers and Project Workrooms

The section earlier in the chapter on records management discusses litigation support centers, some of which are being located off site or in less expensive space. Project workrooms provide a similar function, and keep the firm's conference rooms and public or office spaces from becoming repositories for boxes full of files.

In some firms, project workrooms are known as war rooms. Most project workrooms are about 15' × 15'. They are interior rooms on lawyer floors. Their walls are lined with gray metal shelving units that are ganged together and bolted to the walls. These shelves can store file media in a number of different ways (Bankers Boxes, red ropes or redwells, notebooks, and so on). A voice/data outlet and electrical outlet are typically mounted on one wall near the door to accommodate a computer, printer, or fax machine. One wall may have a white board. There is usually room for a 3' × 6' table for a work area. Paralegals and lawyers come in the room to work on files, and to do a variety of pretrial work. This is not meant to be a conference room; however, it can be used for team meetings about a particular case or assignment. It can also be used as a trial preparation area. Sometimes these rooms are assigned to one particular partner, sometimes on a case-by-case basis. Unfortunately, smaller firms usually do not have these rooms because the core area space is used up by other administrative functions. In larger firms it is typical to have five to ten of these per floor.

Example: See Exhibit 13.5 on page 173.

Food Service

More and more, law firms are getting into the food service business, due to long hours, the nature of 24-7 preparation for deadlines, the tendency to use lunchtime for work-through meetings and to hold partnership meetings at breakfast or after work, and the scheduling of conference rooms for marketing and entertaining in the evening. It is not unusual for a fifty-lawyer law firm to have ten functions a day where food is served. Many larger firms serve three meals a day. (Read more about food service trends in Chapter 5.)

Catering Pantry

For the majority of firms, food is brought in already prepared by off-site catering companies. It is then held at the proper temperature using hot boxes, refrigerators, or freezers until it is plated or served in chafing dishes or steam tables. The kitchen equipment used in catering pantries is not the typical residential line; it is made for commercial use. For example, a commercial dishwasher can wash and sanitize a load of dishes in three minutes. Few firms prepare food on site due to the health codes and the need for special venting. Law firm catering pantries not only accommodate kitchen appliances and preparation space, but storage for china, linens, silver, and glassware. They require storage space to park serving carts, as well as some cabinets or closets that lock.

Service to meeting rooms is typically provided by silent serveries, as described in Chapter 5. A catering pantry should be centrally located within the conference center and near the freight elevator. There should be a direct path to the freight elevator that completely avoids the reception area.

Exhibit 13.6 on pages 174–175 shows a silent servery.

Satellite Coffee Areas

These areas are found on a typical lawyer floor within the core area and preferably near but not in the satellite copy areas. It is also convenient to locate them near the restrooms, so that when people get up to take a break, the two are near each other. The coffee areas have running hot and cold water, sink, coffee maker, garbage disposal, small under-counter refrigerator, under-counter ice maker (separate from the refrigerator), and a trash receptacle (more than one if recycling is a requirement). If the employee lounge (lunchroom) is not on the same floor, the under-counter refrigerator may have a freezer for people bringing frozen lunches. Some firms provide one dishwasher per floor.

Purified water needs to be provided. The least expensive way to do this is in a small unit mounted in a base cabinet that purifies tap water and water going to the coffee pot and ice maker. Big five-gallon water coolers are seldom used, and the bottles (empty and full) take an enormous amount of space. Soft drinks need to be dispensed in some manner. Soft drinks can take a lion's share of space if allowed to. Many firms provide free soft drinks, while others dispense them at a minimal charge through a vending machine. It is best to negotiate with a vending company to supply and refill the machines so you are not encumbered with the space required to store the extras. The least desirable way to dispense soft drinks is through a fountain system similar to those in fast food restaurants. Do not do this! These systems require storage for syrupy bottles and CO_2 tanks. They are messy, require constant service, and the sugar attracts bugs.

We recommend two satellite coffee areas per floor, centrally located for convenience to the greatest number of users. See Exhibit 13.4 on page 172.

Employee Lounge

An employee lounge is a place where employees can go to eat lunch or take a short break. These areas can also function for staff birthday parties or wedding or baby showers. Some firms have a culture where both staff and lawyers use the room. In most cases, just the staff uses the room. An employee lounge is necessary if the firm discourages or does not allow staff members to eat at their desks. Staff members typically cannot afford to or do not want to eat out everyday.

The room should be a departure from the design of the rest of the space. Employees should feel that they have left their offices and are in a different environment. Lighting should not be office-like, but like a nice restaurant or bistro. Furniture should not be institutional, and the colors should be different than those in the office environment. Being in the room should help the staff take their minds off work, and feel like they are out of the office. The space should be divided into two separate areas, one where people can walk in and pick up a soda or cup of coffee or put their lunch in the microwave without disturbing people who are seated in the eating area. We cannot stress this strongly enough! Someone who is eating lunch and reading the newspaper does not want to be distracted by someone running the garbage disposal. In some firms, a TV in the lounge is considered a requisite and a fringe benefit for staff who want to watch soap operas on their lunch hour.

Example: See Exhibit 13.7 on page 176.

Equipment for the employee lounge should include:

- At least one full-size refrigerator/freezer (or more, depending on the number of employees being served)
- Coffeemaker
- Coffee grinder (popular with the reinvention of premium coffee)
- Dishwasher
- Ice maker sized to accommodate staff and future growth
- Microwave ovens (quantity depends on number of staff)
- Garbage disposal
- Vending machines (for soft drinks, snacks, and light foods—quantity depends on 24-7 availability to outside food sources)
- Water purification system
- Trash containers, discreetly built in and distributed throughout the areas
- Locked room for storage and supplies

Lawyer Lounge

In firms where lawyers do not want to eat their lunch with the rest of the staff, there may be a lawyers' lounge where a lawyer can go in the morning and have coffee and a bagel and read the newspaper. The room can have several seating options, such as a living-room setting with sofas and chairs, and a few tables that can be configured for eating as a group or more privately. At lunch, lawyers can have a sandwich delivered from the deli downstairs and have a quiet place to eat or gather with a few other colleagues. It can be a place for sections or departments to have weekly meetings over catered lunches. It can be used after hours by lawyers to discuss the events of the day.

Mock Courtroom

Mock courtrooms appear in various forms, from a model that folds up and stores in a closet to a full-blown half-million-dollar courtroom replica. For rehearsals, moots, and CLE, a mock courtroom can be one of the scenes in a multipurpose room, installed as part of a litigation support center, or set up temporarily in a conference room. Depending on the firm's needs, the microphones and video cameras can be set up permanently or in a mobile operation, with equipment shared by videoconferencing facilities.

Exhibit 13.1
ADMINISTRATIVE MANAGERS' OFFICES

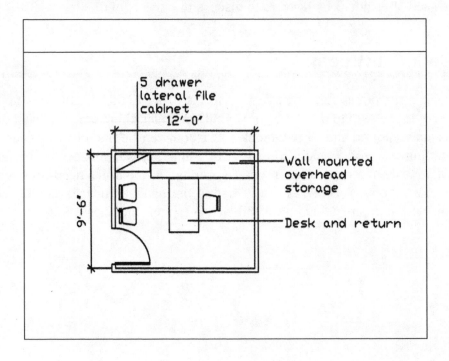

Exhibit 13.2
ADMINISTRATIVE PERSONNEL CUBICLES

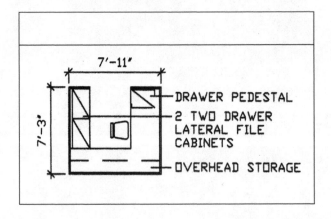

Exhibit 13.3
OFFICE SERVICES CENTER

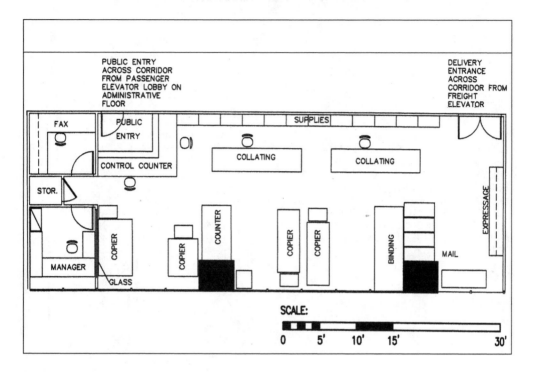

Exhibit 13.4
SATELLITE COPY AREA AND COFFEE AREA

SATELLITE COPY AREAS ARE OFTEN LOCATED NEAR THE FREIGHT ELEVATOR TO BE NEAR DELIVERIES. BESIDE THE COPIER, THE SPACE TYPICALLY ACCOMMODATES SOME OFFICE SUPPLIES, MAIL, HIGH-SPEED COPIER/SCANNER,TYPEWRITER, AND AT LEAST ONE FAX MACHINE. IT MAY ALSO HANDLE EXPRESSAGE AND DELIVERIES. IT MAY BE A MANNED OR UNMANNED STATION.

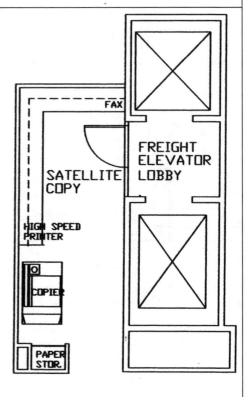

IT IS CONVENIENT TO LOCATE THE SATELLITE COFFEE AREA NEAR THE SATELLITE COPY AREA AS IT SAVES STEPS AND TRAVEL TIME.

A SATELLITE COFFEE AREA WOULD TYPICALLY HAVE A SINGLE SINK WITH HOT/COLD RUNNING WATER, COFFEEMAKER, GARBAGE DISPOSAL, DISHWASHER, UNDERCOUNTER REFRIGERATOR, MICROWAVE AND UNDERCOUNTER ICE MAKER. MOST FIRMS ARE OFFERING SOME TYPE OF PURIFIED DRINKING WATER. THE LEAST SPACE INVASIVE WAY IS TO MOUNT A SMALL WATER FILTRATION SYSTEM IN ONE OF THE UNDERCOUNTER CABINETS. THE LAST ITEM IS TO DETERMINE HOW SOFT DRINKS WILL BE DISPENSED. SOME FIRMS INSTALL VENDING MACHINES THAT ARE EITHER FREE OR AVAILABLE FOR A MINIMAL CHARGE.

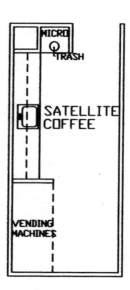

DO NOT FORGET THAT THIS AREA NEEDS TO BE ADA ACCESSIBLE.

Exhibit 13.5
PROJECT WORKROOM

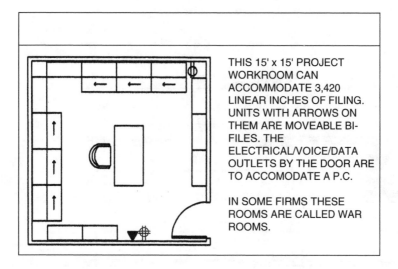

THIS 15' x 15' PROJECT WORKROOM CAN ACCOMMODATE 3,420 LINEAR INCHES OF FILING. UNITS WITH ARROWS ON THEM ARE MOVEABLE BI-FILES. THE ELECTRICAL/VOICE/DATA OUTLETS BY THE DOOR ARE TO ACCOMODATE A P.C.

IN SOME FIRMS THESE ROOMS ARE CALLED WAR ROOMS.

Exhibit 13.6A
SILENT SERVERIES

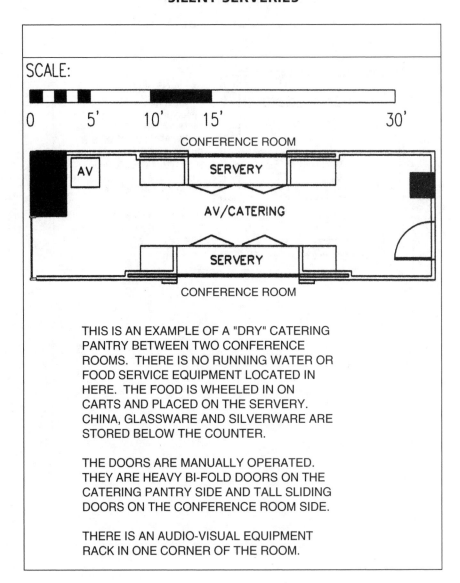

SCALE:

0   5'   10'   15'   30'

CONFERENCE ROOM

AV

SERVERY

AV/CATERING

SERVERY

CONFERENCE ROOM

THIS IS AN EXAMPLE OF A "DRY" CATERING
PANTRY BETWEEN TWO CONFERENCE
ROOMS. THERE IS NO RUNNING WATER OR
FOOD SERVICE EQUIPMENT LOCATED IN
HERE. THE FOOD IS WHEELED IN ON
CARTS AND PLACED ON THE SERVERY.
CHINA, GLASSWARE AND SILVERWARE ARE
STORED BELOW THE COUNTER.

THE DOORS ARE MANUALLY OPERATED.
THEY ARE HEAVY BI-FOLD DOORS ON THE
CATERING PANTRY SIDE AND TALL SLIDING
DOORS ON THE CONFERENCE ROOM SIDE.

THERE IS AN AUDIO-VISUAL EQUIPMENT
RACK IN ONE CORNER OF THE ROOM.

Exhibit 13.6B
SILENT SERVERIES

THIS IS AN EXAMPLE OF A "WET" CATERING PANTRY. IT SERVICES TWO CONFERENCE ROOMS
 BY MOTORIZED DOORS THAT RETRACT INTO THE CEILING.
THE CATERING PANTRY HERE HAS A REFRIGERATOR, FREEZER, TWO DISHWASHERS,
COMMERCIAL ICE MAKER, TWO MICROWAVES, SINK WITH GARBAGE DISPOSAL, COFFEEMAKER.

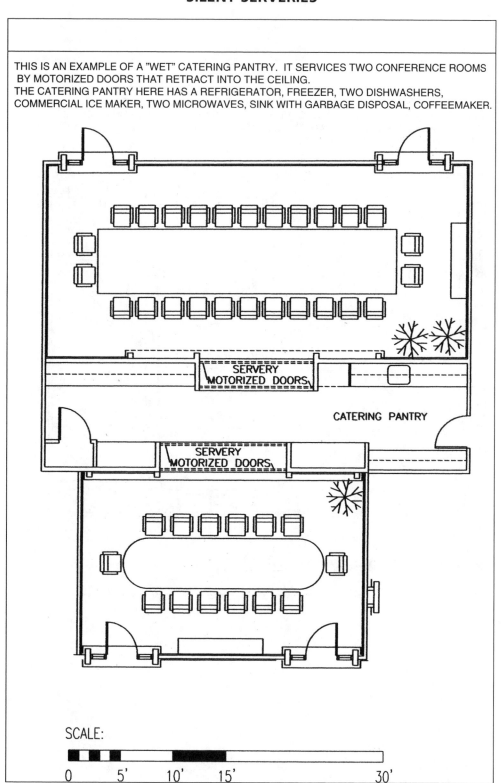

SERVERY
MOTORIZED DOORS

CATERING PANTRY

SERVERY
MOTORIZED DOORS

SCALE:

0   5'   10'   15'   30'

Exhibit 13.7
EMPLOYEE LOUNGE

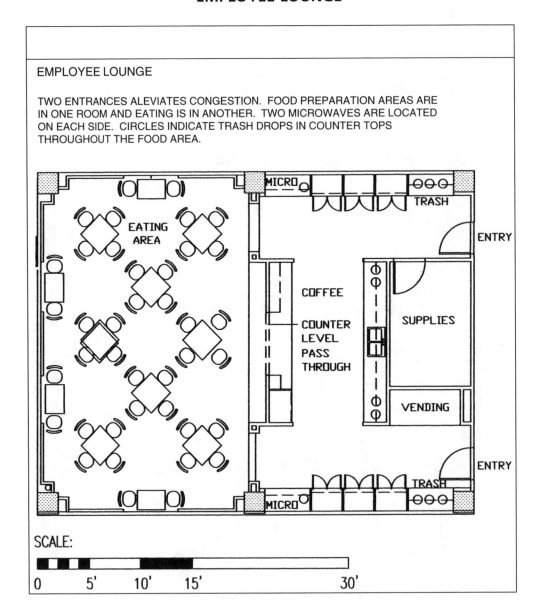

EMPLOYEE LOUNGE

TWO ENTRANCES ALEVIATES CONGESTION. FOOD PREPARATION AREAS ARE IN ONE ROOM AND EATING IS IN ANOTHER. TWO MICROWAVES ARE LOCATED ON EACH SIDE. CIRCLES INDICATE TRASH DROPS IN COUNTER TOPS THROUGHOUT THE FOOD AREA.

EATING AREA

MICRO
TRASH
ENTRY

COFFEE

COUNTER LEVEL PASS THROUGH

SUPPLIES

VENDING

ENTRY

TRASH
MICRO

SCALE:

0   5'   10'   15'   30'

Public Areas 14

Elevator Lobbies

The Firm's Image

If you are a full-floor tenant, you should design and build out the finishes in the elevator lobby to set the image the firm wants to project. If you are not a full-floor tenant, place your entrance at one end of the elevator lobby. This is called having elevator lobby presence, and it also can help make you firm look much bigger than it is. It means that clients do not have to wander through multitenant corridors looking for your suite. Elevator lobby presence usually costs more in rent, but the advantages are usually worth it. If you are a partial-floor tenant, the design and finishes of the existing lobby portrays an image. When shopping for buildings, it is important to keep this in mind and be comfortable with the image the lobby portrays.

Security at Elevator Lobbies

If you are a full-floor tenant you probably need a security camera in the elevator lobby that records traffic 24-7. These cameras are small (about the size of a stack of ten dimes), so they can be discreetly mounted. Many firms elect not to have cameras until an incident happens, and they wish they had a record of it. It is very common to have someone, such as the firm's receptionist, monitor these images throughout the day to see if a person is loitering in the lobby and waiting to gain entry when the door is opened. For multiple-floor firms, the monitor can scan the various floors as a department store monitor does.

You need to consider how after-hours access is handled for clients, staff, and the pizza delivery guy. It may be that after-hours visitors have to call from the base-building security desk on the ground floor and someone from the firm goes down and escorts them up. If people are allowed to go up to the floor after hours, you need a way to know when they are in the elevator lobby, such as a phone that calls into the offices or a doorbell. You also want to consider the safety of the staff members who answer the door after hours. They should be able to see and identify the person before they open the door.

Many municipalities have stringent code requirements for elevator lobbies. Some require a direct corridor to a fire stair. Others require panic buttons that override security systems, allowing anyone to escape into your space at any time. This requirement exists in order to keep someone from being trapped in an elevator lobby during a fire. Have your design professional check the local requirements.

Whether you are a full-floor or partial-floor tenant, the walls of the demising partitions (between your space and the elevator lobby, the multitenant corridors, and the adjacent tenants) need to go to the structure above. This is to prevent someone from popping up ceiling tiles and going over the partition into your space. This also applies to the freight elevator lobby.

Reception Area

Almost without exception, law firms use one centralized reception area. Briefly, the reasons for this are:

- Better security
- Lower personnel costs
- Lower square footage requirements
- Limiting the high-cost area to one instead of several

See Chapter 5 for more reasons.

As the space with the highest level of finishes, the reception area establishes the firm's image. Its design needs to reflect and support the receptionist's control of access to the public areas of the firm. Security and service functions need to be incorporated into the area. Design issues should also consider the wide variety of functions that may be provided in the area, such as phone rooms for visitors to use with cell phones, coat and luggage storage for visitors, secure Internet access, coffee service, and access to restrooms. Accessibility is essential.

A receptionist who is primarily a greeter needs less desk space than a working receptionist. A working receptionist probably needs a printer; it should be hidden from public view. In some smaller firms the receptionist performs duties that do not take as much space as a regular secretary. The receptionist should be in charge of scheduling conference rooms, as well as monitoring when conferences are over so the room can be prepared for a new meeting. Many firms make the mistake of not having someone in charge of cleaning up conference rooms after meetings. Someone (not necessarily a busy receptionist) has to be assigned the task.

Conference Rooms

A conference complex needs support functions. Consider the following:

- Space for a secretary to work and edit documents during a meeting
- A copier, fax, scanner, and high-speed printer
- Space to collate a document
- Caucus room where a small group can break out of a meeting
- Telephone rooms where people can make phone calls, check their e-mail or voicemail, and use their cell phones
- Coat closet and luggage storage
- Visitor offices for visiting lawyers or lawyers from the firm's other offices
- Food service area (at a minimum, an area to prepare beverages, or a catering pantry for food to be brought in and served)
- Audiovisual equipment storage
- Space for floaters who can relieve the receptionist, show people to conference rooms, make copies, help people with travel reservations, call taxis, provide and check beverage setups in conference rooms

Clustered Conference Rooms or Conference Room Complex

Much of our commentary in Chapter 5 on developing trends relates to conference rooms, especially conference-room floors for larger firms and conference room clusters. The distraction and the security issues that arise from having clients in the lawyer office environment leads many firms to establish separate public areas for clients and other people meeting with lawyers. Some of the reasons for the success and popularity of these areas are having an enhanced ability to control and direct visitor traffic, centralizing the support areas for business meetings and avoiding duplication of facilities and related construction costs, and limiting the costs of the highest level of finishes to a smaller area of the firm's space. Also, conference rooms are a fertile area for developments in meeting technology, which we discussed in more detail in Chapter 9.

Basic Planning for Conference Rooms

Before deciding on the sizes for conference rooms, consider some basic concepts. First, in sizing conference room tables and ultimately the room important factor needs to be considered: will chairs be the large swivel tilt kind, or will they be on four legs? Obviously the large chairs take far more space at a table, and fewer seats can be accommodated. A swivel tilt chair needs 36 inches per chair so people can swivel and tilt, while a straight-legged chair that is 23 inches wide needs 28 to 30 inches per chair.

You need at least 54 inches between the edge of the table and the wall behind or a piece of furniture that abuts the wall, although 60 inches is better. This is especially true with swivel tilt chairs. This allows room to walk behind the chair when someone is seated at the table. Remember that many meetings in firms are all-day events, and people tend to push their chairs back from the table and recline back in them.

A conference room also needs a credenza or some type of sideboard or table for a telephone, phone list, and beverage service. The top of the credenza should be of a material that is not easily scratched or marred. If lunches are to be served in the room there should be adequate layout space.

See examples of sizes of conference rooms and the number of seats they accommodate in Exhibit 14.1.

Sizes and Quantities

To determine the sizes and number of conference rooms the firm needs for the new space, keep track of all meetings—the number of attendees, duration, what refreshments were served, and so on. This will also show how many conference rooms are being used simultaneously. Our thoughts on determining the number of conference seats you need per lawyer are in Chapter 5.

Conference rooms need to be designed to accommodate a variety of types of meetings.

- Client meetings: typically the nicest conference rooms with the highest levels of finishes and details
- Discovery: conference rooms that can be set up for quite a long time during the discovery period; typically not highly finished or detailed
- Deposition: conference rooms that need audiovisual capability and properly designed lighting (so the person being deposed does not look like a ghost or a villain)
- Mediations: typically smaller conference rooms—care should be taken to be sure people waiting in these rooms do not wander elsewhere in the firm, so provide some type of entertainment such as magazines or coffee-table books
- In-house conferences: rooms that can be used for section or practice group meetings, CLE seminars, and so on; ideally located on lawyer floors if space permits

Multipurpose Rooms

Nearly every firm over one floor in size needs a multipurpose room to handle larger meetings. These rooms do not have permanent tables, because furniture layouts may vary with each type of meeting. They can be classroom style, theater style, or the whole room can be empty of furniture for a stand-up reception. Multipurpose rooms are usually sized to accommodate the entire partnership in a seated style to allow for a breakfast or luncheon presentation. They may also be sized to handle partners and associates in a theater-style arrangement.

They need to have food service facilities nearby and a silent servery. These rooms need a high level of technology support. We refer you back to Chapter 5, where we mentioned some of these issues, including the recent use of partitions that appear out of the ceiling to divide the room at the touch of a button.

Lighting

Multipurpose rooms should be equipped with a dimming panel with at least five lighting scenes. This means that the various types of light fixtures are programmed to create different lighting scenes or combinations. Consider these types of lighting scenes:

- PowerPoint or slide presentation
- General meeting
- Evening reception
- Video teleconferencing
- Lecture presentation

In addition to various sources of lighting, special attention needs to be given to the type of light fixtures selected. Since this room is used for video teleconferencing at times, light fixtures need to have specially designed baffles so that the lights are not detected by the camera. If this is neglected, the main point of focus in the image will be the light fixtures. There should be several different kinds of lights in this room: dual-ballast fluorescent with special baffles, down lights, and wall washers.

HVAC

Heating and air-conditioning are obviously very important to a multipurpose room. Be sure that your MEP engineer understands that there could be a meeting of twelve or two hundred in this room, so that he or she designs the system accordingly. Also make the MEP engineer aware of the sound systems in the room so the air-conditioning is designed to the appropriate sound levels.

Acoustics

For a room with all these functions, acoustics are very important. The walls need to have sound absorbing materials added to the surface. These are fiberglass with fabric wall covering on top.

Audiovisual Systems

Microphones and speakers are necessary for audio and visual teleconferencing and for sound reinforcement for presentations. These can be discreetly recessed and mounted flush in the ceiling. You need an equipment room behind or near the multipurpose room to accommodate the equipment rack. Plasma screens and rear projection are currently the standards to support these systems. In very large rooms you need multiple screens for viewers in the back. If front projection is the only option, a projector is either recessed above the ceiling on a motorized lift or surface mounted to the ceiling.

There are two ways to design these systems: hire an audiovisual consultant to prepare drawings and specifications for bids, or use an audiovisual vendor who will have technicians design the system using the manufacturer's equipment that they represent. A consultant is a degreed engineer and technicians generally are not, so although consultants are more expensive, you can expect a better product.

In contrast to earlier audiovisual systems that needed to be operated by a technically trained staff member, new systems have their functions programmed into a flat screen mounted in the podium. Anyone can operate the system simply by touching the icons, although a staff member still needs to be trained and familiar with the rudimentary system. We should also mention that recessed motorized projection screens are now being replaced by plasma screens and rear-projection technology, but they remain useful for very large projections. Another aspect of technology used in these rooms is motorized blackout shades on the perimeter windows. Be sure to specify side channels for the shades in order to avoid light leaks.

The multipurpose room can be expensive in terms of the technology bells and whistles. However, a law firm can easily turn this room into a wonderful asset and marketing tool. Let your clients use it for special meetings or events. Let the community use it for functions like the United Way drive kickoff. You will become known as a firm with leading technology that is willing to share it for the good of others.

Furniture Storage Area

Remember that the nature of a multipurpose room is that it is flexible. At 8 a.m. it could be used for a partnership meeting serving breakfast; at 10 there might be a firm-wide meeting on health insurance. At noon it could be used for a section meeting serving lunch. At 3:00 P.M. there might be a CLE seminar, and at 6:00 perhaps a reception for one of your largest clients, who happens to be in town. The room might go through five different furniture configurations in one day. Some setups need tables, some just chairs, and some no furniture at all. The furniture needs to be stored in a room adjacent to the multipurpose room. The tables typically fold down and the chairs stack. There is usually never enough storage room—err on the long side.

Exhibit 14.1A
CONFERENCE ROOM SEATING 8

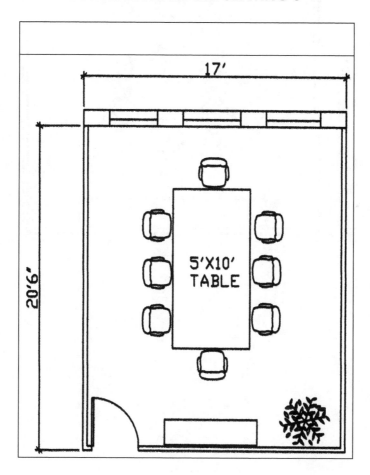

Exhibit 14.1B
CONFERENCE ROOM SEATING 8

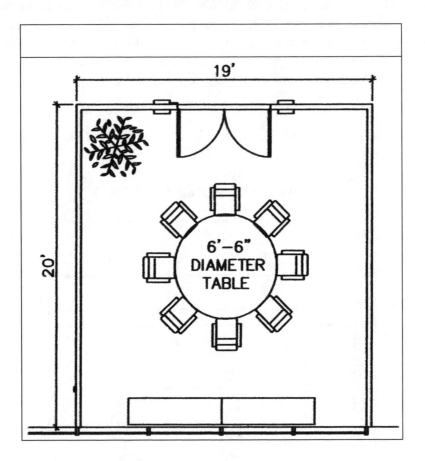

Exhibit 14.1C
CONFERENCE ROOM SEATING 10

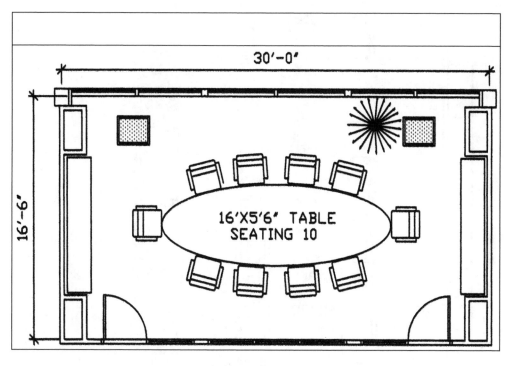

Exhibit 14.1D
CONFERENCE ROOM SEATING 14

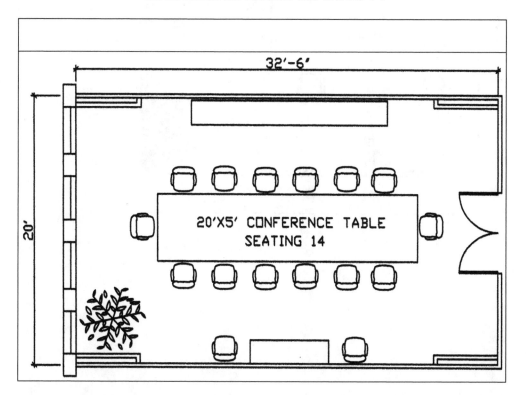

Exhibit 14.1E
CONFERENCE ROOM SEATING 18

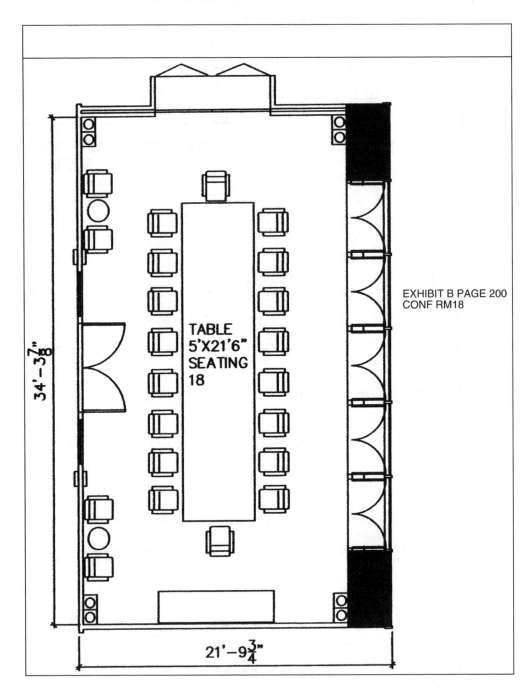

TABLE
5'X21'6"
SEATING
18

34'-3⅞"

21'-9¾"

EXHIBIT B PAGE 200
CONF RM18

Exhibit 14.1F
MULTI-PURPOSE ROOMS

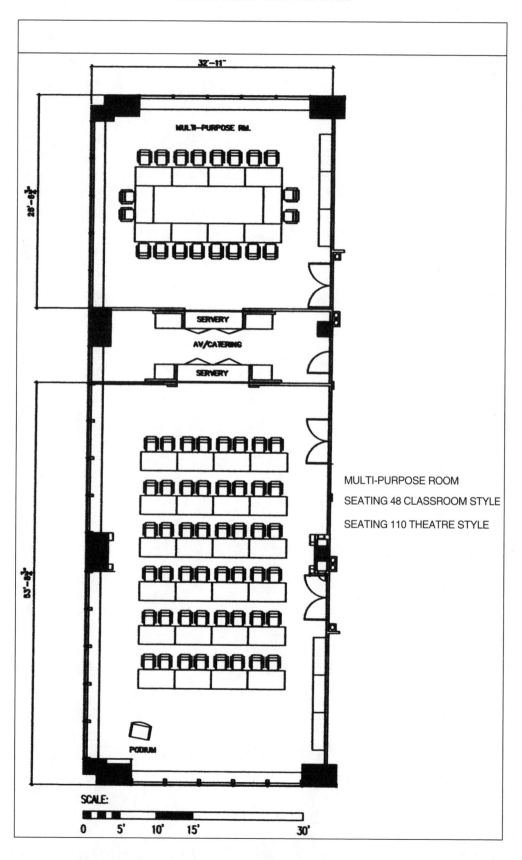

MULTI-PURPOSE ROOM

SEATING 48 CLASSROOM STYLE

SEATING 110 THEATRE STYLE

Finishes in the Lawyer Environment

15

Finishes can be categorized by their uses for ceilings, walls, base, and floors.

Ceilings

In most buildings the space above the ceiling is an air return plenum. Therefore the ceiling must be accessible for the mechanical and electrical maintenance. A nonaccessible ceiling such as drywall or gypsum board like the one in your home is not an option. Most ceilings are a metal grid with acoustical tile that is either laid into the grid or interlocked into the grid. Typically the metal ceiling system supports the ceiling tile and also helps stabilize the partition system. The top track of the wall system is screwed into the ceiling grid. The ceiling grid is typically $4' \times 4'$. The main tees run in one direction and are not meant to be cut. The subtees run at 90 degrees to the main tees and can be adjusted as needed.

The options for the ceiling tiles appear below.

$1' \times 1'$ Acoustical Ceiling Tile

This is called a concealed spline ceiling. No metal grid is visible. It is the most expensive and provides the greatest acoustical privacy. It is more difficult to maintain because it is only accessible at one tile in a $4' \times 4'$ area. These accessible tiles are typically marked with a half-inch white pin. This ceiling system was once considered building standard in class A buildings. Over time, building maintenance people have given the ceiling system a bad name by their neglect in handling maintenance through the ceiling. (In our opinion, their neglect butchers up 2′ × 2′ tile just as much.) This is still an option for high-end spaces such as reception areas and conference rooms.

2′ × 2′ Acoustical Ceiling Tile

This is replacing the concealed spline ceiling as a building standard. The tiles are 2′ × 2′ and set within a 4′ × 4′ grid. They are framed by a metal system where the exposed parts are nominally either ⅝ or ¾ inches wide. There are various quality grades for these systems and the tiles that go in them. Let your design professional educate you on the acoustical and aesthetic merits of each.

Note: Avoid 2′ × 4′ ceiling tile at all cost. It sags over time, and is not appropriate for a law firm.

Options for ceilings in elevator lobbies, reception areas, conference rooms, and other high-end areas continue to be drywall or gypsum wallboard. These can incorporate light coves or other concealed lighting systems. Another material for this application is glass reinforced gypsum (GRG), which can be manufactured to form domes or coffered ceilings.

One final note: When designing an area with a gypsum board ceiling, be sure that all mechanical, electrical, and plumbing items that require access are not located over this ceiling. If they are already there, plan to move them. From an appearance standpoint, not much is worse than a pristine gypsum board ceiling with an access panel stuck in it.

Walls

Wall finishes can be painted drywall or gypsum wallboard, fabric wall covering, vinyl wall covering, millwork wall paneling, stone wall paneling, acoustical wall covering, or whatever the budget allows.

Paint

Paint comes in many quality levels, and you usually get what you pay for. Poor quality in the underlying walls and woodwork can make the best paint look bad, so you should require good floating and sanding on drywall construction and careful filling and cleaning of wood surfaces.

Color is a personal preference. If you are a novice picking the paint color yourself without professional guidance, stay away from strong or saturated colors. You will tire of them easily and they soon appear dated. Stay with light neutrals. Buy a quart or a gallon and try it in the space with the lighting that will be in place.

For walls and ceilings, specify water-based acrylic latex, applied with a roller—not sprayed. Three paint finishes are available. The first is flat, which as the name implies has no sheen. Flat paint does not readily show wall imperfections such as drywall tape joints. However, it mars easily and is not washable. Flat finish is good to use for ceilings, and it is the least expensive.

Eggshell has a very slight sheen and it is our choice for painted walls at law firms. It can show wall imperfections if walls are not properly floated, but it is more mar-resistant than flat finishes. It can be lightly washed, but spot painting touch-ups do not work. For repairs, the whole wall must be repainted. Semigloss finishes have a moderate sheen and, while more commonly used in residential kitchen and bathroom applications, have the advantage of being highly washable. Like eggshell finishes, repairs and touch-ups require painting the entire wall. We consider semigloss to be too shiny for law firms.

For consistency and quality, wall paint should be applied with a roller. For new construction, we recommend one coat of primer and two finish coats. For drywall ceilings, we recommend flat "ceiling white," applied with a low-nap roller.

For painted woodwork, specify one coat of alkyd (oil-based) primer, sprayed, and two finish coats of alkyd semigloss, sprayed. The work should be lightly sanded between coats.

In all cases, primer and paint should come from the same manufacturer to insure compatibility. We recommend using the manufacturer's highest quality paint. It will outlast and outperform less-expensive grades and ensure washability of washable paints.

Fabric

Fabric wall covering can vary greatly in price. Fabric should not be used in confined conditions where people are going to lean up on it or transfer oil from their hands to it. An elevator lobby is a good example of where *not* to use fabric wall covering. Fabric wall covering is by far more tasteful than vinyl wall covering, although vinyl wall covering is more serviceable. Wallpaper is far too fragile for public areas of a law firm.

Acoustical wall treatment is an upholstered wall system that absorbs sound transmission. It is both practical and aesthetically pleasing, but it comes at an expensive price. The thicker the fiberglass used in it, the more sound it absorbs.

Base

Base is the trim that is installed where the wall meets the floor. As a practical matter, it covers up the sins where two trades meet. The least expensive is rubber or vinyl base. It comes in a wide variety of colors and is easily installed. It comes in different heights: 2½, 4, or 6 inches. The 2½-inch is by far the most aesthetically pleasing. Never use the 6-inch. Many landlords and developers offer the 4-inch as their standard. The 4-inch base means that the drywall finishers and the painters do not have to be as careful as they do with a 2½-inch base. The base may be either straight or coved (curved at the bottom). The straight base is used with carpet. The coved is used where there is VCT flooring (so water does not get under the base and wick up onto the drywall). Some landlords and developers say that coved base is their standard everywhere. Again they are taking the easy way out, as the coved portion can cover up a bad carpet installation.

Floors

Floor coverings can vary from sealed concrete to stone. The most common form of floor covering is carpet. Carpet comes in every price range. It may have a pad for more cushion and appearance retention. About half of law firms have carpet with pad and the other half have carpet that is directly glued to the slab. A pad adds to the sound absorption.

Our discussion starts at the high end of floor coverings and works down from there.

Stone Flooring

Next to concrete, two-centimeter (¾″) stone flooring is the most durable and longest-lasting floor covering. It is also expensive but not out of the question for law firms. Stone requires a thicker setting bed, so be sure you have the flooring tolerances to install it.

There is a difference in hardness between marble and granite. Granite is much stronger than marble. Marble has veins or fissure lines along which it can break or crack. Two-centimeter stone with the proper setting bed stands up in a commercial application. Typically two-centimeter stone can be cut in any size (up to certain limits).

One-centimeter (⅜″) material, which is typically available in 12″ × 12″ tiles, is not recommended for commercial use of marble. It breaks and cracks over time. One-centimeter granite is usually fine.

Brick

Brick flooring is very serviceable and affordable. It can be a suitable choice for a historic building. However, taken out of historical context and used in a high rise office building, it conjures up the feeling of a 1970s fad.

Tile

Tile is a very popular material these days. We urge much caution, though, because it can give a residential or bathroom feeling rather than portray a law firm image.

Wood

The density of wood flooring varies by the species of wood. Even the hardest and densest woods do not hold up to the pinpoint pressure applied by women's high-heeled shoes. If you elect to use it, ¾-inch thick solid wood flooring can be sanded and refinished perhaps two times before there is nothing to refinish. The only place wood flooring should be used in a law firm is in private offices, or in historic buildings where the wood floors are original. Wood floors that were installed a hundred years or more ago are usually from a species that was premiere growth wood, original to the forests of the U.S. It was first-growth harvest, and much denser than wood flooring today. This is not to say that high-heeled shoes do not damage it, but the imperfections, dents, and mars are a little more easily forgiven than with new wood floors. If you are in a building with these original old floors, we recommend that area rugs be placed in high traffic areas.

Laminate wood floors are generally most appropriate for residential applications. They are generally inexpensive and can be used in selected smaller areas.

Carpet

Carpet comes in price ranges that fit any budget. Buy the best quality that you can afford and buy it according to the length of your lease or how long you expect to stay in the building. Replacing carpet can be expensive because furniture has to be moved, work has do be done after business hours, and furniture has to be moved back. All of this takes a toll on the other finishes. Walls get marred; doors and door frames are damaged. Electricians and cabling vendors have to undo then redo floor outlets. Large pieces of furniture like secretarial stations and conference tables require skilled workers to move them.

Broadloom versus Carpet Tiles

Broadloom carpet comes in widths from two to twelve feet. The most practical for law offices is twelve-foot goods. Anything narrower has too many seams. Carpet tiles are expensive and not practical for law firms. They are good for airports or areas with very high traffic concentration. They are also required where in-floor electrical duct systems are used.

Appearance Retention

One criterion that should guide you when selecting a carpet is appearance retention. All carpet looks good when it is first laid. Appearance retention is determined by these qualities:

- Fiber
- Construction method
- Dyeing
- Finishing
- Installation
- Maintenance

Fiber

Carpet fiber is either natural (wool) or synthetic (nylon). Carpet, other than area rugs, should never be 100 percent wool. A typical blend is 80 percent wool and 20 percent nylon. The nylon gives wool the durability that it needs. Wool has natural resiliency and springs back. It has natural lanolin and does not give off static shocks. It does not retain stains like nylon and other synthetic fibers. Another attribute of wool is that it looks rich and is not shiny. Wool can be expensive, and is not for every budget.

Nylon has made great improvements over the years. Be sure to get a branded nylon—a fiber that is manufactured by a big-name, reputable company. Unbranded nylons are not worth considering unless you intend to replace carpet soon and can put up with stains until then. Good-quality nylon has surmounted the static problems. Nylon has become the industry standard fiber. We do not recommend acrylics and modacrylics.

A continuous-filament yarn system is best. The alternative is staple yarn, which are short lengths of yarn. With staple yarn, you can lose 10 percent of your carpet to the vacuum cleaner in the first year. The yarn should have at least five twists per inch and the twists should be heat set; otherwise the yarn can "bloom" over time and look matted. This is important for appearance retention.

There are two basic methods of looming carpet: woven and tufted. Woven is best and keeps its appearance longer. You may want to consider this if you are signing a fifteen-year lease. Tufted carpet has come a long way with the primary and secondary backings that hold the tufts in place, and is perfectly acceptable if things like stitches, rows per inch, and other specifications are carefully considered.

Dyeing

There are three basic methods of dyeing carpet. One is skein or yarn dyeing, where the yarn is dyed before the carpet is made. Another is beck or vat dyeing, where the carpet is dyed after it is made. The third type of dye method is solution dyeing, where the fibers are made from plastic pellets that are dyed before the yarn is extruded or spun. The drawback to solution dyeing is that the color range is limited and the fiber has a shiny appearance. The advantage is that it is impervious to many stains and chemicals. It is used heavily in the health care industry.

If your project is large, skein dyed is best because it guarantees a consistent dye lot. You do not have color side-match problems at the seams. It is more expensive than beck dying. Beck dying can be fine if your project is small and all the carpet is dyed at once. Beck dying can work if each floor is dyed at one time and the manufacturer guarantees not having side-match problems. If your project is large, you can get guarantees; if your project is small, listen to your design professional and purchase the best product within your budget. It is not unusual to get ten or more years out of your carpet if you buy carefully in the beginning.

A common misconception is that greater pile heights are better. If you compare a half-inch pile height with a quarter-inch pile height, the longer pile height can fall over on its side and over time look like wear paths. The yarn isn't actually worn out; it just refracts light differently when it is on its side versus when it is standing straight up.

Pattern

Another factor to consider in selecting carpet is pattern versus no pattern. A no-pattern carpet is basically a cut pile, which is what most people have in their homes. In the law firm environment, as opposed to a restaurant or casino, we are talking about a very subtle, tone-on-tone pattern. The carpet can be all one color but appear to be very slightly different colors by the way the pattern makes it look or the way the yarn refracts the light. Pattern can be as subtle as varying the yarn face from a cut pile to a loop or a combination of the two (tip-sheared).

Loop carpet stands up to high traffic where cut pile does not. However, loop carpet does not have the rich feeling of cut pile. An example of an expensive loop carpet is a Berber (which is wool). However, most loop carpet has the look and feel of the carpet used in elementary schools. There are ways to combine loop and cut pile for very attractive and serviceable carpets for higher traffic areas.

Patterns tend to hide wear, dirt, and stains better than a solid-color cut pile. Cut piles are fine for low traffic areas such as private offices. Corridors and high-traffic areas retain their appearance better with a tone-on-tone patterned carpet. We emphasize subtlety in selecting patterned carpet for law firms; the corridors are not huge, expansive spaces that can take the bold and colorful patterns used in places like airports.

Installation

To make your carpet look better for a longer period of time, consider how it is installed and what it is installed over. We have all seen carpet that is rippled and buckled or has stretched. This becomes a tripping hazard. Commercially installed carpet should not be stretched with a conventional perimeter tack-strip system. The standard method for installing carpet is to directly glue the carpet to the substrate. Of course, we are not advocating this method if the building is a historical structure. But if the floor is a concrete slab, as in most commercial buildings, then this is the preferred method. If properly installed with the correct adhesives, the carpet will not ripple and buckle. To add life and appearance retention to the carpet, a cushion or pad is recommended. A thicker pad is not always the better alternative; carpet pad needs to be judged on its density. Today, most good carpets have the pad attached to the carpet at the factory. This produces a product that is monolithic and does not delaminate. It is more expensive, but saves labor at installation. The attached cushion also avoids much damage to the walls, base, doors, and door frames during installation. Traditional broadloom carpet has a backing that is rough and can scratch anything it touches. Adding a pad to the carpet eliminates this problem. It almost pays for itself when it comes to the punch list.

Cleaning

Have your carpet cleaned on a regular basis by a reputable company. Along with cleaning the carpet, the service should use a special machine that lifts the pile of the carpet (called a pile lifter). High-traffic areas such as corridors should be done on a more frequent basis than offices. Before starting on a program, talk to the carpet manufacturer's representative to obtain their recommended maintenance procedures and find out what companies they recommend for a maintenance program. The daily building custodial people do not have the ability to perform this maintenance.

Hard Surface Flooring

Hard surface flooring is used where carpet is not practical, such as in copy rooms, coffee areas, computer rooms, or where there is a high amount of cart traffic, such as file rooms. The most common type of hard surface flooring for a law firm is VCT. It comes in $12'' \times 12'' \times \frac{1}{8}''$ tiles and is laid directly on the slab with an adhesive. It needs to be thoroughly waxed and dried before moving anything on it. One of the frequent mistakes people make is not applying enough wax before moving furniture or equipment on it. Some types of tile need ten coats. Once this is done, mopping and occasional buffing are the daily maintenance. Occasional rewaxing is necessary. VCT is available in a wide variety of colors.

Sheet products are available but the cheap products are not serviceable for a law firm and the expensive products designed for health care are overkill. The only place we see this type of product used in a law firm is if a non-slip floor is desired for a catering pantry. It costs about five times more than VCT.

Building-Standard Finishes

When buildings are new and you are an initial tenant, chances are good that the landlord will offer you a package specifying that they will build out your space using building-standard finishes, and you can select colors within their standard offering. You do not have to take their building-standard finishes; you can elect to use your own. You may want to do a combination, selecting some of their standards and selecting some of your own. Because the landlord purchases in quantity, building-standard pricing structure or unit costs are an incentive.

Building-standard finishes vary by the class of building and by the area of the country. From a practical standpoint, the classification of office buildings as Class A, B, or C is something of a variable, rather than a standard. Generally speaking, Class B buildings are the second tier of quality in a given market. Below are examples of what you might expect.

Finishes in a Class A building in major cities may include:

- Ceiling: 2′ × 2′ acoustical ceiling tile in a 2′ × 2′ fine-line regular ceiling grid
- Walls: 2 coats eggshell (or perhaps flat) latex paint
- Base: 2½-inch straight rubber base
- Floors: 32-ounce cut pile carpet, branded nylon
- Doors: 9-foot solid core wood veneer
- Door frames: 9-foot anodized aluminum
- Hardware: Full mortised

Finishes in a Class B building in major cities or Class A in smaller cities may include

- Ceiling: 2′ × 2′ acoustical ceiling tile in a 2′ × 2′ lay-in ceiling grid
- Walls: 2 coats flat latex paint
- Base: 4-inch cove rubber base
- Floors: 30-ounce carpet, unbranded nylon
- Doors: 8-foot solid core plastic laminate
- Door frames: 8-foot hollow metal
- Hardware: Nonmortised

Advice on Finishes and Colors

We believe that finishes should be classics and not what is current or hot in today's trends. Trends and fads belong in fashion, not in commercial office space. We do not posit that all law firms should have mahogany and dark, saturated colors. Both bright and dark colors are tiring to the eye and make spaces feel small and confined. Keep colors subtle, simple, and neutral—these appeal to a broader range of the general public.

Put your money where it counts. Lawyers are no longer putting wall covering and fancy wood paneling and moldings in their private offices. Save those finishes and their costs for the public areas. The trend is to put higher-quality finishes where they are seen.

Moving to the New Space 16

This chapter has our recommendations for coordinating, timing, and organizing the move. The firm's person in charge of the move should get started early and have great project management skills and a big dose of composure. These attributes, along with some of the techniques we suggest in this chapter, will make moving day an amazingly graceful event.

Civilized Move

Civilized moves happen when we do as much advance preparation as possible before moving day. While we cover plenty of useful techniques in this chapter, we begin by showing you some examples of how firms make the move transparent.

Before moving day:

- Have the Certificate of Occupancy in place and available for inspection
- Have the punch list 100 percent complete
- Have all systems and connections checked out and operational
- Have artwork installed
- Have all new and refurbished furniture and equipment installed
- Have the library, file room, and administrative functions pre-moved

Imagine how much better it is to move the firm into a space where these things have already been done. Our message, then, is simply that the move takes place over a long period of time, and moving day or moving weekend can be near the end of a year-long process. Here are a few words about getting started.

First, organize communications. In a general sense, it seems obvious that communication throughout the firm is vital to keeping the firm operating at full efficiency throughout the project and to make the move to new quarters a positive experience for the firm. Specifically, the person in charge of the move needs to start early, meeting with the firm's moving team. Even the small nuances in picking up things in one office and moving them to another office affect work flow and personal interaction in the new space, so all of your supervisors and managers need to be involved early. These people, in turn, need to work with staff at every level, because people know their jobs and can help the firm hit the ground running on Monday morning when the new office opens. The move immediately affects everyone in the firm, and nearly everyone needs to participate in the move, if only to protect their own work and possessions and to learn how to function in the new space.

In addition to everything that arrives in the moving vans, the move includes replacement of furniture, accessories, systems, and equipment that are delivered directly to the new site and installed there, so success of the move depends on coordination of delivery dates on all the vendor contracts held by the law firm, as well as timely completion by the general contractor.

Planning and Staffing the Move

Our detailed checklist in Chapter 4 in the section on Phase V, Construction and In-House Coordination, contains a timetable and a checklist for the major elements of a move, and it reiterates the urgent need for starting early. A year in advance is not too early to begin serious work on the move. You need a project manager for the move, who will likely be an administrator or a senior manager in the firm. A relatively small portion of firms hire a professional move coordinator. Your move project manager works closely with your design professional, the general contractor, the moving company, and the vendors of major technology and furniture components to coordinate the move. This person should be concerned with the lead times and the coordination required to make the move as seamless as possible. The move project manager should create checklists and a timetable for the move, scheduling the preparations and allowing time to get the work done.

Sidebar

There are two big questions that need to be answered about a move.

1. How much will the move cost?

The moving budget is usually way too low. As a rule of thumb, you can expect the cost to be sixty-five cents to one dollar per square foot for a large or medium-sized firm, and perhaps twice that for smaller firms. The big variables are union labor and building access.

2. How much time will the move take?

This varies according to the size of the crews, the movers' equipment, the number of elevators, and the advance preparation. In our experience, a firm of seven to ten floors can be moved in three days, while a one-floor firm usually takes about a day and a half.

Organizing for the Move

Designing Your Law Office (ABA Law Practice Management Section, 1988) contains excellent advice about selecting a primary moving crew from among the firm's staff: ". . . to work from the beginning to the end of the move. The crew's duties are to assist other employees with packing, to make packing materials available at all times, to answer questions, and to ensure that everything needed is packed before the movers arrive." We see a large scope of responsibility for the crew. The firm's moving crew should meet with the moving company's supervisors for a planning and orientation session before the move. If the two groups can get to know one another and begin to solve problems well ahead of the move, it makes the move go more smoothly. By the all-critical moving day, they recognize each other on sight and have some shared knowledge of the project. The primary moving crew and the move project manager should be the only people in the firm to give instructions to the movers.

When the time comes to move out of the old offices, the goal is to get everything out of the old offices and into the right place in the new offices. On moving day, have your moving supervisors and primary moving crew scheduled to provide coverage at the control headquarters in both the old and new spaces. For the major areas that are being moved, station one primary crew member at the old space and one at the new space while the areas are being moved. The firm's primary moving crew needs to be large enough to work in shifts around the clock if the move happens in that time frame.

Early in the Move Process

Very early in the process, make a list of contacts and include cell and home numbers for the following people:

- New building manager
- Old building manager
- General contractor's representative
- Electrician
- Voice/data cabling company
- Elevator technician (in case of trouble with the elevators during the move)
- The firm's key move personnel
- Moving company
- Vendors
- Installers
- Building engineers
- Security personnel

Your list of contacts will be longer, but these are the essential ones for the move itself. We emphasize that all of these people must be on call throughout the move, even if you move on a holiday.

Develop a list of all items to be moved to the new space.

Determine the working boundaries of the new and existing space with the landlords, and establish an understanding of the times when freight elevators and freight docks can be reserved or scheduled. If loading docks and elevators are not applicable, determine when and how the moving vans can gain access to the existing space and the new space. The how and when can seriously affect the cost of the move.

New furniture needs to be fabricated by the manufacturer or created as millwork and delivered on a precise schedule. Your design professional can suggest furniture vendors and can coordinate the designs for both the architectural millwork and the movable or furniture millwork, such as work stations. If you are reupholstering and refinishing some of your existing furniture, schedule the work before the move. For furniture, the bidding process and manufacturing schedules make it critical to have enough lead time to insure delivery before moving day. These, of course, are items to coordinate with the construction schedule. You should allow no fewer than five months for furniture bids, fabrication, and shipping. Furniture and all other items requiring lead time should be reviewed on a regular schedule until they are installed. New and refinished furniture should be installed before the move day, so as not to compete for the freight elevator.

Throughout the Project: Moving People and Moving Things

Throughout the project, it is essential to communicate about the move with everyone in the firm. Gaining the confidence of everyone and getting people to buy into the process makes things work better. Information helps, and a moving project newsletter can be used to disseminate instructions for preparing for the move, such as packing and unpacking, rules for coordinating the work, and information about the new space. Schedule a move orientation meeting and distribute move information packets. In addition to keeping people apprised of the firm's plans and the progress of the move, you should create a manual for the new space, welcoming and congratulating everyone and providing news, policies, and information about how to function in the new building. This can be produced well in advance of the move. It should include phone lists, information and rules from the landlord, and information about security systems, parking, and the firm's policies and policy changes for the new building. Communication is such an important part of the management of the move that we urge you to find imaginative ways to build cooperation and enthusiasm. Customary ways of building the morale and the gusto that make the process quicker and smoother are specially designed T-shirts and hats (a "uniform" is necessary for the primary moving crew on move day in any case), and a contest to give the move project a name or a logo.

Everything that will be moved needs to be labeled, including all furniture, equipment, accessories, and boxes. If that sounds like a tall order, remember that everyone can label their own furniture and box up the contents of their desks, drawers, and file cabinets. Assign people to pack and label everything in the common areas, and assign people to pack and label everything in the work areas of people who are away from the firm during the move. Supervise this closely, and be sure that nothing goes unlabeled. Your mover will supply a tagging system. Inventory all furniture and equipment and make a list showing where each piece will be placed in the new space. Since many people will be responsible for labeling (maybe everyone will), develop instructions for labeling each type of item, showing where the label should be placed, and make it clear what information goes on the label. Have a deadline for the labeling. Schedule furniture refurbishing and reupholstering as a part of your plan.

Dispose of equipment, furniture, or other items that have not been used recently. Have an in-house tag sale, offering items for sale to people within the firm at low prices, and then make a charitable donation of leftover items.

In the new space, give every office and room a different number, and make large placards for the doors to identify the rooms during the move. For the benefit of non-English-speaking movers, use room numbers and not names. If more than one work station occupies a room, give it a letter following the room number. For every office and space, prepare a sketch or drawing of how the furniture is to be arranged. Paper that is 8½ × 11 inches works fine for the sketch, which needs to be taped on or near the door of every office and room for the benefit of the movers, as does a big, highly visible room number. The paint on the doors and door frames is likely to be brand new and re-painting doors can be very expensive, so ask the general contractor what kind of tape you should use to avoid ruining the finish. Painters' tape (usually blue) is commonly used for this.

Provide a drawing with furniture layouts for each new floor. Mount it on a foam-core board or something similar and place it in the freight elevator lobby or the place where the movers arrive on the floor with their loads. The primary moving crew uses it to direct traffic as everything arrives in the new space. Copies should also go to the move headquarters on each floor.

At least two people need to be stationed at every elevator or arrival point to show the movers which way to go. At least two other people should be walking the corridors looking for movers who appear lost or confused.

Special Plans and Schedules

In addition to hiring a moving company, you need to coordinate delivery of new items and arrange for such things as installing utilities, copiers, and vending machines, as well as specialty movers for computer systems. They require separate arrangements and advance planning. Most moves are scheduled for a Friday, with the intent to have the firm up and running in its new location by Monday. Schedule the move to include a three- or four-day weekend if you can, but be very careful to make sure that you have each one of the contact people we listed earlier in this chapter on call and able to be at the move site within twenty minutes if necessary.

There are some increased risks with moving on a weekend or a holiday. Be sure that your moving company provides top-level supervisors. Some people with more seniority may have earned the right to forego working on weekends and holidays, which could leave the less-experienced people in charge of your moving project. On a related note, if you believe that the moving company or any other vendors' employees may have a problem communicating with your move team, be sure to require English-speaking supervisors throughout the move.

If yours is a multiple-floor law firm and people are going to various floors in the new site, have the movers load things together that are going to the same floor at the new site. Try to keep things together according to their destination.

Here is our list of special needs that should be addressed:

List the things that will need to be moved early, like the library and the file room. Likewise, take note of the vendors who need to install items that are ready before the move.

Review your records storage requirements. Record the number of file drawers or linear feet of other storage needed for every area of files. Develop your plans for moving files to the new office, purging files, and moving files to off-site storage. Take advantage of this time to clean out files! Convince the managing partner to lead by example. You can arrive at the new office with room for files, or with no place to put them.

Your voice/data cabling vendor should be selected early in the building process. Be sure all voice/data and electrical outlets have been tested and are operational before the move.

Schedule deinstallation of the existing systems and reinstallation of new and existing computer equipment and systems. This is a major job for your IT or systems people. If your firm has just one person for this area, bring in temporary staff during the move. Ordinarily, it is an around-the-clock job to get the systems up and running by Monday morning.

Review the terms of all of your equipment leases and arrange for disconnection, moving, and reinstallation, and handle any necessary termination or revision of the agreements. Refamiliarize yourself with the power and communications requirements that you created in Phase I (see Chapter 3) for existing and new equipment, and determine whether leased equipment must be moved by the leasing company.

Moving your phone systems is a five-phase job:

1. If your firm is not able to use existing numbers in the new location, then several months to a year in advance of the move, you need to obtain a block of phone numbers. Remember—try to match the last four digits of the phone numbers to the office numbers. Obtaining a large block of numbers should enable you to do this. Do not forget to plan for growth and expansion. This really does need to be done far in advance of the move.
2. Order your trunk lines. This also requires a lot of lead time if the building does not already have them in place.
3. Arrange for installation of your voice/data cabling. Cabling needs to be installed before the ceilings are closed.
4. Once cabling is in place, the phone system switch can be installed and tested.
5. Have the instruments installed and tested. Try to retain your main numbers and direct-dial numbers.

Contact your plant company to make sure they pick up plants at your old space and deliver new plants to the new one. Rather than reusing plants, it is best to get new plants that can adapt to the lighting conditions in your new location.

Contact all vendors who make deliveries. Give them information about deliveries to the new site. This includes vendors like office-supply companies.

Contact your water, coffee, snack, and food vendors to schedule filling the vending machines. If you stock the kitchen and vending machines before the move, there is a good chance then when you arrive for your first day of business at the new site, the machines will be empty because the movers and various contractors got hungry during the move. This also raises a more serious security issue. If you roll out new computer equipment before the move, be sure to provide some form of security for all the new machinery, as it tends to disappear if left unattended.

Schedule professional demounting and hanging of art and wall-hung items. Art should be moved to a lockable room in the new space. Schedule an installer to come in and hang the art and diplomas after the punch list work is completed.

Collect extra office supplies before the move. As people pack up their desks for the move, most will come across office supplies that they have been hoarding. Near the secretarial stations and in other appropriate areas, provide boxes and invite people to put in extra supplies. Be sure that the boxes are labeled so they are not thrown out as trash.

Review instructions for the library move with your moving company. To save a great amount of library staff time reorganizing things, be absolutely sure your movers understand that the books in the library are to be moved and reinstalled in sequential order. If you are unable to find a mover with book trucks that keep books in order, a carefully executed system of organizing the contents of each shelf into numbered boxes is worth the effort.

Have a detailed plan for your IT department. This department requires special care in a move, and should have a separate detailed plan. Obviously, your technology infrastructure in the new space will be much different. Rollouts of new equipment should be completed and tested before moving day. Avoid implementing major software systems with the move. Determine who is moving electronic and technology equipment. Specialty movers may be necessary. Also, confirm who is guaranteeing that the equipment will function after the move.

Arrange for services for your firm's moving staff. Reserve rooms in a nearby hotel for those who work late or put in all-nighters for the move. Have catered food—pizza, sandwiches, and beverages—brought in throughout the day so people do not have to leave the site. Keep going until everything has been moved to the new location, then take a much-needed rest. If the move goes on nonstop for twenty-four or forty-eight hours, be sure to have your move team replaced every six or eight hours with fresh, rested people.

List of Things to Do for the Firm

Create a schedule showing office numbers, room assignments, and work station assignments.

Keys

Keys for new furniture come in pairs. When new locking furniture and equipment arrives, immediately collect and label one for each lock and save them for opening drawers and cabinets when people lose their keys.

Stationery

Order new stationery products and business cards. Order your printed change-of-address notifications and address them to clients and appropriate recipients. Contact publishers of directories and online listing services; place notices in trade publications. Schedule e-mail and fax notifications to all appropriate recipients, including your vendors.

Intentional changes in work flow, functions, and responsibilities can be established with the move, and the new space may be designed to accommodate changes. In order to make the move more efficient, consider making the changes in routines and responsibilities before the move.

Deliveries

For vendors who deliver office supplies, food, or other items to your office, let them know your new delivery schedules and tell them how and where to make deliveries to your new offices.

Guided Walk-Throughs

Guided walk-throughs of the new and old spaces need to be scheduled at various times for various reasons. Use the list below as a reminder to conduct walk-throughs with vendors or suppliers for the purpose of verifying the condition of the premises and familiarizing people with the spaces and the firm's requirements.

- Bidders, before bids are due
- Vendors, before the move
- Movers, before and after the move
- Installers
- Firm's primary move crew
- Staff and lawyers, just before the move

Move Preparations

This section is about getting ready for moving day. Before you schedule your move, check with local authorities for parades, street closures, or scheduled construction that could impede movers as they travel between buildings or use the loading docks.

Schedule air conditioning as needed for moving during nights and weekends, in both the existing and new facilities.

At the last minute, establish appropriate control headquarters in the old and new offices, where staff, information, and supplies can be found during the move. Refreshments, catering, logging in the movers, first aid, communications, directions, deliveries, interpretation of moving labels, and general information can be centered here. Establish a lost-and-found room here. Setting up this operation may require a staff member to take some materials home and bring them to the new space before the movers arrive.

Schedule deadlines for packing up offices and other spaces, and schedule times when the firm's employees can come back and unpack in order to be ready for work on Monday morning. Usually aim for people to come in at noon or 1:00 P.M. on Sunday to unpack their boxes.

Be sure to check with the management of both your old and new spaces to find out if a security guard or policeman is necessary at move time. Doors will be propped open during the move, so security is a genuine concern.

Disable the security system for your area during the time of the move, because doors will need to be propped open.

Consider setting up an off-site office facility to handle emergency work during the move and to help cover for any delay in transferring systems from one space to the other.

Measure and determine which items will not fit through a normal doorway or freight elevator. Examine the freight elevator lobby and the doors and corridors leading from the freight elevator, and measure the turning radius necessary to get such things as large conference tables, credenzas, and large desks into and out of the elevator, into the corridors, and all the way through all doors, openings, and corners, to their final placements. In addition to measuring elevator doors, check to see whether a hatch in the elevator cab's ceiling can be removed to accommodate taller loads. Plan for disassembly or alternative routes if necessary. Very large items are sometimes hand-carried up the fire stairs, slung under or on top of an elevator (which requires an elevator technician), or hoisted through a window that has been removed.

If you are moving from one building to another, schedule the freight elevators and loading docks in both buildings. Schedule docks and elevators for deliveries from vendors. Check on union requirements. Check to see if elevator operators or security personnel are required. At overtime rates, these can add immensely to the cost of the move.

In both the old and new spaces, schedule the collection and distribution of access cards, parking cards, and keys.

Schedule trash removal and a final cleaning of the old space as soon as the move is complete.

Working with the Moving Company

Begin by making sure that no other vendors or contractors will be in the space while the movers are working there.

Get a certificate of insurance specifically for your move from the mover's insurance company, naming the firm as beneficiary. Your old and new landlords may also require that they are named in the certificate of insurance. Contact your own insurance agent to verify your coverage and to consider special coverage for damage to property. For works of art and high-value items, purchase insurance to cover them beyond the minimum provided by the moving company. At the walk-through before the move, be sure to let the moving company know about any high-value items that require special care in moving.

Determine where packing materials will be delivered and staged. In the destination space, select a space or spaces where cartons can be stacked flat as soon as their contents are removed. Require that movers carry away the empty containers at least once every day for a week after the move, especially the Sunday night after everyone has unpacked. This is often overlooked, since the movers are typically finished on Saturday night. Provide for trash removal at both the old and new offices.

Moving companies provide color-coded labels. Use color coding for specific floors or for specific areas like the library or the central file room. Produce color-coded floor plans in multiple copies for use in the move. Post them in appropriate places like elevator lobbies, and make sure the moving company and all of your move supervisors have copies. Remember that each office and room needs a furniture placement plan attached to the door with contractor-approved tape, as well as a large room-number sign.

Hiring Movers and Installers

Hire your moving company very carefully. Your move is quite literally in their hands, and the wrong company can turn your move into a disastrous event by causing delays and unforeseen costs. Ask your colleagues in other firms for recommendations. Get bids and select from movers with a good reputation for executing moves that are as much like yours as possible in terms of contents, building type, and location. Be sure they are up to the task; price should not be your main consideration here. Learn about the size and type of trucks in their vehicle fleet, and the supervisors and staff. Make sure that the company is big enough to handle your job with ease, but also assure yourself that your own project is important enough to the company that it can command their full attention. Be a discriminating interviewer; remember that even a bad mover or installer may have a few satisfied clients, and use these as their references. You may find it more effective to simply ask which other law firms are their customers.

When you interview their customers, ask about the things that are important for your own move:

- Were they late? Did they delay other processes or waste time?
- Did they know what to do when they arrived? Did they understand your needs in the new space and have the skills to meet them?
- Was their cost estimate accurate?
- Did they have the right equipment for the job?
- Did they have the right personnel for the job?
- Would you hire them again?

Vendor Proposals

As with your other major bid processes, schedule a pre-bid meeting and walk-through with your prospective move vendors. Provide written specifications in your request for proposal (RFP) to show essential information like hours of availability of the elevators, loading dock, and any staging areas for trucks and equipment. Be sure they understand the necessary routes, limitations on sizes for their trucks and equipment, and the exact time when the move will happen.

Your RFP should specify exactly what is to be moved and what packing and unpacking are necessary. You need to become familiar with the moving company's requirements for packing. For example, be sure that you find out how many filing cabinet drawers need to be emptied before the move, because some movers move cabinets with the bottom two drawers filled.

You need to have someone at the moving company as your main contact, a person who knows all about your old and new buildings and the details of your move. This very important person needs to be present for the walk-through interviews. Will your salesperson be present at the move? Ask questions, get written assurances, and be certain that you can reach your moving company contact person throughout the move in case midcourse adjustments are necessary.

With any major construction project, there is a possibility that the move will have to be delayed if the space is not ready by the scheduled moving date. Your agreement with the moving company should specify the measure of damages if the firm is unable to move on the specified date due to construction delays.

You need to be sure that the company has the right equipment, such as rolling book carts to move libraries and file rooms or files, protective materials to prevent damage to your old and new spaces, and trucks that fit your loading dock. We know of more than one occasion when a large, heavily loaded truck backed into a loading dock bay and was too tall to get out once it had been unloaded. The truck's suspension springs, no longer compressed by the weight of the load, made the truck tall enough to be firmly stuck in the bay. Letting air out of the tires allowed the truck to escape with minimal damage, but not without a costly delay and loss of the loading dock at a critical time.

When interviewing the movers, be sure to show them the loading dock or point where they can stage their trucks and check out all rules and physical limitations with freight elevators or stairs. (For example, do you have items that are too big or too tall for the elevator, or is the elevator very slow?) Make the movers responsible for determining which of their trucks fit into the loading docks at both the old and new spaces. In an intrastate move, movers work on an estimated hourly basis. They also come in and estimate weights of all items to be moved. Carefully compare these estimates, remembering that an underestimation of weight can cause an unreliably low estimate of the cost. Have the movers provide with their estimates a preliminary schedule of the sequencing of items to be moved.

Movers must also provide adequate means of vertical and horizontal protection to both existing and new facilities. Before they remove items from the existing space, walk through the space and agree on areas of existing damage. Also, do the same at the new space. The movers need to be held responsible for damage to the existing space and the new space, and for items moved as well as damage in their path of travel to and from the trucks.

For floor protection, this means quarter-inch Masonite on the floors where required by the landlord or the firm. Use Masonite to protect the floors in all major corridors from the truck to the offices. Vertical protection requires padding or other coverings at all points of entry, corners, door frames, and other sensitive architectural or furniture features. A punch list process before and after the move is necessary to make the movers financially (not physically) responsible for repairing damage to doors, door frames, and other parts of the buildings. Be sure that your moving contract provides that any repair be done by your own contractors, not the movers'.

Solo and Small Firm Offices

17

Big Results for Smaller Projects

Solo practice and small firm offices come in a variety of forms. Some are elegant and technologically advanced spaces, while others belong to lawyers who make house calls and keep their records in a closet at home by their laptops. This chapter is primarily about working on smaller projects with smaller budgets. Throughout this book, we have offered advice about how to find and work with first-rate design professionals, but most solo and small-firm budgets never have a nickel for the best designer in town. Nevertheless, we ask you to bear with us briefly because careful use of a good law firm designer can save plenty of money in building costs, square footage requirements, operating costs, and your own billable time.

As we progress through the chapter and talk about how to work with design professionals, we will show you why designers do certain things and how you can take advantage of some of their techniques. By making the best use of whatever level of professional support you can afford (including none), you can get more for your money by using their techniques. In any case, we believe this chapter will help you get the most out of your investment.

Your business plan should have an abiding concern for the effect of aesthetics on the attitudes of your clients and of people who can help you generate clients through referrals or other means. Perhaps even more importantly, your office and its contents are the front-end costs likely to send you out in search of start-up financing. Efficiency and cost control have become watchwords for law office design, but you should also be concerned with service to clients, and this adds more issues to your design plan. To give two examples, clients increasingly require advanced technological capability in their lawyers, which affects the office plan. Also, solo lawyers increasingly split their time among multiple workplaces, such as a home office and one or more shared offices or conference facilities that are more convenient for their clientele. These kinds of issues are important to a prospective lender, so they provide a starting point in the discussion.

Business Plan and Space Plan

We see some distinct advantages in smaller firms and solo lawyers having multiple small offices, especially if you want to cover a region or metropolitan area with convenient locations for a specific clientele. Like any other business, a small law firm needs a written business plan, and a major part of your business plan is a plan for the home for your practice. You can get some help in establishing your planning budget by talking with design professionals, and the same people can help you determine whether your construction budget is realistic. Other people who can help you with your initial estimates for the construction budget are contractors and prospective landlords. Because your office space is typically your second-biggest expense (after staff costs), it would be a serious mistake to shortchange this opportunity to boost your marketing, the efficiency of your practice, and your bottom line. While you will have plenty of other people to satisfy with your planning effort (like lenders, guarantors, building inspectors, code inspectors, subdivision committees, safety and environmental regulators, utility companies, the post office, and your spouse), your own satisfaction is what counts. The plan must help your practice prosper and serve the needs of your clients. Give your review the rigor it deserves.

What Goes in a Plan

Planning prepares you for articulating your needs to other people connected with your project. As we mentioned in more detail in Chapter 1, the plan and its specifications provide the information necessary for estimating office construction and furnishing costs. The plan also becomes the document by which the project is constructed, as well as a guide for maintenance, repairs, and future construction, and a record of what is behind the walls.

We look at all projects, including the smallest, as having distinct phases. The planning phase begins with asking questions about what your practice needs and what you would consider paying for. The programming phase produces the data that you need in order to go shopping for your office space, and it consists of using checklists and interviews to help the space planner know what features are important, what activities will take place in the space, and which of those activities need to be adjacent to others. The planner learns about your room capacity needs and mechanical requirements, as well as priorities for convenience, status, privacy, and support facilities. Armed with an analysis of the data collected, a space planner can compile a design program.

The program may look like a collection of one-page briefs on each of the necessary rooms and spaces, showing required square footage, adjacency requirements, electrical, heating, and air-conditioning requirements, lighting concerns, equipment to be supported, storage requirements, and other factors such as security, privacy, and accessibility that affect the drawings and specifications. This program guides the designer in the task of preparing alternative designs and specifications to fit an available space or to help with the selection of a new location. At the very least, write down your requirements for each of these features as you consider each room. Our checklist below should help you think of spaces and features to program.

Space Requirements Program for a Small Firm

- Number of lawyer offices and their desired sizes
- Number of paralegal offices and their desired sizes
- Number of secretarial stations and their sizes
- Space for office administrator or other support staff
- Conference room seating, facilities, and amenities
- Reception area seating and receptionist station
- Project workrooms (case or war rooms)
- Administration area (service center)
  - Copying, mail, fax
  - Expressage
  - Printing and scanning
  - Binding
  - Deliveries and runners
  - Office supplies and storage
- Filing
  - Centralized or decentralized
- Library and office bookshelves, library work areas
- Technology
  - File server
  - Telephone system
  - Security system

- o Audiovisual equipment
- o Audio teleconferencing
- o Video teleconferencing
- o Technology support staff
- Accounting
  - o In-house or outsourced
- Storage
  - o Coats
  - o Exhibits
  - o Evidence
- Food service
  - o Sink (cold water only or both hot and cold)
  - o Refrigerator (under-counter or full-size, with freezer or icemaker)
  - o Microwave
  - o Under-counter ice maker
  - o Coffee maker
  - o Dishwasher
  - o Water purification system
  - o Drinking water (bottled or direct-plumbed cooler)
  - o Toaster or toaster over
  - o Vending machines (beverages or snacks)
  - o Space for table and chairs in coffee area
  - o Space for canned drinks or bottled water

Working with a Professional

Here are a few reasons why you might consider working with a professional space planner. In many cases, a design professional can save you the cost of his or her fees by freeing up your own billable time. Some landlords have designers or architectural firms that can assist you. A word of caution about using the landlord's design professional: the designer is only doing one job for you, and probably looking to the landlord for a lot more work. Naturally the designer is going to try to please the landlord more than you.

You can bring in your own independent designer and negotiate to have the landlord pay all or part of the design fees. It may be money well spent to use a little cash from your own pocket to accomplish this.

Check the designer's references and ask to see comparable law firms the designer has done. Hiring a design professional can be much like hiring a lawyer or an accountant, and just like with other professionals, you need some up-front talk about fees. There are plenty of competent people available, and you will save time and design costs if you find someone who has designed other law firm offices. A design professional may be an architect, interior designer, or interior decorator. Most law firm renovation involves the services of either an architect or an interior designer. Architects are licensed to design building structural systems as well as the interior components, while interior designers limit their services to the design and construction of the space within the building envelope. For commercial buildings that typically house law offices, both architects and interior designers may retain structural engineers for advice on the building's structural integrity and floor loading. Mechanical engineering firms help with the design and specification of heating and air-conditioning and plumbing systems, and electrical engineers provide the specification of electrical systems. Architectural firms often have interior designers on their staffs, and many interior design firms employ architects. While architects, designers, and interior decorators provide consulting on the aesthetics of a space (such as fabrics, finishes, accessories, and furniture), the practice of interior decorators is limited to these areas. Many interior decorators are affiliated with furniture stores or other vendors. Typical billing arrangements for architects and interior designers are hourly rates or fixed fees. Commissions on their recommended items often augment interior decorators' fees. The net cost of decorators' services may not be evident because furniture and decorative materials often have multiple discount pricing tiers.

Finding a design professional is much like finding a lawyer, with the delightful exception that a law office stands as tangible evidence of the quality of the designer's product. Look at plenty of law offices. The more law offices you see, the better idea you will have of the capabilities of various design practitioners. Lawyers and other people who work in their offices are seldom secretive about who designed the space. They may be quick to point out good and bad features. If you find an office you like, consider interviewing its designer. The national professional associations such as the American Institute of Architects (AIA) and the American Society for Interior Design (ASID) and their local counterparts maintain listings on Web sites, and this may yield some candidates. You will avoid much frustration if you can find a designer who has experience with other law firm projects. This will shorten the designer's learning curve and let you learn from your designer.

Design professionals divide their work into two kinds: commercial and residential. Some do both kinds of work, but the kind you want for your law office is commercial (unless you want your office to look like Aunt Minnie's parlor!). The commercial design practitioner has a professional background in dealing with regulatory matters like ADA and commercial building codes, and the design product is likely to be more responsive to your professional needs. As tempting as it is to do your own design work, do not forget that professional designers can save your personal time, which can be put to better use as billable hours.

Your Practice Reflected in Your Plan

Your business plan should not only include the budgeting aspects of your office, but should also reflect your choice of a home for your practice. Beyond the bare respectability that makes an office appear professional, your office design should target the aspects of your practice that support your clients' expectations of their legal counsel. From the all-important reception area, where clients sit and soak up information about your firm even before you meet, to the conference space, and to your office, take care to make the public spaces reflect your plan in a most professional way.

Chapter 1 of this book discusses creating an image for your firm. The focus of your practice should have a profound effect on your space planning. Do not be tied to trite images of a law firm or lawyers' offices with traditional furniture in dark wood tones with duck prints on the wall. Most of the newer and financially successful firms do not portray that style in their design and furnishings. Think outside the box. Some firms prefer a fresher image that appeals to a younger generation. Your approach to technology may be used to advantage, but keep in mind that the state of the art changes quickly, and you need to avoid showcasing anything that might seem outmoded.

Who are your clients? They need to be comfortable with the professionals whose advice and representation determine their own success or failure. High-technology corporate clients appreciate a clean, modern look that shows off your savvy, active style of lawyering, while an estate planning practice thrives in an atmosphere of personal support and confidentiality. A general practice should have quality furnishings in public areas and a look of uncluttered competence. While your office may reflect your personality and provide evidence of your stability, your qualifications, and perhaps your outside interests, keep in mind the variety of people who come into a law office for your advice and services. Accordingly, you should analyze the sensibilities of your potential clientele carefully.

Also think about who will be referring clients to you. The same issues apply, and you will never know about it if someone did not feel comfortable recommending you.

The real estate watchword of "location, location, location" certainly applies in the sense of convenience for your clients, but a solo or small firm lawyer may provide the advantage of flexibility by having meetings at clients' offices or other convenient locations. Continued rapid development of hand-held communication technology and wireless networks will increasingly give mobile lawyers the ability to work in multiple places. Consider the combinations that will be possible, ranging from a home office from which a lawyer makes house calls to maintaining multiple shared office suites, whether borrowed, leased, or on-call temporary rentals. Larger firms are more and more adopting "hoteling" office arrangements where office space is shared by lawyers from the firm's other locations when they are in town. It may be possible to work out arrangements to borrow space from larger firms.

The location of your office should depend on the demographics of your practice. Do you want to be near your clients? Do you want to go to them or do you want them to come to you? Do you want to be close to a courthouse? Do you want to be downtown? Do you want to be in the suburbs? Do you want multiple locations? It is all a function of where you see your practice. Downtown space, in most cities, is likely to be more expensive than suburban space, but this is not true in every city.

For prestige and quality factors, office buildings are categorized as Class A, B, or C. Classification follows no uniform system, but is derived from a combination of physical aspects of the building and its location. Class A buildings are generally the best buildings in the area where buildings are being compared. They are well located with excellent access and they have the best tenants, building materials, and management. Rental rates follow the A, B, and C classification as well. You can expect a Class A building to be among the nicest in an area.

Finding and Securing an Office Space

From home office to high-rise—all can house a solo practice, and small firms have nearly as many options. Your office may be your second biggest cost item, but it can also be a capital expenditure and an investment in the future of your firm. The most basic decisions about your office require you to determine how you want to allocate your time and money. If you are not overwhelmed with work, you may be able to afford the time necessary to build your office or to buy and renovate an older structure. In any case, avoid underestimating the time these ventures require. When you lease your office space, you buy the luxury of avoiding the time commitment of managing a building, and taking care of taxes, day-to-day maintenance, and security. You do not avoid the cost, but you gain predictability of these major operational expenses.

Finding and securing an office space takes longer than you realize until you have been through it once. Our advice is to start early—a minimum of six months before you expect to occupy the space, but preferably longer. People who have an existing lease should start looking for a new space at least a year before the lease expires. For larger firms, this should be two or three years before the lease expires.

If you are thinking about leasing or renting office space, there are generally two ways to go about it. You can do the legwork yourself, or engage a broker. The broker fees are paid by the landlord, not by the tenant. Brokers typically get 4.5 percent of every dime that you pay over the life of the lease. A broker knows the area, and can advise you about current rental rates.

You should always have alternative office spaces to choose from. Never negotiate with just one landlord. You need at least three options so that you can leverage one against the other in negotiations.

Most landlords have a diagram or a floor plan of the available space. If the landlord does not, feel free to take a tape measure and a notebook and sketch the dimensions. A camera or a video recorder may also be helpful in remembering some of the details. When you look at multiple spaces, they all tend to run together.

Leasing Terminology

Terms you may not be familiar with include rentable square footage versus usable square footage. Usable square footage is the actual square footage of the space, and if you are a full-floor tenant, this includes areas like the square footage in the restrooms and mechanical rooms. Usable square footage is generally considered to be anything that is not a vertical penetration, such as a fire stair, a mechanical shaft, or an elevator shaft.

Rentable square footage is greater than usable square footage because it includes an add-on factor. The add-on factor is different with every building, depending on how efficient each building is. Rentable square footage includes your pro-rata share of common areas such as elevator lobbies and the corridors if you are on a multitenant floor. The typical add-on can be anywhere from 10 percent to 25 percent.

Rental rates may incorporate your build-out cost. One way is to roll construction costs into the cost of the rent, which could substantially raise the amount of rent if it were prorated over the life of the lease. You can also negotiate to have a certain portion of the build-out costs negotiated into the lease and therefore the rent. You can also negotiate a deal where, for example, the landlord pays for build-out costs of up to $30 per square foot, and you pay for costs that exceed that amount.

Most landlords will pay for a free test fit before signing a lease. This gives you an opportunity to compare buildings. You give landlords your project requirements and they have a design professional do a quick plan to see how the space would lay out with your program. If the landlord does not provide this service, you can try doing it on your own. In Chapter 12, we provide some plans and diagrams of typical layouts that you may find helpful.

Lease Arrangements and Negotiations

Look at the space and determine the absolute minimum level of renovation or modification you can live with. Remember that the renovation will affect your rental rate and the length of your lease. Renovations are also important matters for negotiation before the lease is signed.

The document containing your agreement with the landlord about the building improvements, renovation, and physical conditions you receive in exchange for your lease payments is called a work letter. Work letter negotiation is such an important part of larger construction contracts that this book devotes a chapter to the subject (Chapter 8). Many office buildings establish a building-standard set of improvements, which provides a rather Spartan build-out that is generally not suitable for public areas of law offices. Negotiation of terms for the lease and work letter often proceed from the base point of the building-standard improvements, and might include the following:

- Landlord paying for build-out costs above the ceiling, including building-standard light fixtures, ceiling grid and ceiling tile, sprinklers, and mechanical work
- Longer hours, perhaps 7:00 A.M. to 7:00 P.M. and Saturdays, for the provision of air-conditioning to your space
- Free power, heating, and air-conditioning during the build-out
- Free use of the freight elevator and loading dock
- Contiguous expansion space for your offices
- Guarantee of a maintained interior temperature range during specific extreme temperatures in hot or cold weather
- Landlord providing an ADA-compliant building from the parking lot to your office front door
- Sound and heat insulation for all walls, with demising walls between tenants to go to the structure above the ceiling
- Landlord providing a refurbishment if you renew the lease (typically new paint and carpet)
- Janitorial services five days a week
- Signage style and location
- No landlord fee on build-out costs
- A determination of who pays for utilities

Negotiate your lease to provide flexibility for the future of your practice. If your practice is successful, your needs will be quite different than if business is less than you planned. Moving is usually more costly, disruptive, and inconvenient than you imagine it will be, so think about negotiating optional extensions to your lease.

External Effects on Use of Space

Your project is subject to zoning and deed restrictions, building codes, and your landlord's requirements. Zoning ordinances may include historic zoning, which in some cases can create financial incentives for the renovation of distinctive buildings. Minimum parking requirements need to be considered.

As you check your municipal codes and ordinances, you may find that you are referred to a specific edition of the new International Building Codes from the International Code Council. Widespread recent adoption of these codes has produced significant changes as they replace other standard building codes that have been in place for decades. For all except the most minimal work (like painting and carpeting) on your space, building permits are required in most cities and towns. Permits and inspections are required for most of the regulated trades as well.

Insurance carriers impose important limitations on the use of space. For example, owners of buildings that are insured as residential space may not be able or willing to insure part of the building as office space. Other insurance policy limitations may set requirements on alteration, occupancy, or use of buildings because of their location in areas prone to floods, earthquakes, or storms.

Your landlord's requirements and limitations for use of the space are spelled out in the lease you negotiate and in the work letter. The limitations relate to a broad range of construction themes. For example, these documents speak to occupancy, availability of the building to your contractors, utilities, insurance and indemnity, signage, cooperation among contractors and subcontractors, and cooperation and consent of the landlord.

Reusing Space

Whenever you contemplate moving your offices into a building, you will consider whether your budget allows you to gut and rebuild the space, modify the existing space to support your needs, or use the space without modification.

Demolishing and rebuilding office space is costly because unseen conditions from prior building work often cause delays and changes in the job. Asbestos abatement and quirks in building mechanical systems are notorious examples. However, rebuilding is frequently the only way to make the available space look right and serve the needs of your office.

A solo or small law office is not a very big job for most contractors, and most of the bigger and more prestigious contractors are not willing to bid on smaller jobs. And since you may not appear to be a prospect for repeat business, your office may be considerably less important to the contractor than it is to you. Select your general contractor carefully, and make sure the contractor has enough available time, personnel, and resources to get your job done right and on schedule. The horror stories you have heard about subcontractors who don't show up for work are probably true, and your contractor needs to have a good list of subcontractors to call upon when this sort of thing happens.

The working drawings that accompany every building project are not just for the contractor. They provide an important opportunity for you to keep on top of the project at all stages. In order to prevent the designers of your project from taking it in a wrong direction before the plans have been completed, ask your designer for a 50 percent review set. Review the plans carefully, looking for any necessary changes that can be done right away. Also, review the plans carefully when they are 100 percent complete.

In most cases, you need to have an MEP engineering firm provide those drawings and specifications in order to receive a building permit. This can be done less expensively if the MEP subcontractors have licensed engineers on staff that can do the drawings. However, the absence of a system of checks and balances can cause conflicts of interests if one electrician is both designing and building, or one mechanical engineer is designing and his crew is building. If an independent engineer designs, he or she is more likely to design it the correct way and not try to cut corners.

Minor Modifications, or How Many Lawyers Does It Take to Change a Light Fixture?

Minor modifications can provide a very effective and economical treatment for many spaces. Minor modifications are the ones a do-it-yourselfer can do with a bit of instruction from the people at the home-improvement store or from the wide selection of books or Internet sites. Painting, changing the flooring or floor refinishing, or changing light fixtures, door hardware, and window treatments are all simple things that most of us can do with a review of the safety procedures and some advice on materials.

We have a few discouraging words about the prospects for doing minor construction yourself. Most lawyers rent the space their practice occupies. Renting and leasing infuse the strong interest of a landlord into the life of your law practice. Beside the limitations of a lease's general tenancy terms, the landlord has to limit his tenants' activities to protect against liability claims. Whether an insurance carrier requires it or the landlord wants to avoid a potential liability, most leases do not permit the tenant to perform the construction necessary to turn a space into a law office. Do-it-yourself law office construction is the exception rather than the rule. After all, what landlord wants to chance having the work done by somebody who might damage the building and endanger other tenants?

But of course there are the exceptions, and smaller commercial properties and residential conversions are more likely to have fewer limitations in their leases. Among the many advantages of owning your own building may be the flexibility to build your office using a sensibly planned combination of your own work and that of specialists in the building trades. In any case, you should protect yourself with appropriate insurance coverage. For building an office in the home you own, be aware of zoning and building regulations, a homeowners' association's rules for conducting business in your home, and the requirements of a subdivision's architectural committee.

Many easy-to-find Internet sites provide instructions for specific renovation tasks. To find materials, equipment, and fixtures for your building projects, a standard source is **http://www.sweets.com**.

Using the space as it is can be an economical solution to your space needs. In order to get the most advantage from paying for little or no renovation, be sure you are not taking too much space. Touch-ups and extra cleaning for floors and walls are good investments. Keep your clients' first impressions in mind. The entrance to your space should be as attractive as you can make it, and that includes door hardware and finish, signage, and lighting.

Use of Space and Layouts

In Chapter 12, we reviewed lawyer office layouts and provided some diagrams of typical lawyer spaces and work space for lawyers' support staff. The generally accepted standard space requirements for lawyers' offices have been shrinking over the past two decades. More lawyers are meeting with clients and opposing counsel in conference rooms, not in their offices. In large and small firms, paralegal offices are typically determined by configuring the remaining space after lawyer offices are designed.

For a solo practitioner, who of necessity is the management committee, head of the litigation section, and inside counsel to the firm, clutter happens. The same can be said of many lawyers. For this reason and others, we recommend a conference room for meetings with clients and other lawyers. A conference room is easier to keep presentable than your office. A well-furnished small conference room can double as a library or an overflow waiting room, and it allows you to reduce space requirements for lawyer offices. A useful variation is to separate the office from the conference room with double doors so that the two can be combined for large meetings. Be sure to have plenty of clearance for chairs around the conference table. Five feet from the edge of the table to the wall is standard practice.

A sole practitioner or a very small firm is a microcosm of a large firm in that it needs most of the same support activities that a large firm needs. This includes an area for administrative items such as copying, faxing, scanning, mail deliveries, and expressage. Carefully consider your coffee service area and facility. The minimum that most offices can get by with is bottled water, a small refrigerator, and a microwave, and these do not require plumbing. Plumbing for commercial buildings is expensive. You can estimate that building a small coffee bar in an office building adds a minimum of approximately $10,000 to costs for the space.

Other support areas include filing areas and library facilities. Filing needs vary widely from one office to the next. While formal library spaces have shrunk to zero in many law offices, bookshelves and administrative functions for handling printed information should remain a part of your planning.

We have a Top Ten List of mistakes often made in planning smaller office spaces, and the top seven really stand out. They are:

1. Taking more space than is needed. Your lease negotiation should include your options for expanding your office into contiguous space within the building.
2. Not taking advantage of vertical space. Consider all of the wall space that is underutilized and use it to store files, books, and notebooks. Space is expensive.
3. Forgetting to plan for storage areas.
4. Not negotiating for contiguous expansion options.
5. Not negotiating to have the thermostat installed in your offices rather than in a neighbor's office.
6. Not negotiating for some less-expensive space in the building (maybe in the basement) for storage of less-active files.
7. Not starting early enough. This applies to almost every phase of the process.

Furnishings: New, Used, Rented, or Refurbished

Furniture is readily available in new, used, or refurbished condition. Your design professional should know about sources for each.

For new furniture, never pay the full list price. You should expect to get it for about 70 percent of the catalog list price. Most office furniture dealers do not show you price lists; your job is to shop around and compare price and quality. In furniture stores, however, you should expect to pay the full sticker price.

For the start-up firm, the most economical route is to purchase good used office furniture. The used furniture market is saturated due to the turnover in the corporate community in the last decade. It pays to shop around. Larger cities are the best resource, and there's always eBay. Refurbished furniture can provide a wonderful result for the money, especially if you can select high-quality classic pieces from good manufacturers. Avoid residential furniture. Your conference room should not look like a dining room.

Rental furniture can be expensive, but if that is your only alternative, try negotiating price and terms with the supplier. Before negotiating, you need a realistic plan of how long a rental term is required. This drastically affects the monthly charge. Also consider the lease-to-purchase option. Be aware that rental furniture is usually not high-grade or even medium-grade quality.

The Move-In

Moving into your first solo office can be your easiest move ever, but when you have clients, pending matters, and a need to make a smooth transition from one office to another, you need a good plan.

Develop a list of all items to be moved to the new space. Determine with your new and existing landlords when freight elevators and freight docks can be reserved or scheduled, or when and how the moving vans can gain access to the existing space and the new space. The how and when can greatly affect the cost of the move. (For more advice on hiring movers, see Chapter 5.)

When interviewing the movers, be sure to show them the loading dock or point where they can stage their trucks and what the situation is with freight elevators or stairs. Make them responsible for determining which of their trucks will fit into the loading docks at both the existing building and the new space. In an intrastate move, movers work on an estimated hourly basis. They also come in and estimate weights of all items to be moved. Carefully compare these estimates. Have the movers provide with their estimates a preliminary schedule of the sequencing of items to be moved. Movers must also provide adequate padding or other means of protection to walls, floors, and door frames in both existing and new facilities. Before they remove items from the existing space, walk through the space and mutually agree on areas of existing damage. Do the same at the new space. The movers need to be held responsible for damage to the existing space, new space, and items moved, as well as their path of travel from their trucks to the intended space. This means they must use quarter-inch Masonite or a similar hefty protection on the floors if required by the landlord or yourself. Also, vertical protection is needed at all points of entry; and at corners, doorframes, and other sensitive architectural or furniture features. Determine who is moving electronic and technology equipment. Also, confirm who is guaranteeing that the equipment will function after the move. Work closely with utility companies and your computer advisors to insure a seamless transition from your old office to the new one. Library books need to be moved and reinstalled in sequential order, but in practice, this rarely happens.

Technical Considerations in a Nutshell

Electrical and Cabling

Check outlet locations and wall switches with your furniture plan. Are receptacles where they are needed? At a minimum, you should add a dedicated circuit for the file server, your phone system, and other critical electronics, and you may want to do the same for your copier and printer. A great many things can affect the quality and reliability of your electrical supply. An uninterrupted power supply (UPS) system can provide increased protection for your data and can allow your server or computer to shut down gracefully in the event of a power interruption.

For your phone system, add voice cabling unless you are able to get by with a wireless phone system. These are generally less reliable than wired phones. If you have a wireless network, you may be able to avoid buying some of the data cabling. Depending on your building and numerous external influences, a wireless network could save some expenses for data cable. However, in most cases you do not save much, because the cost of pulling a second cable for data along with the voice cable is relatively small. Today, most firms are pulling two Cat 5 cables to each location. One is typically used for voice and the other for data. Both, of course, may be used for data, depending on how the cables are terminated. You should regard data security very seriously when you think about wireless networking. When you consider a space for your office, see how well your mobile phone works throughout the space. Sometimes interference that affects your phone affects a wireless network as well.

Lighting

In any office, lighting has a significant effect on physical fatigue and eye strain, which translates to efficiency and profits. Review the section on lighting in Chapter 10. Significant functional and aesthetic advantages can frequently be created at low cost by minimizing glare on your work and by changing the color of light in your office space.

An Overview of the Project

Putting it all together, the following checklist offers our suggestions for coordinating the planning, construction, and quality control for a smaller office.

- Have a business plan in place.
- Determine what technology will be used. These decisions impact the amount of space you need. Consider the following:
  - Copiers
  - Personal computers (including laptops and docking stations)
  - Printers
  - Scanners
  - Faxes
  - File server

- o Telephone system
- o UPS systems
- o Internet service provider
- o Network
- o Security system
- o After-hours or independent heating and air-conditioning system
- Write a program for space requirements:
  - o How many lawyer offices; what sizes?
  - o How many paralegal offices; what sizes?
  - o How many secretarial stations; what sizes?
  - o Conference room
  - o Reception area seating—how many seats? Receptionist station?
  - o Project workrooms
  - o Administrative area (service center)
  - o Copy, mail, and fax, receiving and outgoing
  - o Expressage
  - o Printing and scanning
  - o Binding
  - o Deliveries and runners
  - o Filing (centralized or decentralized)
  - o Accounting (in-house or outsourced)
  - o Coffee area
  - o Storage
  - o Library
  - o Technology needs
- Find space options (have three or more).
- Negotiate with prospective buildings.
- Get landlords to do free test fits to see which building works best and is the most efficient.
- Negotiate lease with the selected building.
- Have final plans prepared.
- Review drawings. Making changes now is much less expensive than after construction has started.
- Get multiple bids.
- Award contracts; receive construction schedule from contractor and begin construction.
- Coordinate owner-provided items; be sure voice and data cabling are pulled at the appropriate time *during* construction.
- Start shopping for furniture. (Actually, this can go on at a much earlier time in case you find a color scheme you like that can influence the carpet and wall color selection in step 8. Take preliminary space plans with you so you know the furniture will fit the space.)

- Schedule a weekly meeting with the contractor and landlord to review the work, progress, and the construction schedule. Make them demonstrate each week that they are on schedule.
- Establish delivery dates and times with any vendors that are delivering or installing owner-furnished items. These items are typically delivered after construction is completed. However, delivery times need to be established far in advance. Also, check with the landlord to see if the freight elevator needs to be reserved. Consider these items:
  - Telephone system
  - Computer-related equipment
  - Furniture
  - Copiers and fax machines
  - Movers
  - Signage
- When the construction is complete and the space has had its final cleaning, walk the space with the contractor and show the contractor the items on your punch list. This is a written list that documents any items that were not satisfactorily done and need to be corrected. Examples could be:
  - Marred walls, doors, or frames
  - Final coat of paint not covering
  - Damaged ceiling tile
- Document the space room by room. The contractor should repair these items before you move in. If time does not permit this, allow the contractor to do it after move-in. You may negotiate coverage of move-in damage at no extra cost.

The Economics of Building Your Law Office

18

Holding costs down is probably much easier if you have all the time in the world, but time is our most valuable commodity. Our best advice for keeping costs down is to stay on schedule, and the best way to do that is to begin early. It is easy to underestimate the time required for the first attempt at a new job, so we hope you use our checklists as reminders of how long it takes to accomplish the necessary tasks. We recently read an article by a weekend sailor who claims he carefully lists his best estimates of the time required for every aspect of each task before he performs needed maintenance on his sailboat. He calculates the total time and multiplies it by a factor of 2.5, which produces a fairly useful estimate of the time it really takes. Relocating an office can likewise take much more time than you think. The economic advantages you get from an early start include having more opportunities to compare vendors, being first in line and ahead of others who compete for products, services, and subcontractors, being able to negotiate with less time pressure, and having more choices throughout the project. We begin this chapter with some guidelines for building your initial project budget, and we show some sample budgets for different sizes of office projects.

Typical Law Firm Build-Out Costs

The cost of a law firm build-out is generally discussed either as cost per useable square foot or cost per rentable square foot. The processes involved in moving into a new space or of modifying existing space are too varied to warrant actual dollar guidelines, but we do suggest some factors to consider as you shop for prices and quality. With care and verification, you may want to consider our general estimates for a build-out from the bare slab.

Moving into Existing Space

This can be as easy as taking the existing space exactly as it is. At a bare minimum, consider having the carpets cleaned, repainting public areas, rekeying the front door, and adding new graphics and signage. Determine if the existing voice/data cabling will work. If you will be using a file server, you probably want to add a dedicated circuit with an isolated ground. Will the existing electrical outlets accommodate your printer or copier? Any painting and carpet work needs to be done before you move in. It is surprising how often we see furniture being moved to accommodate the work on the space. It adds both cost and inconvenience.

Modifying Existing Space

The range in this case can run the gamut from changing fabric wall covering in the reception area to greatly modifying the core areas for better efficiency. For perimeter offices, the size may not always be exactly what is desired, but leaving walls in place can save a lot of money. The economics of this sort of renovation are affected by the factors discussed above and by whatever minor construction is needed. Do not forget the substantial costs of demolition, and remember to include a larger allowance for contingencies as suggested below.

Building Out from Bare Slab

Building out a law firm from bare slab means that the building is new or the space you are considering has never been built out. Alternatively, the space may have been built out before but the landlord has demolished the previous build-out. Typically, an office building provides a level of construction that is ready for the tenant's construction, so we assume that it meets the descriptions that follow.

The condition of the premises is that the concrete slab or floor is bare. The perimeter window wall system is complete and installed. The gypsum board is installed above or below the window wall. The base-building core is complete. The restrooms and drinking fountains are complete.

The following systems are installed in a primary distribution system, but are not completed to be project specific:

- Heating and air-conditioning system
- Electrical system, complete to the electrical closet, and primary distribution system installed on the floor
- Life safety system (includes fire suppression system [sprinklers] and fire extinguisher cabinets if required)
- Lighting and finishes in the elevator lobby (if this is a multitenant floor)
- Handicap accessibility for base building, access to building, and parking

In addition, the ceiling grid may or may not be installed, and the building should have its Certificate of Occupancy.

The cost to build out a law firm from bare slab can range anywhere from $30 per square foot to over $150 per square foot. These costs are for construction only and do not include fees, furniture, and other items typically referred to as "soft costs." Costs vary drastically depending on the area of the country. Figures quoted here are not for larger cities or areas that have a high cost of living index. Even our range, which increases by a magnitude of five from low to high, may be too narrow. Therefore, we suggest that you see Chapter 19 for examples of law firm budgets that are categorized as low, medium, and high.

On Schedule and On Budget

Time is money—and quality. Throughout the book, we have emphasized starting early enough to allow for scheduling all the time-consuming parts of the work. Delays cost money by compressing the schedule and requiring other parts of the job to be done in less time and at a higher cost. If you think playing catch-up on a building project is an option, consider the costs of overtime, bigger crews, too many crews in the space at one time, and too many users for the freight elevator. The work on your office must be done in order, allowing materials to dry, set, cure, or be installed before the next task. Inspections and inspectors must be scheduled at various stages of completion. A general contractor, when faced with a delay in one phase of the job, may work ahead in other parts of the schedule. However, this compresses the time available for other vendors and contractors who are forced to reschedule to accommodate the general contractor's changes. In addition to causing awkward situations between your vendors and contractors, speeding up the job increases the chance that parts of the work will need to be redone due to shortcuts and the carelessness that happens with a rush job.

Alternates

Alternates are a way of creating a menu for shopping for pricing. Before the construction documents are issued for pricing, an alternate list is developed and incorporated into the documents. The contractor prices this list and submits it with the final pricing. This list allows the firm to choose among various pricing options. Some representative examples: (1) in lieu of rubber base in all partner offices, provide a four-inch painted wood base; (2) in lieu of the specified fabric wall covering in reception area, provide painted drywall; (3) in lieu of carpet with attached pad, provide carpet without attached cushion.

It saves time and money if the alternate list is structured in a written format so that the contract documents do not have to be changed and reprinted.

Hiring Your Team and Creating Requests for Proposals

We have suggested that you hire a number of consultants, contractors, and vendors, and we have recommended that you choose from among the ones who come highly recommended and have recent experience in building law firm spaces. Shopping for the people and companies to work on your project can make all the difference in its success, and is worth the effort. In hiring some of the vendors and team members, you save time by meeting with your initial list of prospects as a group. This applies to furniture vendors, moving companies, and interior plant companies.

However, for some vendors and members of your team, you also need to see examples of their work. This includes architects, designers, engineers, audiovisual vendors, millwork contractors, and, of course, general contractors. Arrange tours of projects they have done.

First, create a request for proposals or invitation to bid, looking for the professional help you need to execute a general concept. For just about every job, there are expensive ways and cheap ways, fast ways and slower ways, and high-quality and so-so quality jobs. Prospective contractors need to know as much about your project as possible in order to show you what they can do to help you, and the RFP is your first opportunity to tell them what you require and what is important for a satisfactory outcome. Putting a lot of thought into your RFP will be rewarding, whether you are hiring a consulting engineer, a designer, or a mover. Chapter 19 contains examples of documents related to project budgets, beginning with a sample RFP.

Second, you will generally save time and avoid some miscommunications with your prospective general contractors and their subcontractors if you invite them all to a pre-bid conference where you can answer questions and make sure they address their proposals to the same specific requirements. For general contractors and subcontractors, this is scheduled a week or two after the contract documents have been sent to your prospects. At this meeting, place copies of the building's rules and regulations by the sign-in sheet. Be certain that every prospective bidder has a copy, and have a landlord's representative there to answer questions. For all of your bidders, the building regulations are very important, because they govern such things as availability of elevators, utilities, permissible times of access to the building, means of exit and entrance, required protection of the building floors and walls, trash and dumpsters, and a host of other items that affect how the work is done and what it costs.

This is the time when you need to be sure that the bidders understand your rules, as well as the landlord's. You want to be sure that your bidders plan no surprises that compromise the operation of your firm during construction, especially if you are expanding your offices on the same floor of the building. You need to set clear, written limits on noise, odors, dust, cleaning, and access to the spaces. Your requirements for temporary walls, sound insulation, and interruption of utilities, air-conditioning, and filtering need to be established before bidding, or you will pay more for them when they become change orders. Explain details of any "swing" space you have negotiated with the landlord. Swing space is space for the law firm to occupy while its current space in the building is being renovated. If multiple floors are being built at different times, a firm may negotiate contractor's swing space to house materials acquired for the entire project that are being consumed as construction proceeds through different spaces. In any case, the rules, regulations, and access are as important for the swing space as they are for the construction areas, and they cannot be neglected at this stage. Chapter 19 contains an example of a pre-bid document.

Upon receiving proposals, narrow the candidates to a short list. You will learn from the bidders and their proposals, and your awareness of possible approaches may increase as you assess the bidders' professional abilities. The short list of a manageable number of bidders are then allowed to compete as finalists for the job. Depending on the type of service you are buying, compare them carefully.

Be sure to get the following information:

- Who will be in charge? Be sure they will be available when you need them, throughout the project. Prefer principals or senior managers of the firm.
- The qualifications of the personnel for the project—the crews, designers, engineers, and laborers whose work you will be paying for. Carefully examine the résumés and references of key personnel (the professionals) and particularly of the construction superintendent. Distinguish between permanent staff and temporary workers.

- What work they have done that is like your project.
- What other law firms have hired them to do this type of work.
- How they intend to go about the work on your project. Do they contemplate a radical approach?
- What other work they will be doing at the same time they are doing yours. Will other work compete for their attention?
- The volume of their work for each of the last five years, and how this compares to the current volume of their work.
- How much work they are capable of staffing. Are they big enough to do your job easily? Or, on the other hand, is your job too small to command their attention when you need something done?

Check the Budget at Every Phase

A master budget needs to be established and tracked throughout the project. The law firm administrator or the design professional can be assigned this task. The budget needs to be updated and presented to the committee at least once at the end of each of the first three phases of the project. During Phase IV, when multiple packages are out for bid, this process may need to occur several times. During Phase V, since all pricing is in contract form at this point, this task amounts to monitoring the process and recording any change orders.

Contingency

Any budget must have a contingency. A contingency is basically a percentage of the contract amount that is carried as a bottom line for unforeseen hiccups. Early in the process (Phase I and Phase II), a typical contingency may be 15 to 18 percent. After preliminary pricing has been received at the end of Phase III, the contingency may drop to 10 to 12 percent. After final pricing has been received at the end of Phase IV, the contingency may drop to 7 to 10 percent. The percentages may be higher for a small-scale project. If the project is a remodel or there is existing construction in place, the percentage of the contingency may be higher due to unforeseen conditions. For example, some old flooring material is scheduled to be demolished, and it is determined that the adhesive used to install it contains asbestos and abatement is required; or when the ceiling tile is opened up, and a large plumbing line is running exactly where some lighting fixtures are planned for the reception area and the type of lighting fixtures must be changed.

The contingency should be a number that is carried in your budget. It should not be carried as a line item in the contractor's numbers. It is also a good idea to carry the contingency on the bottom line of the budget and not just on the construction portion. The other soft costs do not have the potential for as great a change as the construction cost, but unexpected things always arise. Of course, the firm may decide to make changes, which can add any amount to the cost of the project.

What the Landlord Will and Will Not Pay For

In Chapter 8 in the section on work letter negotiation, we discussed in detail what the landlord should be expected to pay for. As a reminder, here is a quick summary of major items:

- All demolition
- Everything above the ceiling (electrical, mechanical, fire suppression, and so on), ceiling grid, ceiling tile and building standard lighting fixtures
- All utilities during construction
- All freight elevator costs during construction
- Common demising partitions
- A turnkey build-out to the firm's design intent and specifications, or an allowance for the build-out
- Guarantee that the space will be ready to occupy by a certain date
- Professional fees including architectural and design, structural and MEP engineering (typically, the landlord pays for only a small portion of these fees)
- Moving costs
- Brokerage fees (if a broker is used)
- Building-standard window coverings

Having the landlord responsible for the complete build-out carries a double-edged sword. If the landlord has to guarantee that the space is built out without incurring additional charges to the tenant, or if he has to guarantee a schedule, he will protect his interests first, not those of the tenant. Likewise, if you are required to use the landlord's contractor to build out the space, the contractor will be mindful to look out for the landlord's interests first, since he knows that his repeat business comes from the landlord.

These are what a landlord will typically *not* pay for (soft costs):

- Furniture (or any item that you can move with you)
- Cabling (this is changing now that most people are standardizing on what type of cabling they use)
- Graphics and signage
- Art, accessories, plants
- Window coverings (beyond the building standard)

Things to Watch Out For

Change Orders

Change orders are changes to the contract price for additional work or changes to the scope of work. For example, if a contractor identifies something that does not work or that needs to be remedied, you need to ask if this change will result in a price increase. Sometimes things need to be moved slightly to avoid conflict. If an item has not been installed, then it is reasonable to assume that moving it slightly will not result in a price change.

Do not let change orders pile up. To keep things on schedule, you might need to allow the contractor to proceed with changes before they can be priced. It is reasonable to expect that a change order will not take longer than a week to price unless the scope is large. It is best to devote a portion of the construction meeting to a discussion of the status of change orders. Contractors quite often do not deal with change order pricing in a timely manner, and at the end of the project suddenly present you with thousands of dollars in changes.

Deal with change orders as they occur. Once something has been closed up, it is difficult to reopen a wall to see if something was moved because there really was a conflict.

Also, be direct with the contractor. If the contractor makes a suggestion to change something, figure out whether the change is in your best interest or the contractor's best interest, and whether there is a cost associated with the change.

Watch out for contractor mark-up on change orders. When the project documents go out for pricing, stipulate in the general conditions that the contractor is not allowed fee markup on any change order up to, for example, $50,000. Or stipulate that the contractor is not allowed a markup until the change orders reach a collective total of, for example, $100,000. These amounts vary, depending on the project's scope.

For 99 percent of all build-outs, change orders are an inevitable part of construction. Be mindful and not neglectful.

Contractor Markup

Your contractor needs to make a fair profit, and a careful review of the proposed contract can keep the profit in a fair and appropriate range. The contractor negotiates a fee for the work, generally about 3 to 5 percent of the contract amount. The general conditions section of the contract recites a pass-through of the general contractor's specifically agreed expenses in carrying out the obligations of the contract. These expenses are the costs to the contractor of getting the work done, and they include such items as his construction trailer, salaries, insurance, tools, utilities, and transportation.

General conditions items may be viewed as the cost of having the contractor there on the job, although they include a share of costs with the construction company's offices. These administrative and overhead items usually amount to about 5 percent of the value of the contract. Once the contract is in place, the contractor, of course, tries to hold these costs down in order to generate more profit. It is common for contractors to pump up the project costs in the general conditions portion of the contract by overstating expenses, and you should review those sections carefully, looking for expenses that the contractor can forego. Likewise, we urge you to review the subcontractors' contracts to insure that the general contractor is not overstating the amounts of those contracts in drafting a bid for the project.

Standard legal form books illustrate ways to structure contracts and monetary agreements with the contractor. The AIA has made available a selection of standard contract documents that includes widely used standard forms and provides a starting point for drafting. They are available online, by CD-ROM, and as a component of AIA's *The Architect's Handbook of Professional Practice.*

In our discussion here, we assume that you have one general contractor who holds the subcontractors' contracts. There may be contracts that the law firm wishes to hold directly with other contractors, rather than with the general contractor. Examples are voice/data cabling contracts or millwork fabrication contracts (for such items as secretarial stations and custom conference tables) where the product is brought in at the end of a project after the space is basically finished. There is often no need to put these items under the general contractor's scope and have their costs marked up with general conditions costs and fees.

Definition of Substantial Completion

A construction contract carries a definition of the phrase "substantial completion," because this event triggers other events, such as the beginning of the warranty period. It protects the tenant from having to assume certain responsibilities before construction is completed, and it defines how complete the space is when the tenant takes possession or initially occupies it. Unfortunately, this phrase is not at all clear on its face. Be very careful how this term is defined, as a contractor's idea of completion can be very different from your expectations of how finished the space is when you open up for business. Your contract should identify who will certify that the work is substantially complete, as well as providing ground rules for the punch list process. If work needs to be done after you move in, have a clear understanding that work is to be performed on an after-hours basis at no additional cost, so that you can conduct business without such disruptions as workmen hanging on ladders with noisy drills, or the smell of adhesives or paint.

Miscellaneous Costs

As you review your initial budget, be sure to include these items, which are typically not included in the general contractor's contract:

- Cabling
- Audiovisual systems
- Security systems
- Professional fees
- Furniture
- Freestanding millwork
- Special window coverings
- Special floor coverings (area rugs)
- Library shelving
- Moveable file systems
- Graphics and signage
- Art
- Accessories
- Plants and plant containers
- Moving costs
- Office Equipment
- Stationery and business cards

See the next chapter for examples of budget documents for building out the space, as well as examples of furniture budgets.

Samples of Budget-Related Documents 19

A. Request for Proposal

We include this sample RFP as an example of a document used to qualify bidders, consultants, and vendors.

B. Budget Documents for Building Out a Law Firm Space

We present samples of the following budget types for use in planning. They are, of course, specific to a project and subject to changing prices.

Exhibit 19.2: Preliminary Budget
Exhibit 19.3: Preliminary Pricing Budget
Exhibit 19.4: Construction Administration Budget
Exhibit 19.5: Furniture budget

Exhibit 19.1
A SAMPLE REQUEST FOR PROPOSALS

RE: Request for Proposal, MEP Engineering Services
          Law Firm of XXX and XXX

Dear Mr.

Interior Space Design, Incorporated (I.S.D.) as planning consultant to XXX and XXX, requests your response to provide a proposal for mechanical, electrical and plumbing engineering services based on project criteria identified in this letter.

The law firm, XXX and XXX, currently occupies levels 92, 93, and 94 of Shorter Tower at 202 North Sixth Street in Pottsville. They have renewed their lease and will demolish most of the existing floors. The shaded walls show existing partitions to remain. They will also take all of level 95 and 24 and half of level 96. As you can see from the enclosed plans level 95 will be a conference floor. That floor will have a very high level of build out. Level 24 is an administrative floor and will have a " building standard" level of build out. The typical attorney floors (92, 93, 94 and 96) will have a moderate level of build out. We have enclosed the reflected ceiling plans and furniture plans for each floor.

The engineering firm submitting a proposal must represent that they are knowledgeable of this building's systems and will effectively coordinate the tenant's requirements into these systems.

1.   <u>**Schedule**</u>

    The project schedule is outlined as follows:

6 Feb 02	I.S.D. issues documents to engineers for engineering
15 Feb 02	50% review of engineering documents by I.S.D.
19 Feb 02	100% review of engineering documents by I.S.D.
21 Feb 02	Issue final architectural and MEP drawings and specifications for final pricing
6 Mar 02	Receive and review pricing
18 Mar 02	Issue for construction
14 Jun 02	Substantial completion level 24
27 Sep 02	Substantial completion level 96
25 Oct 02	Substantial completion level 95
10 Jan 03	Substantial completion level 94
4 Apr 03	Substantial completion level 93
13 Jun 03	Substantial completion level 92

2.   <u>**Drawings and Specifications**</u>

    The engineering drawings are to be prepared using a computerized drafting system. I.S.D. will provide backgrounds indicating all lighting, power and communication symbols. In no case are the above-referenced symbols to be redrawn by the engineers. The engineers shall prepare their applicable notes, switching, circuits, ductwork, etc. All ductwork shall be shown to scale to avoid conflicts with lighting fixtures. The engineers shall endeavor to coordinate new work and existing conditions to avoid light fixture conflicts.

    The architectural reflected ceiling plans shall indicate type and exact location of all light fixtures, locations of light switches, ceiling materials, and associated details. After mutual coordination for placement with the engineer's drawings, the architec-

Exhibit 19.1 **243**

Exhibit 19.1 A Sample Request for Proposals (continued)

tural reflected ceiling plans and the engineers' lighting plans shall include exact location of exit signs, fire speakers, and smoke detectors. The engineers' plans shall also incorporate the required circuiting thereof. The architectural drawings include a lighting fixture schedule which indicates the manufacture, model number, lamp type, volts and wattage. The engineering lighting plans shall indicate all circuits, switching and adequately sized dimmers.

The architectural power and communication plans shall indicate all receptacles, multi-outlet strips, communication outlets and mounting heights. Also all client and general contractor supplied equipment shall be indicated by location on the architectural power and communication plans and referenced to the architectural equipment schedule. The client has provided manufacturer's technical specifications which supply volts and amps. The engineering drawings shall indicate circuits for all devices.

The engineering drawings shall include a power plan, lighting plan, a mechanical plan and a plumbing plan for each floor plus mechanical and electrical detail sheets as required. The engineers are to provide mechanical, electrical and plumbing specifications on their drawings.

3. **Scope**

The project shall include a personal computer at every office and work station. PC's are to be daisy chained to the same circuits. Printers are not to share the same circuits as PC's.

There will be a moderate amount of incandescent lighting on level 95.

There will be two copier rooms on each typical attorney floor.

The computer room shall consist of file servers, hubs and the telephone switch. An existing UPS system will be used. It will require its own air conditioning system.

The engineers shall provide a connected load summary to determine watts per square foot.

There will be one employee lounge on level 24 and one catering pantry on level 35. There is one coffee bar on each of the typical attorney floors with associated plumbing (refrigerator, ice maker, dishwasher, coffee maker and garbage disposal).

The existing restrooms on levels 92, 93, 94 and 95 will be demolished of all fixtures and finishes. They will be built back new. We have selected the fixtures which will be specified on the engineers' drawings.

We will request that the engineers review the final pricing as received from the MEP subcontractors.

4. **Submittals**

The engineers will be required to review and respond in a timely manner to all submittals and shop drawings involving their scope of work. The engineers shall review the final air balance report for compliance with the contract documents.

5. **Site Visits**

The engineers shall be required to review related work in place and prepare a field report indicating any problems or discrepancies observed. These site visits shall occur:

a. before preparing the working drawings to observe as built conditions,
b. before drywall is two sided,
c. before the ceiling is closed in,
d. at substantial completion to prepare a punchlist of related work.

Exhibit 19.1 A Sample Request for Proposals (continued)

The proposal submitted should be addressed to Mr. George G. George at Shorter Tower at 202 North Sixth Street in Pottsville, NE 73123 with a copy to I.S.D. The proposal should include all of the above-referenced services under the Basic Fee. A list of Additional Services and Estimated Reimbursable Costs should also be included. The agreement of services shall be between XXX & XXX and the engineering firm. Invoices shall be sent directly to XXX & XXX with a copy to ISD.

A copy of the preliminary plans is enclosed. We look forward to receiving your proposal by 00/00/00 (approximately one month). Should you have any questions, please call.

Sincerely,

Suzette S. Schultz
Principal

Exhibit 19.2 **245**

Exhibit 19.2
A SAMPLE PRELIMINARY BUDGET

ISD Interior Space Design, Inc.

NAME OF LAW FIRM: **DATE:**
    Tenant Improvement Costs - Refurbishment
    Revised Estimate

Professional Costs		
Construction Manager	230,000	
Architectural	450,000	
Engineering	103,200	783,200
General Conditions		249,000
Demolition		330,000
Concrete		5,000
Metals		92,500
Wood & Plastics		1,756,503
Doors-Windows-HRDW		455,500
Finishes:		
Drywall	650,000	
Tile & Stone	336,000	
Acoustical	195,000	
Flooring	405,600	
Paint & Paper	293,000	1,879,600
Specialties		49,100
Equipment		61,000
Conveying		90,000
Mechanical		1,375,000
Electrical		950,000
Network Cabling		145,000
Total		8,221,403
Contingency		752,320
Grand Total before Deductions		8,973,723
Per Rentable Sq. Ft.		93.95
Deductions:		
Limited Buildout on Floor 99 (use current finishes only build		
necessary offices)		(334,950)
Remove Expansion Joints		(15,000)
Remove Structural Steel Reinforcement for Floor 99		(20,000)
(part of File Room will have to be located in the basement)		

Exhibit 19.2 A Sample Preliminary Budget (continued)

Doors to be flush standard/paint grade, in lieu of custom millwork on attorney floors	(71,000)
Delete Millwork Covers on Fan Coil Units	(15,000)
Reuse and relocate doors and hardware for the 99th floor	(13,300)
Double up of etched glass in budget above	(30,000)
Partitions to go 6″ above ceilings in lieu of full height on floors 99 and 99 (same as current)	(28,000)
Reuse Ceiling Grid on 99	(17,000)
Reduce grade of wall treatment in smaller multipurpose room	(1,500)
Change aluminum frames with electrostatic paint finish to be a factory per-finish	(10,000)
Reduce refrigerator specifications	(14,000)
Do not revise finish or location of the elevator call buttons/lanterns	(42,000)
Reduce the number of HVAC zones (floors 99-99) from 25 to 20 zones	(50,000)
Deduct for not installing chiller on 99th floor	(53,000)
Reuse existing 2×4 fluorescents in lieu of new type A on Floor 99	(33,600)
Use MC Cable in lieu of hard wire for the branch circuit devices (requires Landlord approval)	(42,000)
Use MC Cable in lieu of hard wire for fire alarm devices (requires Landlord approval)	(11,000)
Use a modular wiring system for the applicable light fixtures	(76,000)
Deduct electrical at chiller	(23,000)
Total Deductions	(900,350)
Less Contingency Reduction	(90,035)
Total Deductions and Contingency Reduction	(990,385)
Revised Total	7,983,338
Per Rentable Sq. Ft. Likely Other Reductions	83.58
Final Pricing Based on Final Plans—Est. 5% reduction	(323,719)
Reduction of Contingency	(290,303)
Possible Revised Total	7,369,316
Per Rentable Sq. Ft.	77.15
Building Allowance	5,730,900
Amount to be Funded by the Law Firm	1,638,416
Amount Budgeted	716,363

Exhibit 19.2   **247**

Exhibit 19.2 A Sample Preliminary Budget (continued)

Amount Exceeding Original Budget	922,054
Alternates That will be Provided for Consideration:	
Down grade detailing and wood species	Not Priced
Delete muntins in transoms; utilize full piece of glass	Not Priced
Delete custom wood shutters and go to a more standard wood or metal blind	(40,000)
Delete or minimize spline ceiling and use 2×2 or 2×4 grid	(6,000)
Use Lower Grade ceiling grid	Not Priced
Utilize carpet instead of stone on 99-99	(30,000)
Reduce quantity and quality of wall coverings	Not Priced
Eliminate electrostatic painting of convector covers on 95, 98–99	(16,000)
Remove and replace blinds for exterior windows ($88 per window)	Not Priced
Change Plumbing Fixture types	Not Priced
Eliminate dual switching of the type A fixtures	(5,700)
Eliminate dimmer package on the 99th floor	Not Priced
Deduct to change light fixtures to type B or C.	(11,356)

Exhibit 19.3 Preliminary Pricing (Design Development) Budget

PRELIMINARY PRICING BUDGET

ISD Interior Space Design, Inc.

PRELIMINARY PRICING BUDGET
NAME OF LAW FIRM: DATE:

GENERAL CONSTRUCTION			
Estimated General Construction	33	52,000	$1,716,000
Structural Reinforcement for Library			
(If required)		25,000	25,000
Total Estimated General Construction			**$1,741,000**

FREE STANDING MILLWORK FURNITURE	Unit Cost	
12 Associate "C" Workwalls &		
6 partner w.w. (type A)		166,500
8 New double secretarial stations	14,000	112,000
18 New printer units at secretarials	1,100	19,800
20 New side panels at modified sec'y.	500	10,000
units		
2 Receptionist desks	7,500	15,000
3 New library tables	4,000	12,000
TOTAL FREESTANDING MILLWORK		**$ 335,300**

FREESTANDING MILLWORK TOUCH UP	
Estimate to touch up existing	4,500.00
sec'y & workwalls	
TOTAL ESTIMATED MILLWORK TOUCH UP	**$ 4,500.00**

FURNITURE		
File cabinets, overfiles &		176,147.57
library shelves		
		0.00
Library shelves (7 hi) Incl. above		0.00
Library shelves (3 hi) Incl above		0.00
12 Library chairs	650	7,800.00
2 Refurbished systems furn.	3,000	6,000.00
for billing		
2 Refurbished systems furn.	3,000	6,000.00
for file clerks		
1 Refurbished systems	3,000	3,000.00
furn. for librarian		
2 Additional word	2,500	5,000.00
processing stations		
2 Furniture for legal assistant offices	4,500	9,000.00
2 Reception sofas	3,500	7,000.00
2 Lunchroom tables	300	600.00
8 Lunchroom chairs	250	2,000.00
1 New moveable filing system	45,000	45,000.00
TOTAL NEW FURNITURE		**$ 267,547.57**

Exhibit 19.3   **249**

Exhibit 19.3 Preliminary Pricing Budget (continued)

CONSULTANT FEES					
Architectural fees	1.75	52,000	91,000		91,000
M.E.P. Engineering	0.48	52,000	25,000		25,000
Structural Engineering			5,000		5,000.00
TOTAL CONSULTANT FEES				$	**121,000.00**
(Excludes reimbursables)					

MISCELLANEOUS				
Graphics Allowance			5,000	5,000
Voice/Data cabling	1.00	52,000	52000	52,000
Moving Costs	0.80	52,000	41600	41,600
Art Installation Allowance			720	720
TOTAL MISCELLANEOUS				**$99,320**

SUBTOTAL			**$ 2,568,668**
CONTINGENCY (8%)			**$205,493**
TOTAL ESTIMATED COSTS	53.35	52000 S.F.	**$ 2,774,161**

OPTIONS:

1. Includes new file cabinets and overfiles.
2. Includes 12 associate workwalls and 6 partner (type A) workwalls and table desks.
3. If used moveable filing system can be found, it could save approximately $19,000.
4. We have assumed that you will take your existing library shelving.
5. Add $10,000 if landlord will not provide window coverings on level 9.

NOT INCLUDED:

New phone switch, stationery printing, art, plants, accessories, draperies, furniture other than indicated above, security system furniture other than coffee area (no microwaves, projection screens, marker boards).

Built-in partner workwalls.

The construction estimate assumes the reuse of existing building standard doors and aluminum frames.

The space will not have the same level of acoustical integrity that the existing XXXX office has.

Exhibit 19.4 Construction Administration Budget

Construction Administration Budget

This becomes the final construction budget. Bids are in and accepted. The Construction Administration budget is subject to Items of Change, which form the basis of Change Orders. The cost of Change Orders is generally absorbed by the project's contingency fund or separate funding needs to be applied.

 Interior Space Design, Inc.

XXX Law Firm	DATE
REVISED PRICING BUDGET	PROJECT #

GENERAL CONSTRUCTION

General Construction (Base Contract)	1,786,422
Items of Change (to date)	50,000
Owner supplied lighting	16,000
Total Estimated General Construction	**$1,852,422**

FREE STANDING MILLWORK FURNITURE

14	Associate "C" Workwalls	$103,800.86
4	Partner "A" Workwalls	$ 44,042.03
21	New double secretarial stations	$302,966.98
	New library end panels and surrounds	$14,907.70
4	New library tables	$ 7,613.27
	Relocate reception desks	$ 101.79
Total Freestanding Millwork		**$ 473,432.63**

MISC. MILLWORK

1	Conference Table		5,988.00
2	Receptionist desks	1,875	3,750
	Modify 2 reception desks (estimate)	2,000	4,000
	Estimate to touch up existing workwalls & reception desks		1,800.00
Total Misc. Millwork			**$ 13,738**

FURNITURE

	File cabinets & overfiles		209,923.99
	Two drawer file cabinets	36 × 50	1,800.00
	Library shelves		7,902.42
16	Library chairs	650	10,400.00
1	Recover existing sofa for 29 reception		1,687.84
2	Additional word processing stations	2,500	5,000.00
5	Desks for legal assistant offices	1,100	5,500.00
1	Reception sofa		2,381.50
6	Lunchroom tables		1,976.69
24	Lunchroom chairs		6,894.57
1	New moveable filing system	28,569	28,569.34
25	Side Chairs		7,848.00
Total New Furniture			**$ 289,884.35**

Exhibit 19.4 **251**

Exhibit 19.4 Construction Administration Budget (continued)

CONSULTANT FEES				
Architectural fees	1.75	52,000	91,000	91,000
Additional services				10,000
M.E.P. Engineering				22,293
Structural Engineering			5,000	5,000.00
Total Consultant Fees				**$ 128,293.00**
(Does not include reimbursables)				

MISCELLANEOUS				
Graphics Allowance			5,000	5,000
Southwestern Bell			0	4,392
Moving Costs (estimated)	0.80	52,000	41600	41,600
Art Installation Allowance			720	720
TCI Cable				426
Mail Slots				6,333
Total Miscellaneous				**$ 58,471**

SUBTOTAL			**$2,816,241**
CONTINGENCY (5%)			**$140,812**
TOTAL ESTIMATED COSTS	56.87	52,000 S.F.	**$2,957,053**
OTHER FIRM			**−253,000**
FURNITURE PURCHASES			
REVISED ESTIMATED COSTS	52	52,000 S.F.	**$2,704,053**

NOT INCLUDED:

Stationery printing, art, plants, accessories, draperies, furniture other than indicated above, equipment other than coffee area (no microwaves), fabric wallcovering, marker boards.

1. Does not include missing window coverings on level 90.
2. Does not include special bookshelves.
3. Does not include icemaker for catering pantry.
4. Does not include new hardware.

Exhibit 19.5
FURNITURE BUDGET

 Interior Space Design, Inc.

FURNITURE AND MISCELLANEOUS BUDGET

Qty.	Area	Item	Unit Cost	Total Cost
	Reception			
2		Sofa	2,500.00	5,000.00
8		Side Chairs	800.00	6,400.00
2		Receptionist chairs	550.00	1,100.00
1		Custom area rug	20,000.00	20,000.00
1		Reception desk	12,000.00	12,000.00
1		Writing desk	7,000.00	7,000.00
1		Writing desk chair	1,200.00	1,200.00
3		Nova p.c. screen	500.00	1,500.00
4		Side tables	500.00	2,000.00
		Subtotal		**56,200.00**
	Conference Room A			
1		Table	23,000.00	23,000.00
1		Credenza	10,000.00	10,000.00
18		Chairs	1,500.00	27,000.00
4		Side chairs	700.00	2,800.00
2		Side tables	500.00	1,000.00
		Window covering allowance		3,500.00
		Subtotal		**67,300.00**
	Conference Room Seating 14			
2		Tables	16,500.00	33,000.00
3		Credenzas	8,500.00	25,500.00
28		Conference chairs	1,200.00	33,600.00
1		Add for one smart table	4,000.00	4,000.00
		Subtotal		**96,100.00**
	Conference Rooms Seating 12			
3		Tables (smart)	19,000.00	57,000.00
3		Credenzas	10,000.00	30,000.00
36		Chairs	1,200.00	43,200.00
		Subtotal		**130,200.00**
	Conference Rooms Seating 12			
2		Tables	15,000.00	30,000.00
2		Credenzas	10,000.00	20,000.00
24		Chairs	1,200.00	28,800.00
		Subtotal		**78,800.00**

Exhibit 19.5 **253**

Exhibit 19.5 Furniture Budget (continued)

Conference Rooms Seating 10

1	Table	11,500.00	11,500.00
1	Credenza	10,000.00	10,000.00
10	Chairs	1,200.00	12,000.00
	Subtotal		**33,500.00**

Conference Rooms Seating 8

3	Table	10,500.00	31,500.00
3	Credenza	10,000.00	30,000.00
24	Chairs	1,200.00	28,800.00
1	Add for one smart table	3,000.00	3,000.00
	Subtotal		**93,300.00**

Multi-purpose Rooms

40	Tables	800.00	32,000.00
175	Chairs	550.00	96,250.00
3	Credenzas	15,000.00	45,000.00
6	Storage dollies	600.00	3,600.00
1	Millwork Podium	5,000.00	5,000.00
	Subtotal		**181,850.00**

Employee Lounge

3	Two top tables	300	900.00
7	Four top tables	350	2,450.00
26	Chairs	310	8,060.00
1	Banquette	4000	4,000.00
	Subtotal		**15,410.00**

Library

6	Single faced library shelves		1,890.00
70	Double faced library shelves		29,750.00
5	Library table w/ Nova pc screen		25,000.00
10	Chairs	650.00	6,500.00
6	Double end panels	775.00	4,650.00
1	Library reference desk	10,000.00	10,000.00
1	Moveable shelving unit	40,200.00	40,200.00
	Subtotal		**117,990.00**

Project workrooms

350	Gray metal shelf units	110	38,500.00
	Use old conference room furniture		0
	Subtotal		**38,500.00**

Exhibit 19.5 Furniture Budget (continued)

Training room

6	Tables	800.00	4,800.00
8	Chairs	525.00	4,200.00
1	Credenza	2,500.00	2,500.00
	Subtotal		**11,500.00**

Central files

2	Task seating	525.00	1,050.00
4	Pedestals	400.00	1,600.00
1	Moveable shelving unit	30,360.00	30,360.00
8	Workstations	3,200.00	25,600.00
	Subtotal		**58,610.00**

Miscellaneous

6	Vestibule console tables	800.00	4,800.00
2	Visitor offices	20,000.00	40,000.00
	Subtotal		**44,800.00**

Associate Offices

61	Workwalls	5,500.00	335,500.00
61	Two drawer lateral files	475.00	28,975.00
61	Metal pedestals	400.00	24,400.00
61	Desk chairs	850.00	51,850.00
61	Guest chairs	500.00	30,500.00
	Subtotal		**471,225.00**

Paralegal Offices

24	Repaint existing five drawer lateral files		2,400.00
24	Pedestals	400.00	9,600.00
24	Desk chairs	650.00	15,600.00
24	Repaint existing two drawer lateral files		1,440.00
	Subtotal		**29,040.00**

Secretarial Stations

56	Task seating	525.00	29,400.00
28	Secretarial stations MW 300		420,000.00
321	Posting shelves at file wall		38,520.00
	Subtotal		**487,920.00**

Administration

10	Accounting cubicles	3,200.00	32,000.00
7	Managers office p.lam. workwalls	22,400.00	22,400.00
8	IS cubicles	3,200.00	25,600.00
	Subtotal		**80,000.00**

Exhibit 19.5   **255**

Exhibit 19.5 Furniture Budget (continued)

	GRAPHICS BUDGET		
6	XXX, XXXX & XXXX, PLLC	1,500.00	9,000.00
200	Attorney, paralegal & misc.	111.00	22,200.00
56	Secretarial	35.00	1,960.00
23	Conference rooms (d.n.d.)	125.00	2,875.00
21	Elevator call lanterns	1,000.00	21,000.00
8	Elevator call buttons	1,200.00	9,600.00
	Misc.		1,000.00
6	Exiting graphics	1,200.00	7,200.00
	Subtotal		**74,835.00**

	MISCELLANEOUS		
56	Planters at secretarials	225.00	12,600.00
	Plants	Leased	0.00
60	Planters	750.00	45,000.00
	Accessories allowance	20,000.00	20,000.00
	Art allowance	250,000.00	250,000.00
	Subtotal		**327,600.00**

Total furniture, graphics & misc.   **$2,494,680.00**

Glossary

AC Alternating current. The standard form of electrical energy used in this country.

abatement Process of removal or encapsulation of asbestos, generally to avoid airborne concentrations of the material.

acoustical wall treatment Stretch fabric system with fiberglass infill. This absorbs sounds.

addendum Written document amending obligations of the parties, made before executing the contract.

air handling fixture A ceiling-mounted light fixture that can also function to supply and return conditioned air.

air plenum The space between the ceiling and the floor above. It is used for returning air to the mechanical room. It is also used for ductwork, lighting, cabling, sprinklers, and plumbing lines. Anything going into the plenum typically has to be rated.

alkyd oil-based paint Paints made with a synthetic alkyd resin. Newer paints combine solvents, oils, and binders in various combinations, resulting in paints with different qualities.

ambient lighting Fluorescent lighting that is directed toward the ceiling, causing light to bounce off the ceiling for an even distribution of lighting and very low source of glare.

amp or ampere Unit used to measure the amount of electrical current.

antistatic Conductive carpet for computer rooms and similar operations

as-is A term used in leases to describe the physical condition of a space. Typically a tenant takes a space as-is, meaning that no improvements are required or that the tenant is responsible for making any improvements.

ASTM American Society for the Testing of Materials.

astragal The vertical strip that conceals the gap between a pair of doors.

attached cushion Carpet cushion or pad that is attached to the back of the carpet after the carpet is made.

Axminster A type of woven carpet, generally wool and usually patterned.

257

background sound system Also known as sound masking or white noise. A system of electronic sound producers installed in the plenum that create artificial noise, thus masking intelligible speech.

baffle A screen or object that deflects air, sound, or light.

baluster The vertical support of a handrail.

balustrade A series of balusters.

base An applied material where the wall meets the floor, commonly made of vinyl, rubber, wood, or stone.

base building The existing shell condition of a building before the installation of tenant improvements.

bays The space between two column lines in a building. A window that extends out from the exterior wall.

blocking Wood reinforcement inside walls between studs to support wall-hung items such as overhead cabinets.

BTU British thermal unit, the quantity of heat needed to raise one pound of water one degree Fahrenheit at sea level. This is a standard of measurement for sizing mechanical systems and heat output from equipment.

building grid The module that corresponds with the building structural columns and windows. This refers to the space between the columns and the space between the window mullions.

CAC Ceiling attenuation class, a rating system for a ceiling structure's efficiency as a barrier to airborne sound intrusion between two closed rooms, over the speech frequency range.

candle power/candela Candlepower measures the directional intensity of light, measured in candelas.

carpet construction Refers to how the carpet was made. Generally, carpets are woven or tufted.

case work Cabinetwork or millwork.

Cat 6 Category 6 cable, currently the industry standard for voice and data cabling.

CDs Construction documents. The plans and specifications used for building a project; also called working drawings.

chair rail Molding attached to the wall that prevents chairs from damaging the wall when they are pushed back.

change order A written document that alters or amends items in the contract documents.

chase A space used horizontally or vertically for running conduits and cables or for exhausting air.

circuit breaker A switch in the electrical panel. It can be tripped or automatically shut off if power consumption exceeds its rated value.

clerestory Glass windows occurring generally above seven feet from the finished floor.

closure Mechanical hardware that automatically closes a door or holds it open.

coaxial Type of cable previously used for computer cabling. It is still used for some television cabling.

coffers Recesses in ceilings, walls, and domes.

cold cathode Type of lighting similar to neon.

conductor Wire used to carry electrical current to the electrical outlet.

conduit Metal or plastic tubes that are used to pull electrical and communication wires through. In most construction, plastic does not meet building codes.

connected load The sum of the ratings of the electricity-consuming equipment connected to an electrical supply system.

convector A type of mechanical system usually located below exterior windows that provides heat and air-conditioning by convection.

core area (also referred to as building core) The area which occupies base building elements such as fire stairs, elevators, mechanical rooms, electrical rooms, columns, and restrooms.

cornice Top portion of the entablature.

cove An area of the ceiling often used to conceal indirect lighting.

cove base Rubber or vinyl base with a curved bottom edge used with resilient flooring so water does not extend under the base of the wall.

creep factor The horizontal distance between panels in systems furniture workstations.

cut pile A type of carpet made with the fibers sheared at the same level so that the cut ends of the yarn are exposed.

dead load The weight of walls, partitions, doors, and structural members such as columns, floors, and roofs. Any other permanent items of building construction including MEP and service items.

decibel (dB) A unit for expressing relative intensity of sounds on a scale from 0 dB for the average least-perceptible sound to 130 dB for the average pain level.

demand load The total power required by a facility.

diffused lighting Lighting that is not obviously from one particular light source.

diffuser A metal grille or louvered device typically mounted in the ceiling that dispenses supply air or return air.

direct glue A means of attaching carpet directly to the flooring substrate using an adhesive material.

direct lighting Light fixtures mounted in the ceiling plane to dispense light directly down to the work surface.

double rubs A term used to describe fabric that has been tested under an abrading system to withstand a given number of rubs before it becomes abraded or unusable. The test is one of the industry standards; fabrics used commercially need to withstand a minimum of 15,000 double rubs.

down light A recessed lighting fixture, typically incandescent, that is used typically for lighting reception areas and elevator lobbies. The opening aperture is typically six inches.

electrical metering Refers to separate metering as opposed to calculations of connected load; used for determining electrical costs in the work letter.

electric strike Electrified hardware used on a door, typically when a security system is used. Power is shunted to the strike and free exit is achieved without setting off an alarm.

employee lounge A place where employees can eat their lunch. See examples in chapter 13.

ergonomics The interface between the human body and equipment.

fascia Vertical form or panel; also privy ionic architrave.

fenestration The design arrangement in proportion of openings into a building, such as windows and doors.

fillet or filet A flat piece of molding separating two other pieces of molding.

fir-down A dropped ceiling made out of gypsum board. This condition typically occurs above cabinets, at portals, archways, and wall openings.

fire rating ASTM has certain ratings of materials based on fire resistance. This pertains to walls, ceilings, floors, and doors. There are fire-rating requirements based on building occupancy types.

flash patch To repair the unlevel floor condition of an existing floor.

flexible metal conduit (FMX or Greenfield) Used to protect electrical and voice/data wiring, often when some flexibility or movement is required. A true conduit, but appears similar to BX, or armored cable.

floor monument An electrical receptacle mounted on top of the floor through the slab that contains electrical outlets or voice/data outlets.

fluorescent lighting This uses ultraviolet wavelengths. This is the most common light source in office buildings due to long lamp life, low heat output, and general overall efficiency to provide a lot of light for less money.

fluting–vertical The vertical grooves on the shaft of a column.

foot candle A photometric unit, measurable with a light meter, consisting of the amount of illumination produced by a standard candle at a distance of one foot.

freestanding millwork Millwork that is installed after all finishes are in place. This includes secretarial stations, receptionist desks, conference tables, credenzas, podiums, etc. This is typically a contract between the tenant and the millwork contractor and is not run through the general contractor.

fusible link A metal link that melts at low temperatures, causing safety devices to close such as for fire doors and rolling grilles.

gallery desk Typically found at a reception area or secretarial station. The vertical sides extend up beyond the work surface and have a horizontal ledge. This is to hide desk clutter and to accommodate a space for signing a document.

general contractor The prime contractor that holds the subcontracts from subcontractors.

graphics Another term for signage.

grid Framework for a suspended ceiling system. Also, the system of modules created by spacing of the building structure, such as columns and windows.

grounding Connecting an electrical device to earth or some conductor that serves in place of earth.

ground-isolated An isolated ground is a type of electrical circuit that helps protect computers and electronics. In addition to helping protect against power surges, it provides a clean grounding path to the service panel and reduces electromagnetic noise.

grounds Wood or metal reinforcement in the walls to support cabinets or other wall-hung items. Also referred to as blocking.

guardrail A railing system, typically mounted forty-two inches above the floor around openings at stairs and balconies.

halogen Type of light source similar to quartz, providing clear white light.

hand The field and lay of a fabric.

handed A term used with hardware and doors where a door is meant to swing one way. Typically when you approach a door, the hand that is most likely to use the door lever or knob describes if it is a right hand or left door. The same is true in reverse door openings where it becomes a right-hand reverse or left-hand reverse.

high hat An incandescent or fluorescent down light that is recessed or semirecessed in the ceiling

HVAC Heating, ventilation, and air-conditioning.

interior room Any room or office not on the perimeter window wall.

internal stair A stairway used for connecting floors of multiple-floor law firms so people don't have to wait for elevators.

junction box A steel electrical box, usually mounted within wall cavities that contain connections for electrical receptacles or devices.

laminated glass Two or more layers of glass separated by layers of film. Laminated glass has better acoustical insulation properties than single-layer tempered glass. The plastic film layer between the two layers of glass keeps the glass from creating shards or splinters if it is broken.

lamp A term used in the lighting industry to mean light bulb.

lintel The horizontal support member that spans an opening.

life safety system Emergency lighting, alarms, sprinkler systems, strobes, smoke detectors, and similar equipment that may interface with elevators and security systems.

loggia The gallery behind an open arcade or colonnade.

low voltage lighting Lighting that operates at a substantially lower voltage via a step-down transformer.

lumen A photometric unit. In the context of LCD projectors, the more lumens, the more light output, and the brighter the image.

masking sound See *background sound system*.

mastic Any of a number of adhesives, most commonly used for setting tile.

millwork Any cabinetwork, running trim, wood doors, and wood frames, or paneling—basically anything made from a high-quality wood rather than plastic laminate. This can be either paint grade or stain grade.

mock-up An original full-sized model for evaluation, generally used for demonstration and development of such things as office furniture systems or millwork. A mock-up is usually made with inexpensive materials to demonstrate fit and functionality.

movable shelving A form of high-density shelving that eliminates multiple aisleways being used at the same time

mullion A vertical member that divides windows into panes or lights.

mutton A thin wood member that divides windows into panes or lights.

nosing The overhang on a stair tread.

NRC Noise reduction coefficient, the unit of measure for sound absorption of a particular surface material such as ceiling tile, acoustical wall treatment, or carpeting. The higher the number, the more effective the sound absorption.

open office (also referred to as systems furniture) Furniture systems that are demountable, and made up of low partitions, work surfaces, storage units, and accessories that can be reconfigured for flexibility.

parabolic A type of deep-celled metal light fixture trim that allows for even distribution of light in a $2' \times 4'$ or $2' \times 2'$ light fixture, eliminating much of the glare from previous generations of fixtures.

pedestal A drawer unit mounted below a work surface that typically has two small drawers and one file drawer. Also called a box-box-file pedestal.

PL A type of fluorescent light source.

plastic laminate A resin-impregnated surface applied to millwork and other flat surfaces, often referred to by the trade name Formica.

plenum The space above the ceiling and below the slab above. This is typically used for returning air to the mechanical room. This space is also used to run ductwork, recessed lighting fixtures, sprinkler lines, and plumbing lines. The space has a particular fire rating.

project workroom A room used by lawyers, paralegals, and secretaries. This is also referred to as a war room and used for storing files and as a workroom. Typically the walls are lined with shelves, and contain a work surface, telephone, and a space for a computer.

prototype A functionally representative rendition of a piece of furniture or millwork, fabricated late in the development cycle, before production; a version that serves as the basis for evaluation, demonstration, and further development.

punch list A written list of construction items that are either unacceptable or incomplete, given to the general contractor for correction.

PVC Polyvinyl chloride, used mostly for pipes and plumbing fixtures and castings. This material is not used often in high-rise construction due to fire codes.

raceway An area where voice/data and electrical cables are run vertically or horizontally within systems furniture.

receptacle An electrical outlet device mounted in the wall; usually houses two or four electrical outlets.

reveal A recessed area between two surfaces.

RFP Request for proposal.

riser Vertical component of a stair or a vertical pipe.

saddle Flooring transition strip from one type of floor surface to another. The material can be wood, stone, rubber, or metal.

service center Combined services functioning in one area such as central copy, central fax, central supply, central mail, messenger receiving, and dispatching.

soffit A dropped ceiling, usually made out of gypsum board. This condition typically occurs above cabinets, at portals, archways, and wall openings.

soft costs These include fees, furniture, art, accessories, plants, signage, and in general, costs not covered by the landlord.

sound masking See *background sound system.*

STC Sound transmission coefficient. This is an old means of testing sounds passing through or over a partition. This has been replaced by the CAC test.

stringer The vertical structural component of a stair that supports the treads and risers and is positioned 90 degrees to the treads. It is most frequently a steel channel.

structural glass Glass that does not require vertical mullions. This can be supported by the head and the sill, and is typically anywhere from $^3/_8$ to $^3/_4$ inches thick.

subcontractor A contractor whose contract is held and coordinated by the general contractor.

systems furniture Furniture systems that are demountable, made up of low partitions, work surfaces, storage units, and accessories that can be reconfigured for flexibility.

task lighting A lighting source that provides illumination for a specific work surface task area.

tempered glass Glass that has been processed by reheating after fabrication and cutting, which gives it a high degree of strength and safety features. However, it cannot be cut after it has been tempered.

terrazzo A type of floor finish with marbled chips added to the cement mortar and poured in place. After it has set, it is then ground and polished, and is an extremely durable floor finish.

tread The horizontal stepping surface of a stair.

troffer A mechanical device that can be mounted to the back side of a fluorescent light fixture, enabling the fixture to have supply air handling capabilities.

UL Underwriters Laboratories, Inc. refers to itself as "an independent, not-for-profit product-safety testing and certification organization."

under floor duct system A raised floor system that allows for air-conditioning, electrical, and voice/data wiring to be run under the floor. Raceways are embedded into the floor on a grid pattern that allows access to components via access panels.

VAV Variable air volume system.

VCT Vinyl composition tile.

veneer 1) A flitch that has been applied to a wood substrate to be used for millwork panels or furniture, etc. 2) A topical surface application of a different material to a substrate.

voice/data The communication cables that provide voice and/or data service to the user locations.

volt and watt Volts measure electrical pressure, while watts measure the total amount of electricity in a system at a given time. The formula volts × amperes = watts.

wall washer A directional wall light fixture, typically used for illuminating artwork or other featured items.

watts per square foot This refers to the building's ability to supply power to the tenant. Law firms require a rather high range, such as 7.5 watts, so they should try to negotiate available wattage based on rentable square feet, rather than usable square feet.

weft The left to right fiber in fabric or carpet, or the top to bottom fiber in fabric or carpet.

white noise See *background sound system*.

window wall The perimeter of the building, usually used for lawyer offices only.

wired glass Rolled glass with wire mesh imbedded in it to hold it together for fire safety.

working drawings See *CDs*.

work letter A part of the lease document that describes landlord cost and responsibilities and tenant cost and responsibilities for the build-out of the lease space.

yarn-dyed Yarn dyeing is a process of dyeing the skeins in the yarn stage before a carpet is manufactured.

Abbreviations

&	AND
∡	ANGLE
@	AT
℄	CENTERLINE
Ø	DIAMETER; ROUND
#	NUMBER; POUND
ACT	ACOUSTICAL TILE
ADJ	ADJUSTABLE
ALT	ALTERNATE
AL or ALUM	ALUMINUM
ANOD	ANODIZED
APPROX	APPROXIMATE
ARCH	ARCHITECT (URE)/ DESIGNER
AUTO	AUTOMATIC
AVG	AVERAGE
A/V	AUDIO VISUAL
AWT	ACOUSTICAL WALL TREATMENT
BB	BASE BUILDING
BD	BOARD
BLDG	BUILDING
BLKG	BLOCKING
BOT	BOTTOM
BTWN	BETWEEN
B/B	BACK TO BACK
CAB	CABINET

C_L	CENTERLINE
CLG	CEILING
CLO	CLOSET
CLR	CLEAR
CMU	CONCRETE MASONRY UNIT
COL	COLUMN
CONC	CONCRETE
CONST	CONSTRUCTION
CONT	CONTINUOUS
CONTR	CONTRACTOR
CPT	CARPET
CT	CERAMIC TILE
CTR	CENTER
D	DEPTH
DBL	DOUBLE
DET	DETAIL
DF	DRINKING FOUNTAIN
DIA	DIAMETER
DIAG	DIAGONAL
DIM	DIMENSION
DN	DOWN
DR	DOOR
DWG	DRAWING
EA	EACH
EL or ELEV	ELEVATION
ELEC	ELECTRIC (AL)
ENGR (G)	ENGINEER (ING)

EQ	EQUAL	LTS	LIGHT
EQ or EQUIP	EQUIPMENT	MAR	MARBLE
	RE: EQUIPMENT	MAX	MAXIMUM
	SCHEDULE	MECH	MECHANICAL
EXH	EXHAUST	MET or MTL	METAL
EXT or EXST	EXISTING	MFR	MANUFACTURER
FAB	FABRICATE	MIN	MINIMUM
FD	FLOOR DRAIN	MISC	MISCELLANEOUS
FE	FIRE EXTINGUISHER	MTD	MOUNTED
FEC	FIRE EXTINGUISHER	MUL	MULLION
	CABINET	MW	MILLWORK
FHC	FIRE HOSE CABINET	NA	NOT APPLICABLE
FIN	FINISH (ED)	NAT	NATURAL
FL or FLR	FLOOR	NIC	NOT IN CONTRACT
FLUOR	FLUORESCENT	NO or #	NUMBER
FT	FEET/FOOT	NTS	NOT TO SCALE
FURN	FURNISH	OC	ON CENTER
FUT	FUTURE	OD	OUTSIDE DIAMETER
FVC	FIRE VALUE CABINET	OFC	OFFICE
FWC	FABRIC WALLCOVERING	OPHD	OPPOSITE HAND
GA	GAGE/GAUGE	or OPP. HD.	
GALV	GALVANIZED	OPNG	OPENING
GC	GENERAL CONTRACTOR	OPP/OP.HD	OPPOSITE/OPPOSITE
GL	GLASS		HAND
GR	GRANITE	PC	PERSONAL COMPUTER
GRG	GLASS REINFORCED	PF	PLUMBING FIXTURE
	GYPSUM		RE: PLUMBING SCHED.
GWB GYP. BD.	GYPSUM WALLBOARD	PL	PARALEGAL OFFICE
HC	HOLLOW CORE	PLAM	PLASTIC LAMINATE
HDWD	HARDWOOD	or P.LAM.	
HDWE or HDW	HARDWARE	PLAS	PLASTER
HM	HOLLOW METAL	PLMG	PLUMBING
HORIZ	HORIZONTAL	PLYWD	PLYWOOD
H or HT	HEIGHT	POL	POLISHED
HVAC	HEAT, VENTILATING	PTD	PAINTED
	& AIR CONDITIONING	PTN	PARTITION
IN	INCH	PWR	PROJECT WORKROOM
INCAND	INCANDESCENT	QT	QUARRY TILE
INCL	INCLUDE (D) (ING)	QTY	QUANTITY
INSUL	INSULATION	R	RADIUS
INT	INTERIOR	RA	RETURN AIR
JAN	JANITOR	RB	RUBBER BASE
JT	JOINT	RE	REFER/REFERENCE
JUNC	JUNCTION	REFL	REFLECTED
J-BOX	JUNCTION BOX	REQD	REQUIRED
L	LONG/LENGTH	REV	REVISION
LAM	LAMINATE (D)	RH	RIGHT HAND
LAQ	LACQUER	RM	ROOM
LF	LINEAR FOOT	RND	ROUND
LH	LEFT HAND	SC	SCALE
LIN	LINEAR	SCHED	SCHEDULE (D)
LT. FIX.	LIGHT FIXTURE(S)	SIM	SIMILAR
LTG	LIGHTING	SPEC	SPECIFICATION

SQ	SQUARE	VCT	VINYL COMPOSITION TILE
SS	STAINLESS STEEL	VEN or VR	VENEER
ST	STONE	VERT	VERTICAL
STD	STANDARD	VIF	VERIFY IN THE FIELD
STL	STEEL	VWC	VINYL WALLCOVERING
STOR	STORAGE	W	WIDTH
STRUC	STRUCTURE (AL)	WD/WD.VR.	WOOD/WOOD VENEER
SYM	SYMMETRICAL	WT	WEIGHT
TEL	TELEPHONE	W/	WITH
THK	THICK (NESS)	W/O	WITHOUT
TYP	TYPICAL		
UNO	UNLESS NOTED OTHERWISE		

Typical Drawing Symbols

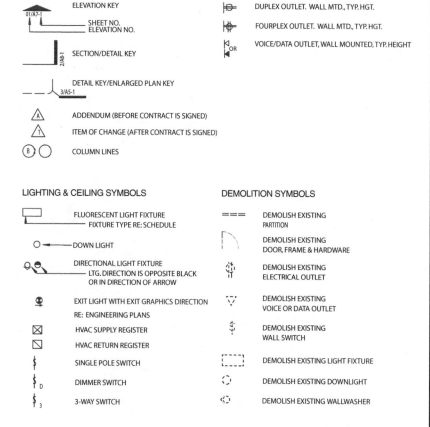

GENERAL SYMBOLS

ELEVATION KEY

01/A7-1

SHEET NO.
ELEVATION NO.

2/A8-1   **SECTION/DETAIL KEY**

DETAIL KEY/ENLARGED PLAN KEY
3/A5-1

A   **ADDENDUM (BEFORE CONTRACT IS SIGNED)**

1   **ITEM OF CHANGE (AFTER CONTRACT IS SIGNED)**

B   **COLUMN LINES**

POWER & COMMUNICATION SYMBOLS

DUPLEX OUTLET. WALL MTD., TYP. HGT.

FOURPLEX OUTLET. WALL MTD., TYP. HGT.

OR   **VOICE/DATA OUTLET, WALL MOUNTED, TYP. HEIGHT**

LIGHTING & CEILING SYMBOLS

FLUORESCENT LIGHT FIXTURE
FIXTURE TYPE RE: SCHEDULE

O   **DOWN LIGHT**

DIRECTIONAL LIGHT FIXTURE
LTG. DIRECTION IS OPPOSITE BLACK
OR IN DIRECTION OF ARROW

EXIT LIGHT WITH EXIT GRAPHICS DIRECTION
RE: ENGINEERING PLANS

HVAC SUPPLY REGISTER

HVAC RETURN REGISTER

SINGLE POLE SWITCH

D   **DIMMER SWITCH**

3   **3-WAY SWITCH**

DEMOLITION SYMBOLS

=== **DEMOLISH EXISTING**
PARTITION

DEMOLISH EXISTING
DOOR, FRAME & HARDWARE

DEMOLISH EXISTING
ELECTRICAL OUTLET

DEMOLISH EXISTING
VOICE OR DATA OUTLET

DEMOLISH EXISTING
WALL SWITCH

DEMOLISH EXISTING LIGHT FIXTURE

DEMOLISH EXISTING DOWNLIGHT

DEMOLISH EXISTING WALLWASHER

267

Bibliography

Online Bibliography

"The Infography: Law OfficeDesign"(**http://www.infography.com/content/240887819435.html**).

Books

Albrecht, Donald, et. al., ON THE JOB–DESIGN AND THE AMERICAN OFFICE (Princeton Architectural Press, 2000).

Antonelli, Paola, WORKSPHERES: DESIGN AND CONTEMPORARY WORK STYLES (Museum of Modern Art, 2001).

Ching, Frank D.K. and Francis D. Ching, ARCHITECTURE: FORM, SPACE, AND ORDER (Wiley, 2nd edition 1996).

Cohen, Uriel, Mary Gorman, William Robinson, Anthony Schnarsky and Gerald Weisman, IMPROVING THE LAW OFFICE: PRINCIPLES FOR DESIGN (University of Wisconsin-Milwaukee, 2000).

Fabbrizzi, Fabio, OFFICE DESIGN (ARCHITECTURE TOOLS) (TeNeues, 2002).

Frankel, Elana, DESIGN SECRETS: OFFICE SPACES (Rockport, 2001).

Henderson, Justin and Vernon L. Mays, OFFICE DESIGN SOURCE-BOOK: SOLUTIONS FOR DYNAMIC WORKSPACES (INTERIOR DESIGN AND ARCHITECTURE) (Rockport Publishers, 2003).

Karlen, Mark, SPACE PLANNING BASICS (Wiley, 2nd edition 2004).

Knackstedt, Mary V., THE INTERIOR DESIGN BUSINESS HANDBOOK: A COMPLETE GUIDE TO PROFITABILITY (Wiley, 3rd edition 2002).

Kohn, A. Eugene and Paul Katz, BUILDING TYPE BASICS FOR OFFICE BUILDINGS (Wiley, 2002).

Mays,Vernon, OFFICE & WORKSPACES: AN INTERNATIONAL PORTFOLIO OF 43 DESIGNERS (Rockport, 2001).

Marmot, Alexi Ferster and Joanna Eley, OFFICE SPACE PLANNING: DESIGNS FOR TOMORROW'S WORKPLACE (McGraw-Hill, 2000).

Matthew, Stewart, OTHER OFFICE: CREATIVE WORKPLACE DESIGN (Frame Publishers, 2004).

Montes, Christina Montes, NEW OFFICES (Harper Design International, 2003).

Myerson, Jeremy and Phillip Ross, 21ST CENTURY OFFICE (Rizzoli, 2003).

Null, Roberta L., UNIVERSAL DESIGN: CREATIVE SOLUTIONS FOR ADA COMPLIANCE (Professional Publications, Inc., 1996)

Piotrowski, Christine and Elizabeth A. Rogers, DESIGNING COMMERCIAL INTERIORS (Wiley,1999).

Piotrowski, Christine, PROFESSIONAL PRACTICE FOR INTERIOR DESIGNERS, (Wiley, 3rd Edition 2002).

Rayfield, Julie K., THE OFFICE INTERIOR DESIGN GUIDE: AN INTRODUCTION FOR FACILITY AND DESIGN PROFESSIONALS (WILEY,1994).

Yee, Roger, CORPORATE INTERIORS No. 5 (Visual Reference Publications, 2003).

Zelinsky, Marilyn, THE INSPIRED WORKSPACE: INTERIOR DESIGNS FOR CREATIVITY AND PRODUCTIVITY (Rockport, 2002).

Zelinsky, Marilyn, NEW WORKPLACES FOR NEW WORKSTYLES (McGraw-Hill,1997).

Articles

Accessibility

"Don't Overlook Needs of Employees with Dwarfism." *Successful Job Accommodations Strategies,* March 26, 2004.

"Provide Wheelchair Users With Adjustable Workstations." *Successful Job Accommodations Strategies*, June 25, 2004.

"Reasonable Accommodations For Disabilities, Not The Disabled." *The Recorder*, May 22, 2002.

"Take Steps To Accommodate Obese Workers." *Successful Job Accommodations Strategies,* March 26, 2004.

Art Collections

Shane, Corinne. "Law Firms in Vanguard of Corporate Art Collecting; Paintings, Prints, Photographs & Sculpture." *Law Firm Partnership and Benefits Report*, September 1996.

Economics

Adler, Sam. "Opulence Sends Wrong; Austerity, Efficiency Ascendant in Firm Décor." *Law Firm Partnership and Benefits Report*, December 1996.

Altonji, Joeseph B. "Think Before You Sign; Firms Should Ask Some Hard Questions About The Future Before Entering Into a New Lease." *Legal Times*, March 29, 2004.

Axelroth, Joan L. "Despite All the Talk of Online Research, Physical Libraries Continue To Exist–And With Good Reason." *New Jersey Law Journal*, December 11, 2000.

Bamberger, Joanne Cronrath. "Office Design Revisited; Law Firms Learn That Onyx Walls and Flat-Screen Monitors Send a Message." *Legal Times*, June 14, 2004.

Brants, Lucy. "Setting Up Shop Inexpensively." *Legal Times*, October 21, 1996.

"Good Design, Within Limits; How Three Firms Made Tight Budgets Go A Long Way." *Legal Times*, March 16, 1992.

Indik, Martin K. "For Small and Big Firms; Why Pay More? Tips for Avoiding Paying More Than Necessary." *Law Firm Partnership and Benefits Reports*, April 1998.

Jacobson, Cary A. "Designing For An Efficient Law Firm." *Illinois Legal Times*, February 1991.

McGregor, Lynn. "Good Office Design Can Cut Costs, Boost Productivity." *The Lawyers Weekly*, March 8, 2002.

"Making Work Spaces More Functional." *U.S.A. Today Magazine*, March 1997.

Martin, Robert. "Maximizing Space: A New Priority for Law Offices." *New York Law Journal*, November 19, 1991.

"Office Design Sends Message, So Be Creative and Conservative." *Miami Daily Business Review*, December 30, 1996.

Peck, Wendy. "Designing Law Firms; New Offices Around The Country Are Making The Most of Smaller Spaces." *Legal Times*, September 16, 2002.

Peck, Wendy. "Efficiency Is the Watchword When Designing Law Firm Office Space; New Offices Around the Country are Making the Most of Smaller Spaces." *New Jersey Law Journal*, May 19, 2003.

Polo, Steve. "Design Your Offices For Maximum Efficiency; Profitability Increases When Facilities, Technology and Organizational Strategies are Aligned with the Vision of the Firm." *New Jersey Law Journal*, November 3, 2003.

Polo, Steve. "Maximum Efficiency; Law Firms Of The Future Will Look More Like Their Corporate Clients." *Legal Times*, October 6, 2003.

Ponce, Pedro E. "Frugality and Function Add Up To D.C. Bar's Winning Style; core Group Wins Prizes For Offices Design." *Legal Times*, November 14, 1994.

Sunoo, Brenda Paik. "Office Design Can Increase Productivity." *Workforce*, April 1998.

Ergonomics

Dennis, Donald A. "Smart Practices: Become An Industrial Athlete: Ergonomic Don's Guide To Preventing Office Injuries." *Law Practice Management*, May 2000/ June 2000.

"Designing/Redesigning the Workspace." *Successful Job Accommodations Strategies,* February 21, 2001.

Laiserin, Jerry. "Ergonomics in the Digital Office." *Architectural Record*, October 2001.

Melia, Marilyn Kennedy. "Turn Down the Lights For Office Safety." *Safety & Health*, January 1994.

" Practice Perfect- Reply All; Offices Go Ergonomic; Firms Address What Could Be A Pain In the Neck Or Wrist Or . . ." *Texas Lawyer*, July 31, 2000.

Peck, Richard L. "The Office As 'Therapy Assistant'" *Behavioral Health Management*, July/ August 1996.

Sunoo, Brenda Paik. "Office Design Can Increase Productivity." *Workforce*, April 1998.

"Use This Checklist To Set Up Your Work Station." *Managing Today's Federal Employees*, April 4, 2001.

Vandagriff, David P. "Be Comfortable, Get Organized: Ergonomic Keyboard and Case-Management System Stress Ease Of Use." *ABA Journal*, February 1996.

Mobility

Easter, Terri H. "Making Room For More; Crowell & Moring Adopts Hotelling, Hot Desks, Group Space, and Telecommuting." *Legal Times*, October 9, 2000.

Harhai, Stephen J., "Technology In Practice; Personal Technology: An Out-Of-The-Office Experience." *Law Practice Management*, April 2003.

The Process

Altonji, Joeseph B. "Think Before You Sign; Firms Should Ask Some Hard Questions About The Future Before Entering Into a New Lease." *Legal Times*, March 29, 2004.

Levin, Arnold Craig. "Design By Consensus; Involving the Partners Is Not Only Necessary, It Can Actually Be Done." *Legal Times*, October 6, 2003.

Lowe, Douglas H. "A Checklist for the Basics of Law Firm Design." *Texas Lawyer*, April 8, 1991.

Lowe, Douglas H. "Think Before You Design The Office; From Firm Image, To Cost, To Comfort, To Effiecency: Options Abound." *Legal Times*, November 11, 1991.

Peck, Wendy. "Efficiency Is the Watchword When Designing Law Firm Office Space; New Offices Around the Country are Making the Most of Smaller Spaces." *New Jersey Law Journal*, May 19, 2003.

Polo, Steve. "Design Your Offices For Maximum Efficiency; Profitability Increases When Facilities, Technology and Organizational Strategies are Aligned with the Vision of the Firm." *New Jersey Law Journal*, November 3, 2003.

Rodgers, James G. "Planning of Law Firm Libraries Is In Transition." *New York Law Journal*, September 24, 1990.

Miller, Marjorie A. "Designing Your Law Office; The Design Process." *Law Practice Management*, January 1990/ February 1990.

Wallace, Mary Colette. "Complexity of New Office Designs: Thinking Through Your Future Workplace." *Searcher*, November/ December 2000.

Technology

"For Technology Crystal Ball, Look To FutureLawyerOffice.com." *Corporate Legal Times*, November 2001.

Easter, Terri H. "Making Room For More; Crowell & Moring Adopts Hotelling, Hot Desks, Group Space, and Telecommuting." *Legal Times*, October 9, 2000.

Harhai, Stephen J., "Technology In Practice; Personal Technology: An Out-Of-The-Office Experience." *Law Practice Management*, April 2003.

Hickman, Don. "Starting From Scratch; When You Open a New Law Office, the Task of Selecting Hardware and Software–and Getting it Up and Running in Time–is Daunting." *New Jersey Law Journal*, June 23, 2003.

Laiserin, Jerry. "Ergonomics in the Digital Office." *Architectural Record*, October 2001.

Polo, Steve. "Design Your Offices For Maximum Efficiency; Profitability Increases When Facilities, Technology and Organizational Strategies are Aligned with the Vision of the Firm." *New Jersey Law Journal*, November 3, 2003.

Robbins, Mary Alice. "Firm Interiors Evolve With the High-Tech Times." *Texas Lawyer*, August 2, 2004.

General Topics

Adler, Sam. "Applying Feng Shui Concepts to Firm Décor." *Law Firm Partnership and Benefits Report*, December 1996.

Arcidi, Phillip. "Sure-shot Modernism; Two Office Interiors." *Progressive Architecture*, December 1991.

Axelroth, Joan L. "Despite All the Talk of Online Research, Physical Libraries Continue To Exist–And With Good Reason." *New Jersey Law Journal*, December 11, 2000.

Baron, Angela S. "New or Renovated Space Needs To Be Designed With Systems in Mind." *The National Law Journal*, October 14, 1991.

Blau, Frank. "Office Layouts Should Leave Room for Growth; Designing Space for Computers." *The National Law Journal*, March 5, 1990.

Brants, Lucy. "Setting Up Shop Inexpensively." *New Jersey Law Journal*, November 4, 1996.

Brennan, Aoife, Jasdeep S. Chugh and Theresa Kline. "Traditional Versus Open Office Design: A Longitudinal Field Study." *Environment and Behavior*, May 2002.

Brydone, Eleanor. "It's Imperative to Put People First When Designing a Law Office." *The Lawyers Weekly*, November 2, 2001.

Buchholz, Barbara B. "Law Office Design Competition; The Look Of A Winner." *ABA Journal*, August 1996.

Buchholz, Barbara B. "Winning With Style: Light-Filled Interiors, Bold Statements of Form Following Function, and Rooms With Views Make the Difference in This Year's ABA Journal Design Competition." *ABA Journal*, August 1995.

Butler, Jonathan P. "Law Office of the Future Emphasizes Technology." *The National Law Journal*, May 26, 1997.

Canfield, Curt A. "Getting the Most From an Information System." *New York Law Journal*, August 1, 1995.

Canfield, James L. "The Right Consulting Firm Is Key To Selecting the Right Technology." *New York Law Journal*, September 5, 1995.

Cage, Wayne. "Morphing Interiors; As the Practice Of Law Changes, So Does The Configuration of the Modern Firm's Offices, Where Fine Furnishings Are Being Supplanted By Functionality and Flexibility." *Texas Lawyer*, April 15, 1996.

Chanen, Jill Schachner. "Into the Woods: Designing, Handcrafting Fine Furniture Opens New Vistas For Atlanta Lawyer." *ABA Journal*, June 1995.

Chanen, Jill Schachner. "Launching Into A New Space: Work Style And Personnel Needs Take Over In Office Floor-Plan Design." *ABA Journal*, January 2001.

Collins, Bruce D. "Lawyers Need a Room of Their Own." *Corporate Legal Times*, January 2003.

Crockett, Jim. "The Office: A Living Lab?" *Consulting-Specifying Engineer*, April 2000.

"Dream Building For Environmentalist." *Futurist*, July/August 1991.

"Designing Your Office Space For Work In Progress." *Miami Daily Business Review*, April 3, 2000.

Donald, Mark. "Space Rebels; Going Where Few Have Gone, More Lawyers Break The Workspace Barrier." *Texas Lawyer*, August 2, 2004.

Fearnley, Joshua. "New Office Design Concepts Reflect The Changing Workplace." *Legal Times*, April 19, 1999.

Fiegenschuh, Ron, Janet Rankin and Kelly Dougherty. "Designing A New Office." *Legal Times*, March 12, 2001.

Fiegenschuh, Ron, Janet Rankin and Kelly Dougherty. "Renovate or Relocate? Deciding Whether To Stay Or Move Begins With Defining The Firms Goals." *Legal Times*, March 12, 2001.

Fine, Brenda. "Lawyers' 'War Room' Debuts; Hilton Offers World of Savings." *National Law Journal*, September 29, 1997.

Fujara, Larry J. "Avoiding Problems In Relocation." *Legal Times*, May 1991.

Gallagher, Leigh. "Death to the Cubicle!" Forbes, September 7, 1998.

Gladwell, Malcolm. "Designs For Working" *New Yorker*, December 11, 2000.

Goetz, Lewis J, and Nestor Santa-Cruz. "Design Solutions To Law Firms' Evolving Needs." *Legal Times*, April 5, 1999.

Graff, Brett. "Forget the Dilbert Drones and the Boss Corner Digs. South Florida Office Space Today is Designed for Sharing Information." *Miami Daily Business Review*, November 10, 2000.

Hablutzel, Margo Lynn. "New Products: Portable Office Modules." *Law Practice Management*, October 1993.

Hablutzel, Margo Lynn. "New Products: "Windows" For Windowless Offices." *Law Practice Management*, March 1993.

Harhai, Stephen J., "Technology In Practice; Personal Technology: An Out-Of-The-Office Experience." *Law Practice Management*, April 2003.

Harris, Carolyn G., "Coming of Age in New York; Philosophical Debate Over Designation of Modern Building." *New York Law Journal*, February 19, 1997.

Hildebrant, Bradford W. "Planning the Library Environment." *New York Law Journal*, November 13, 1990.

Hill, Lee. "Architects Give Firms A Step Up in Design; Fancy Flights of Stairs? Maybe. But No Flights of Fancy in These Stair Layouts." *New York Law Journal*, June 26, 2003.

Jansz, Pamela. "Mobility Is the Key to Disaster Planning; A Mobile Office System Can Be Had With Laptops, Cell Phones, Pagers and Daily Data Backup." *New Jersey Law Journal*, September 16, 2002.

Jones, Tom. "Sketching Out Future With Space." *National Law Journal*, October 14, 2002.

Kerlow, Eleanor. "Arnold And Porter Calls Shots on Design; One Deal Fell Through, But Firm Brings Know-How To New Project." *Legal Times*, June 8, 1992.

Kerlow, Eleanor. "Designs For Two Firms Offer A Study In Contracts; At Howrey & Simon, Mood Is High Tech." *Legal Times*, March 15, 1993.

Kerlow, Eleanor. "Functionality With Flourishes." *Legal Times*, September 21, 1998.

Kerlow, Eleanor. "Living Through Dust and Noise; Dickstein, Shapiro Survives Its Renovation." *Legal Times*, March 19, 1990.

Kerlow, Eleanor. "Milgram Thomajan Mixed Creativity, Cost-Consciousness." *Legal Times*, March 16, 1992.

Kerlow, Eleanor. "When Style Meets Budget; Financial Limits Don't Mean Boring Design; Seyfarth, Shaw Spent Wisely For Comfort." *Legal Times*, March 19, 1990.

Krocheski, Jake J., and Holly M. Moyer. "Relocating? A Solid Plan Reduces Inconvenience." *New York Law Journal*, April 12, 1994.

"Law Firm Librarians on Design, Staffing, Spending" *National Law Journal*, July 14, 2003.

"Law Office Design Competition; The Final Word In Offices." *ABA Journal*, August 1997.

Lehman-Smith, Debra. "Forging A Happy Union Between A Grand Old Lobby and Modern Law Offices." *Legal Times*, September 13, 1999.

Lieber, Ronald B. "Cool Offices." *Fortune*, December 9, 1996.

"Lighting and Productivity." *Society*, May/June 1995.

Lowe, Douglas H. "Think Before You Design The Office; From Firm Image, To Cost, To Comfort, To Effiecency: Options Abound." *Legal Times*, November 11, 1991.

Mahinka, Stephen Paul. "A Beautiful Space; Morgan Lewis' New Home Has Dramatic Aesthetics, Real Efficiencies." *Legal Times*, March 18, 2002.

"Making Work Spaces More Functional." *U.S.A. Today Magazine*, March 1997.

Manning, Allison and Stephan Roussan. "Keep Clients Informed of Matters Through Private Web Site Pages." *New York Law Journal*, September 9, 1997.

"Morgan Lewis Opens New Building In Washington, DC." *The Metropolitan Corporate Counsel*, February 2002.

Morgenstern, Barbara L., "A Port In A Storm: Personalizing Office Décor Creates A Comfort Zone For Clients." *ABA Journal*, October 1995.

Morgenstern, Barbara L. "Room For Compromise: To Reap The Benefits Of Office Sharing, Get Details Straights Upfront." *ABA Journal*, May 1997.

Nielsen, Shelia. "Organization By Design; Overcoming Chaos In Your Office And Work Habits." *Legal Times*, February 19, 2001.

"Office Furniture & Design." *New Jersey Law Journal*, November 11, 1996.

Peterson, Martha and Allen Kanter, "Law Firms Try a Democratic' Use of Office Space." *The National Law Journal*, October 15, 1990.

Polo, Steve. "Maximum Efficiency; Law Firms Of The Future Will Look More Like Their Corporate Clients." *Legal Times*, October 6, 2003.

Rogers, James G. "Space Odyssey: Law Offices For The 21st Century, The Age Of Technology Has Significantly Transformed Office Renovations And Relocations." *The National Law Journal*, January 30, 1995.

Sapino, Brenda. "Tinsman & Houser Rises From the Ashes; San Antonio Firm Wanted Wow' In Its Design, and Got it." *Texas Lawyer*, October 8, 1990.

Shepard, Ritcheyna A. "How To Build a Mid-Size Firm From Scratch." *New York Law Journal*, October 31, 2000.

Shepherd, Ritchenya A. "Zero to 44 in 3 years." *The National Law Journal*, November 6, 2000.

Slind-Flor, Victoria. "Is Your Office In Harmony?" *The National Law Journal*, July 13, 1998.

Studley, Jamienne S. "Is What You See What You Want To Convey?" *Texas Lawyer*, June 1, 1992.

Studley, Jamienne S. "Office Design Reflects a Firm's Values, Culture." *The Recorder*, May 22, 1992.

Tatum, Michael D. "Radical New Concept: Places People Really Want to Work." *Interiors*, July 1997.

Vandagriff, David P. "Be Comfortable, Get Organized: Ergonomic Keyboard and Case-Management System Stress Ease Of Use." *ABA Journal*, February 1996.

Wilson, Sally R. and Thomas C.E. Jones. " Designing Lawyers, In the New Economy, Interiors Are Planned With Efficiency and Comfort In Mind." *Legal Times*, October 9, 2000.

Wilson, Sally R. and Thomas C.E. Jones. "Making Time For Design; Plan The Interior Of Your Firm With Efficiency and People in Mind." *Texas Lawyer*, January 15, 2001.

Zemsky, Bill. "A Design Solution to the Office Paper Explosion" *The Recorder*, January 24, 1992.

Zemsky Bill. "Go With the Flow—of Paper, That Is; When Designing an Office, Don't Forget the Documents." *Legal Times*, March 16, 1992.

Zemsky, Bill. "Go With The Flow–Of Paper, That Is; When Designing an Office, don't Forget the documents." *Texas Lawyer*, October 12, 1997.

Index

Selected Books from . . .
THE ABA LAW PRACTICE MANAGEMENT SECTION

Law Office Procedures Manual for Solos and Small Firms, Third Edition

By Demetrios Dimitriou

This newly revised edition provides you with everything you need to develop and compile a succinct, comprehensive procedures manual, geared toward the unique management issues of a solo or small firm. This step-by-step guide offers direction on setting policy and procedures for your firm, and provides sample language and documents, both in the text and on the accompanying CD-ROM, to allow for easy customization. Proper implementation of sound policies and procedures will help ensure your firm operates effectively, efficiently and productively, resulting in optimal delivery of legal services to your clients.

The Essential Formbook: Comprehensive Management Tools for Lawyers, Vols. I-IV

By Gary A. Munneke and Anthony E. Davis

Useful to all legal practitioners this series will help you establish profitable, affirmative client relationships while avoiding unnecessary risks. And, all the forms are available on accompanying discs, making it easy to modify them to match your specific needs.

Volume I, Part I, addresses **Partnership and Organizational Agreements**, providing information about law firm management structure models, ethics, and general counsel. **Part II—Client Intake and Fee Agreements—**walks you through the intake process, including how to effectively gather information on new clients, manage the client selection process, make judgments, and use engagement and nonengagement letters.

Volume II, Part I, discusses **Human Resources**, and covers the hiring process, training and development, compensation, and discipline and termination. **Part II** covers **Fees, Billing, and Collection** and includes information on measuring billing practices, hourly billing, pricing legal services, alternative fee agreements, engagement letters, and managing the billing process.

Volume III, Part I, covers **Calendar, Docket and File Management**, including document backup, retention, destruction, and security. **Part II** outlines **Law Firm Financial Analysis**, including financial analysis of risks that all law firms confront.

Volume IV, Part I addresses **Disaster Planning and Recovery**, and offers guidance on both planning for disaster and on recovery after such an event, including contributing to the disaster relief of others. **Part II** covers **Risk Management and Professional Liability Insurance** and examines in detail professional liability insurance for lawyers.

Winning Alternatives to the Billable Hour: Strategies That Work, Second Edition

Edited by James A. Calloway and Mark A. Robertson

Find out how to initiate and implement different billing methods that make sense for you and your client. You'll learn how to explain—clearly and persuasively—the economic and client service advantages in changing billing methods. You'll discover how to establish a win-win billing situation with your clients no matter which method you choose. Written for lawyers in firms of all sizes, this book provides valuable examples, practical tools, and tips throughout. The appendix contains useful forms and examples from lawyers who have actually implemented alternative billing methods at their firms.

How to Start and Build a Law Practice, Platinum Fifth Edition

By Jay G Foonberg

This classic ABA Bestseller—now completely updated—is the primary resource for starting your own firm. This acclaimed book covers all aspects of getting started, including finding clients, determining the right location, setting fees, buying office equipment, maintaining an ethical and responsible practice, maximizing available resources, upholding your standards, and marketing your practice, just to name a few. In addition, you'll find a business plan template, forms, checklists, sample letters, and much more. A must for any lawyer just starting out—or growing a solo practice.

The Lawyer's Guide to Marketing on the Internet, Second Edition

By Gregory Siskind, Deborah McMurray, and Richard P. Klau

The Internet is a critical component of every law firm marketing strategy—no matter where you are, how large your firm is, or the areas in which you practice. Used effectively, a younger, smaller firm can present an image just as sophisticated and impressive as a larger and more-established firm. You can reach potential new clients in remote areas, at any time, for minimal cost. As with any other promotional tactic, the use of the Internet needs to be thoughtfully integrated into your overall marketing strategy. *The Lawyer's Guide to Marketing on the Internet*, Second Edition, can show you how to effectively and efficiently market your law practice on the Internet.

The Lawyer's Guide to Fact Finding on the Internet, Second Edition

By Carole A. Levitt and Mark E. Rosch

Written especially for legal professionals, this revised and expanded edition is a complete, hands-on guide to the best sites, secrets, and shortcuts for conducting efficient research on the Web. Containing over 600 pages of information, with over 100 screen shots of specific Web sites, this resource is filled with practical tips and advice on using specific sites, alerting readers to quirks or hard-to-find information. What's more, user-friendly icons immediately identify free sites, free-with-registration sites, and pay sites. An accompanying CD-ROM includes the links contained in the book, indexed, so you can easily navigate to these cream-of-the-crop Web sites without typing URLs into your browser.

The Lawyer's Guide to Marketing Your Practice, Second Edition
Edited by James A. Durham and Deborah McMurray
This book is packed with practical ideas, innovative strategies, useful checklists, and sample marketing and action plans to help you implement a successful, multi-faceted, and profit-enhancing marketing plan for your firm. Organized into four sections, this illuminating resource covers: Developing Your Approach; Enhancing Your Image; Implementing Marketing Strategies; and Maintaining Your Program. Appendix materials include an instructive primer on market research to inform you on research methodologies that support the marketing of legal services. The accompanying CD-ROM contains a wealth of checklists, plans, and other sample reports, questionnaires, and templates—all designed to make implementing your marketing strategy as easy as possible!

Through the Client's Eyes: New Approaches to Get Clients to Hire You Again and Again, Second Edition
By Henry W. Ewalt
This edition covers every aspect of the lawyer-client relationship, giving sound advice and fresh ideas on how to develop and maintain excellent client relationships. Author and seasoned practitioner Henry Ewalt shares tips on building relationships and trust, uncovering some unlikely ways to make connections in addition to traditional methods. Marketing techniques including brochures, newsletters, client dinners, and sporting events are discussed. Other topics that are covered include client intake, client meetings, follow-up, dissemination of news, fee setting and collection, and other client issues.

The Lawyer's Guide to Creating Persuasive Computer Presentations, Second Edition
By Ann Brenden and John Goodhue
This book explains the advantages of computer presentation resources, how to use them, what they can do, and the legal issues involved in their use. You'll learn how to use computer presentations in the courtroom, during opening statements, direct examination, cross examination, closing arguments, appellate arguments and more. This revised second edition has been updated to include new chapters on hardware and software that is currently being used for digital displays, and all-new sections that walk the reader through beginning skills, and some advanced PowerPoint® techniques. Also included is a CD-ROM containing on-screen tutorials illustrating techniques such as animating text, insertion and configuration of text and images, and a full sample PowerPoint final argument complete with audio, and much more.

The Lawyer's Guide to Strategic Planning: Defining, Setting, and Achieving Your Firm's Goals
By Thomas C. Grella and Michael L. Hudkins
This practice-building resource can be your guide to planning dynamic strategic plans and implementing them at your firm. You'll learn about the strategic planning process and how to establish goals in key planning areas such as law firm governance, competition, opening a new office, financial management, technology, marketing and competitive intelligence, client development and retention, and more. The accompanying CD-ROM contains a wealth of sample plans, policies, and statements, as well as numerous questionnaires. If you're serious about improving the way your firm works, increasing productivity, making better decisions, and setting your firm on the right course, this book is the resource you need.

Collecting Your Fee: Getting Paid from Intake to Invoice
By Edward Poll
This practical and user-friendly guide provides you with proven strategies and sound advice that will make the process of collecting your fees simpler, easier, and more effective! This handy resource provides you with the framework around which to structure your collection efforts. You'll learn how you can streamline your billing and collection process by hiring the appropriate staff and drafting a bill that the client is motivated to pay. In addition, you'll benefit from the strategies to use when the client fails to pay the bill on time and what you need to do to get paid when all else fails. Also included is a CD-ROM with sample forms, letters, agreements, and more for you to customize to your own practice needs.

Marketing Success Stories: Conversations with Leading Lawyers
Edited by Hollis Hatfield Weishar and Joyce K. Smiley
This practice-building resource is an insightful collection of anecdotes on successful and creative marketing techniques used by lawyers and marketing professionals in a variety of practice settings. These stories of marketing strategies that paid off will inspire you to greater heights. You'll gain an inside look at how successful lawyers market themselves, their practice specialties and their firms. In addition to dozens of first-hand accounts of success stories from practitioners, you'll find advice from in-house counsel and others who give candid feedback on how strategic marketing influences their decision to hire a specific firm. Learn how to make new contacts, gain more repeat business, increase your visibility within the community, and learn many other action steps with this worthwhile addition to your law firm's marketing library.

30-Day Risk-Free Order Form
Call Today! 1-800-285-2221
Monday–Friday, 7:30 AM – 5:30 PM, Central Time

Qty	Title	LPM Price	Regular Price	Total
_____	Collecting Your Fee: Getting Paid From Intake to Invoice (5110490)	$ 69.95	$ 79.95	$_____
_____	The Essential Formbook, Volume I (5110424V1)	169.95	199.95	$_____
_____	The Essential Formbook, Volume II (5110424V2)	169.95	199.95	$_____
_____	The Essential Formbook, Volume III (5110424V3)	169.95	199.95	$_____
_____	The Essential Formbook, Volume IV (5110424V4)	169.95	199.95	$_____
_____	How to Start and Build a Law Practice, Platinum Fifth Edition (5110508)	57.95	69.95	$_____
_____	Law Office Procedures Manual for Solos and Small Firms, Third Edition (5110522)	69.95	79.95	$_____
_____	The Lawyer's Guide to Creating Persuasive Computer Presentations, Second Edition (5110530)	79.95	99.95	$_____
_____	The Lawyer's Guide to Fact Finding on the Internet, Second Edition (5110497)	69.95	79.95	$_____
_____	The Lawyer's Guide to Marketing Your Practice, Second Edition (5110500)	79.95	89.95	$_____
_____	The Lawyer's Guide to Marketing on the Internet, Second Edition (5110484)	69.95	79.95	$_____
_____	The Lawyer's Guide to Strategic Planning (5110520)	59.95	79.95	$_____
_____	Marketing Success Stories, Second Edition (5110511)	64.95	74.95	$_____
_____	Through the Client's Eyes, Second Edition (5110480)	69.95	79.95	$_____
_____	Winning Alternatives to the Billable Hour, Second Edition (5110483)	129.95	149.95	$_____

*Postage and Handling	
$10.00 to $24.99	$5.95
$25.00 to $49.99	$9.95
$50.00 to $99.99	$12.95
$100.00 to $349.99	$17.95
$350 to $499.99	$24.95

**Tax
DC residents add 5.75%
IL residents add 8.75%
MD residents add 5%

*Postage and Handling	$_____
**Tax	$_____
TOTAL	$_____

PAYMENT

❑ Check enclosed (to the ABA)

❑ Visa   ❑ MasterCard   ❑ American Express

_____
Account Number   Exp. Date   Signature

Name _____ Firm _____

Address _____

City _____ State _____ Zip _____

Phone Number _____ E-Mail Address _____

Note: E-Mail address is required if ordering the
The Lawyer's Guide to Fact Finding on the Internet
E-mail Newsletter (5110498)

Guarantee

If—for any reason—you are not satisfied with your purchase, you may
return it within 30 days of receipt for a complete refund of the price of the
book(s). No questions asked!

Mail: ABA Publication Orders, P.O. Box 10892, Chicago, Illinois 60610-0892
♦ Phone: 1-800-285-2221 ♦ FAX: 312-988-5568

E-Mail: abasvcctr@abanet.org ♦ Internet: http://www.lawpractice.org/catalog

About the CD

The accompanying CD contains the following material from the book:

- Sample Bid Analysis (Exhibit 3.1)
- Comprehensive Checklist and Schedule (pp. 25-38 in the book)
- Equipment Inventory Form and Letter (Exhibit 6.1)
- Furniture Inventory Form and Letter (Exhibit 6.2)
- Law Firm Planning Questionnaire (Exhibit 6.3)
- Building Criteria Questionnaire (Exhibit 7.2)
- Building Evaluation and Report (Exhibit 7.3)
- Project Checklist for Solo and Small Firm Offices (pp. 227-229 in the book)
- A Sample Request for Proposals (Exhibit 19.1)
- A Sample Preliminary Budget (Exhibit 19.2)
- Preliminary Pricing (Design Development Budget) (Exhibit 19.3)
- Construction Administration Budget (Exhibit 19.4)
- Furniture Budget (Exhibit 19.5)

The files are in Microsoft® Word® format.

For additional information about the files on the CD, please open and read the "**readme.doc**" file on the CD.

NOTE: The set of files on the CD may only be used on a single computer or moved to and used on another computer. Under no circumstances may the set of files be used on more than one computer at one time. If you are interested in obtaining a license to use the set of files on a local network, please contact: Director, Copyrights and Contracts, American Bar Association, 321 N. Clark Street, Chicago, IL 60610, (312) 988-6101. **Please read the license and warranty statements on the following page before using this CD.**

CD-ROM to accompany

The Complete Guide to Designing Your Law Office

WARNING: Opening this package indicates your understanding and acceptance of the following Terms and Conditions.

READ THE FOLLOWING TERMS AND CONDITIONS BEFORE OPENING THIS SEALED PACKAGE. IF YOU DO NOT AGREE WITH THEM, PROMPTLY RETURN THE UNOPENED PACKAGE TO EITHER THE PARTY FROM WHOM IT WAS ACQUIRED OR TO THE AMERICAN BAR ASSOCIATION AND YOUR MONEY WILL BE RETURNED.

The document files in this package are a proprietary product of the American Bar Association and are protected by Copyright Law. The authors, Suzette S. Schultz and Jon S. Schultz, retain title to and ownership of these files.

License

You may use this set of files on a single computer or move it to and use it on another computer, but under no circumstances may you use the set of files on more than one computer at the same time. You may copy the files either in support of your use of the files on a single computer or for backup purposes. If you are interested in obtaining a license to use the set of files on a local network, please contact: Manager, Copyright and Licensing, American Bar Association, 321 N. Clark Street, Chicago, IL 60610, (312) 988-6102.

You may permanently transfer the set of files to another party if the other party agrees to accept the terms and conditions of this License Agreement. If you transfer the set of files, you must at the same time transfer all copies of the files to the same party or destroy those not transferred. Such transfer terminates your license. You may not rent, lease, assign or otherwise transfer the files except as stated in this paragraph.

You may modify these files for your own use within the provisions of this License Agreement. You may not redistribute any modified files.

Warranty

If a CD-ROM in this package is defective, the American Bar Association will replace it at no charge if the defective diskette is returned to the American Bar Association within 60 days from the date of acquisition.

American Bar Association warrants that these files will perform in substantial compliance with the documentation supplied in this package. However, the American Bar Association does not warrant these forms as to the correctness of the legal material contained therein. If you report a significant defect in performance in writing to the American Bar Association, and the American Bar Association is not able to correct it within 60 days, you may return the diskettes, including all copies and documentation, to the American Bar Association and the American Bar Association will refund your money.

Any files that you modify will no longer be covered under this warranty even if they were modified in accordance with the License Agreement and product documentation.

IN NO EVENT WILL THE AMERICAN BAR ASSOCIATION, ITS OFFICERS, MEMBERS, OR EMPLOYEES BE LIABLE TO YOU FOR ANY DAMAGES, INCLUDING LOST PROFITS, LOST SAVINGS OR OTHER INCIDENTAL OR CONSEQUENTIAL DAMAGES ARISING OUT OF YOUR USE OR INABILITY TO USE THESE FILES EVEN IF THE AMERICAN BAR ASSOCIATION OR AN AUTHORIZED AMERICAN BAR ASSOCIATION REPRESENTATIVE HAS BEEN ADVISED OF THE POSSIBILITY OF SUCH DAMAGES, OR FOR ANY CLAIM BY ANY OTHER PARTY. SOME STATES DO NOT ALLOW THE LIMITATION OR EXCLUSION OF LIABILITY FOR INCIDENTAL OR CONSEQUENTIAL DAMAGES, IN WHICH CASE THIS LIMITATION MAY NOT APPLY TO YOU.